"She was bloated, disfigured, very beat up. They showed us the body exactly as they found it. Not where it was, of course. It was lying on a slab, but the stocking was still around her neck, her face was bloated, a paper towel was stuck in her mouth with pieces hanging out and she was bloody, black and blue, she was dirty. You could see everything that had happened to Joyce that night."

H

BEYOND OBSESSION

RICHARD HAMMER

AVON BOOKS ▲ NEW YORK

AVON BOOKS
A division of
The Hearst Corporation
1350 Avenue of the Americas
New York, New York 10019

Copyright © 1992 by Richard Hammer
Published by arrangement with the author
Library of Congress Catalog Card Number: 91-24395
ISBN: 0-380-71037-4

Published in hardcover by William Morrow and Company, Inc.; for information address Permissions Department, William Morrow and Company, Inc., 1350 Avenue of the Americas, New York, New York 10019.

The William Morrow edition contains the following Library of Congress Cataloging in Publication Data:

Hammer, Richard, 1928—
    Beyond Obsession / by Richard Hammer.
        p.   cm.
    1. Murder—Connecticut—Case studies.   2. Trials (Murder)—
Connecticut—Hartford County.   3. Aparo, Joyce.   4. Coleman, Dennis.
5. Aparo, Karin.   I. Title.
HV6533.C8H36   1992   91-24395
364.1′523′097462—dc20   CIP

First Avon Books Printing: March 1993

AVON TRADEMARK REG. U.S. PAT. OFF. AND IN OTHER COUNTRIES. MARCA REGISTRADA.
HECHO EN U.S.A.

Printed in the U.S.A.

RA   10 9 8 7 6 5 4 3 2 1

Why, what could she have done,
        being what she is?
Was there another Troy for her to burn?

                —W. B. YEATS
                    "No Second Troy"

My only love sprung from my only
        hate!
Too early seen unknown, and known
        too late!

                —WILLIAM SHAKESPEARE
                Romeo and Juliet

Author's Note

This is a work of nonfiction. The reader will find in it events that defy logic, actions that would not be credible in fiction, people whose motives seem often irrational and not easily explained, sometimes beyond simple explanation or even any explanation at all. But life does not follow formulas, and neither people nor events behave as we would wish them to or as we believe and expect they should. Yet this story is a true one, the events did happen and these people are real.

The story is a mystery, its solution still debated. There are a number of events about which the major participants told conflicting versions, sometimes vastly and critically different. In most instances I have presented both versions, to give the reader the opportunity to make up his or her own mind on which seems most reasonable, on which seems most clearly to arise from what went before and from the personalities of the antagonists. I have, though, tried to set down guideposts, which the reader should take merely as my view. If there are solutions to the unanswered questions that hover over the outcome, they lie in the story itself and how the reader interprets it. As will become clear, different people have read the evidence in different ways.

Some mention must be made about the section dealing with the trials of Dennis Coleman and especially of Karin Aparo. A trial, contrary to television and fictional presentation, is a study in tedium. It is long stretches of legal argument and repetitious and befuddling questions and responses, broken now and then, but not often, by an illuminating colloquy. There are few surprises, for any good lawyer should know the answer to a question before he or she asks it, and there are almost never one of those dramatic climaxes so dear to fiction. These trials were different only to the extent that witnesses gave widely conflicting testimony.

In setting down what seemed to me the high points and critical moments in direct examination and cross-examination in these trials, I have tried to edit out the repetitions and obfuscations. On occasion I have juxtaposed testimony that was separated by hours or days because such testimony essentially dealt with the same event or was otherwise directly related. To the greatest extent possible, though, nothing has been taken out of context or put into a frame that it did not have in the courtroom, and the questions and answers are as they were given by attorneys and witnesses.

A final note: This book, like any work of nonfiction, could not have been written without the help of a great many people. And so I must thank all those people in the town of Glastonbury, Connecticut, and other places in the state who went out of their way to talk to me and share their memories and opinions. Most did not want their names mentioned, and I have not done so. The same is true of various police officers and other public officials from the town and the state who did talk to me, though they were under a court order to prevent them from doing so, under the assumption that the cases finally would be resolved and the order lifted by the time this book appeared, though it remains in effect to this day.

Though I spent a considerable period of time with Dennis Coleman, three of the principals in this story refused to talk about it. They were Karin Aparo, Christopher Wheatley and Kira Lintner. What appears in relation to them, then, is a result of what they said in court or to the police or elsewhere and what those who knew them imparted to me. Without the cooperation of those friends, who spoke openly to me, any understanding of these three, and others, would have been impossible.

Several people deserve my special appreciation for the unstinting help they provided. Because some are mentioned during the course of this book, I will not cite them here. But I must particularly thank M. Hatcher Norris, the attorney for Dennis Coleman. I would have been lost without his generous assistance. He was the first person I spoke to, and he shared his experiences, pointed me in a number of directions, opened innumerable doors and was always available when I needed him for advice. James Cavanaugh, who headed the state police investigation of the murder and has since retired, dug into his recollections and turned over to me masses of letters, diaries, photographs and other documents. Dr. Eugene Goldberg, a psychoanalyst, and Dr. Robert Broad, a psychologist who has dealt exensively with disturbed adolescents, both friends of mine, took the time to explore facets of this story with me, to provide me with their insights and head me toward various studies that proved essential to understanding the participants in this story.

I must also thank Martin Gross, who came upon this

story and brought it to me. Without him, I would never have written this book. Finally, there is my wife, Arlene, who listened for a year while I tried to fathom what had happened, whose insights helped me find what I hope were the right directions and who took the time from a very busy schedule to read this book in manuscript from its very first words and offered her invaluable suggestions and corrections gently. If there are faults in this work, they are mine. Whatever merit it has, I share with her.

PART ONE

"I WILL 'DO THE DEED' "

1

August 5, 1987

Joyce Aparo was missing. The forty-seven-year-old former social worker, who was one of the most valued employees of Athena Health Care Associates, hadn't shown up for work on this hot and rainy Wednesday morning. It was not like her. A single mother raising a sixteen-year-old daughter after three bad marriages, she was dedicated to her work. She was never late.

At first nobody was concerned. About six weeks before, somebody had rear-ended the 1986 Volkswagen Jetta that Athena leased for her. She had suffered whiplash, and since then the pains in her neck had been growing progressively worse. Finally she had decided to see a chiropractor. One of the partners in Athena had arranged an appointment with the best man in Waterbury, Connecticut, where the company maintained its offices. The doctor was a very busy man, his calendar full, appointments scheduled weeks in advance. As a favor he agreed to make time for her. Joyce was due there at ten in the morning, so perhaps, without telling anyone, she had decided to go straight to his office from her home in Glastonbury, about thirty miles to the east, rather than show up at the Athena office first.

But just after ten Michael Zaccaro, one of Athena's founding partners and a very close friend of Joyce's, called the doctor's office to check. Joyce wasn't there.

Mrs. Aparo, the receptionist said, had not appeared for her appointment, and she had been about to call to find out if anyone at Athena knew whether she was merely late or, in fact, intended to cancel. Zaccaro said he had no idea why Joyce was late, and he was sure she intended to keep the date. He would try to find out what was holding her up.

Zaccaro dialed the number of the Aparo condominium on Butternut Drive, in the northern part of Glastonbury. There was no answer. Perhaps, he thought as he hung up, Joyce had been held up in traffic. Then his phone rang.

A little before seven that morning in Bernardston, a village near the border where Massachusetts meets Vermont and New Hampshire, Police Chief Peter Brulotte, a burly, weathered middle-aged man, was preparing his breakfast. Suddenly there was a knock at his door. His sergeant, the only other cop on the town's police force, stood outside. A car had just been discovered half in a stream at the bottom of the slope right beside Brulotte's house. It hadn't been there when the chief went to sleep. Sometime during the night somebody had driven it off the road, down the slope, into the stream, and then gone his or her way without disturbing the police chief's slumber. Brulotte and his sergeant hurried out into the morning's damp heat. In the stream they found a white 1986 Volkswagen Jetta, its license plates removed. The inside of the car had been stripped, too. There were no insurance certificates, registration or gasoline credit cards, but the key was still in the ignition. Somebody, Brulotte thought, had gone to an awful lot of trouble to dump a nearly new car and was trying to make identification of the owner as difficult as possible. All that was left were a couple of audiocassettes in the well by the driver's seat. Either the car had been stolen and then ditched, Brulotte thought, or the owner had simply abandoned it for some unexplained reason.

Brulotte copied the VIN (vehicle identification number) of the Jetta from the plate on the dashboard and then drove to his office in the town hall on South Street. It was just after eight in the morning. He began making calls, one to the Massachusetts motor vehicle bureau, another to the national registry of stolen cars. He waited. The reports came back. Nobody in Massachusetts had ever registered a car with that VIN, and there were no reports of that particular car on the stolen car computers.

Brulotte drove the twenty-odd miles into Greenfield, the closest city of any size, and went to the local Volkswagen dealer. Was there any way, he asked, to find out about a car through its VIN? There was indeed. "They apparently have an elaborate computer system," he recalled, "where they could tell where this car was last serviced and who owned it by the VIN number." The dealer punched the number in, and what came back were the name and number of a Connecticut leasing agency. Brulotte called. He was told that the car had been leased by a company in Waterbury, Athena Health Care Associates.

It was a little after ten in the morning when Brulotte called Waterbury.

"It sounds like one of our cars," Zaccaro told him. "It sounds like Joyce Aparo's car."

How, Brulotte asked, could he reach this Joyce Aparo? Zaccaro gave him her phone number in Glastonbury.

But, Zaccaro said, he didn't really think Brulotte would have much success if he called it, though he certainly ought to try. Athena people had been calling for the last hour and hadn't gotten anything but unanswered rings. There was, though, somebody who might know where Joyce was, her teenage daughter, Karin. In all likelihood Karin was in Rowayton, staying with her violin teacher, Albert Markov. Karin, a promising violinist, or at least that's what her mother told everyone, had been studying with Markov for the past year at the Manhattan School of Music in New York and since the end of the term in June had been spending much time at the Markov home in Rowayton, taking private lessons. Joyce had left the Markovs' number with Athena in case of emergency. Zaccaro passed that number along to the Bernardston police chief.

What Zaccaro didn't tell Brulotte, though, was his immediate reaction to the news that the Jetta had been abandoned. Damn it, he thought, Joyce had hired somebody to steal the car and dump it somewhere. Or maybe she had even done it herself and was now making her way back to Connecticut. Ever since her accident she had been complaining about the car. It didn't run right. The people who had fixed it had done a terrible job. Every time she got into the car she told them that she was afraid something was going to happen. It had become a lemon, she said, and she had asked Athena's lawyer, R. Jeffrey Sands, to look into the state's lemon law to see if somehow the car could be turned back. She didn't want that Jetta anymore, she had told Zaccaro several times. Could he please arrange for her to get another one? She had even asked both Zaccaro and Sands about the insurance on the car, whether it would cover a replacement if the Jetta were stolen. That, thought Zaccaro, familiar with the way Joyce Aparo's mind worked, must be what was behind all this.

He called Jeff Sands at his office in Hartford's prestigious law firm of Wiggin & Dana and recounted the morning events. "Do you think," he asked, "that maybe Joyce took the car up there and ditched it and maybe she's making her way back here somehow or other and then she's going to report it to the police? Do you think that could be it?"

"Yeah," Sands said. "It must be some crazy stunt like that to dump the car and collect on the insurance. That would be just like Joyce."

After Chief Brulotte got no answer at the Aparo number, he dialed again. This time he dialed the number of the Glastonbury Police Department.

It was a little after ten in the morning when Officer Keith O'Brien of the Glastonbury police got a call from the dispatcher. He was to proceed to 3 Butternut Drive in the town's Milestone Commons, an area of culs-de-sac that had been developed over recent years into a number of moderately expensive town house condominiums. There he was to check on the whereabouts of a Joyce Aparo. O'Brien reached the condominium a few minutes later, went to the front door and knocked. Nobody answered. He called in the news, or lack of it, then waited while the desk officer tried to phone the Aparo number. After a dozen rings he hung up and radioed O'Brien that obviously nobody was home. O'Brien left a note in the mailbox asking Mrs. Aparo to call police headquarters when she returned, and then he drove back to headquarters.

An hour and a half later, just after noon, Lieutenant David Caron, who headed the town's police patrol unit, told O'Brien to go back to Butternut Drive and try again. There was still nobody home. Officer O'Brien tried the front door. It was unlocked. He walked inside. The five-room apartment was empty. He made a cursory search. To his eye, nothing seemed out of place. One of the two bedrooms, containing a four-poster bed with a frilly canopy, desk, dressers and bookcase cluttered with photographs, papers and stuffed animals and dolls, was undisturbed. The bed was made; everything was as neat and orderly as what was obviously a teenager's room could reasonably be expected to be. In the other bedroom the bed was unmade, obviously having been slept in, the sheets tousled. The bed had been shoved away from the wall, and a blanket and several pillows were on the floor beside it. Perhaps, O'Brien reasoned, that was the way the woman liked to sleep. He went to the phone and called Caron to report what he had observed. Caron decided he wanted to take a look for himself and told O'Brien to hang around till he got there.

Ten minutes later Caron arrived. Together, they wandered about the apartment. Like the front door, the sliding glass doors on the north side, facing onto Griswold Street, a main thoroughfare in that part of town, though hardly a heavily traveled one, were unlocked. The policemen looked in Joyce Aparo's bedroom again. They glanced about the living room; on the coffee table were a ten-dollar bill and a Texaco gasoline credit card, a concert program and some other papers. On the floor between the kitchen and the living room were some garbage bags, the open box the bags had come in and a blue, orange and yellow afghan that, they later learned, Joyce Aparo had crocheted. "It was strange the way the bedroom was," O'Brien says, "the bed unmade and shoved away from the wall, pillows on the floor, things like that, but to tell the truth, my curiosity was not piqued."

Finished with their search, finding nothing to indicate to them that anything untoward might have happened there, O'Brien and Caron left the apartment and locked the door behind them. Back at the station, Caron called Brulotte in Bernardston and reported to the police chief that there was nothing suspicious at the Aparo residence.

About eleven-thirty, with still no news of Joyce Aparo, Mike Zaccaro dialed the Markovs' number in Rowayton. It was not something he wanted to do; he had no desire to alarm sixteen-year-old Karin. Albert Markov answered. Karin Aparo was indeed there. She took the phone. She had been with the Markovs since the previous Friday, she told Zaccaro. She and her mother had driven down from Glastonbury at the start of the weekend, had gone to a party at one of Athena's nursing homes in Greenwich and then driven with the Markovs to Binghamton, New York, where the Markovs' twenty-four-year-old son, Alex, a violinist with a growing international reputation, gave a weekend concert. They had driven back from Binghamton late on Monday night, reaching the Markov home at about four on Tuesday morning. Joyce was up early and had left in her Jetta about eight-thirty to check on a new nursing home in Old Saybrook and from there had driven back to Glastonbury. Karin had stayed on in Rowayton. She had originally intended to return home Tuesday, but Joyce had told her to stay over an extra day. She and her mother had spoken over the phone at about six and then again about eight or nine on Tuesday evening and everything had seemed normal. When Zaccaro told Karin about the car, she said she had no idea why or how it might have come to rest in northern Massachusetts. As for her mother, she had no idea where she might be. She seemed only moderately concerned.

Just before twelve, only minutes after Zaccaro's call, Karin placed one herself, to the Tallwoods Country Club in Hebron, a few miles southeast of Glastonbury, where her boyfriend of the past year, nineteen-year-old Dennis Coleman, was spending the summer working as a short-order cook at the concession stand. Later she said the reason she called him was that he lived in Glastonbury and she thought he might have heard something. Dennis told a different story about the reason for that series of calls and what was said between them.

Karin never told Dennis that she had also been called by Chief Brulotte and that she had repeated to him the story she'd given Zaccaro before giving a description of her mother.

About two-thirty that afternoon an eleven-year-old boy was walking his dog along Route 10, Bald Mountain Road, in Bernardston. As they neared a small bridge over the Fall

River, the dog suddenly began tugging at the leash, trying to break loose and race down the slope under the bridge. There was something lying there just at the edge of the river. The boy, holding the leash, let himself be dragged down the slope. He got about twenty feet from that something when he stopped. It was a body. He didn't stay long enough to find out anything more. He turned and raced up the slope, ran home and told his stepfather of his discovery. The stepfather called Chief Brulotte and described the scene.

The chief got into his car and headed for the river. When he reached it, there was nothing to be seen. Wrong bridge. He drove another half mile, to a second bridge over the river. This was the right bridge.

On the riverbank under it, covered with some leaves and brush, was the body of a dark-haired woman in her mid-forties. She had on only a nightgown, one shoulder strap dangling low on her arm. There were bruises all over her body, some apparently from a struggle before she died. There were abrasions and a layer of dirt coating her arms, legs and body, obviously from her having been dragged across rough ground to this spot. Her face was bloated as well as badly bruised, nearly unrecognizable. She had been strangled, and the panty hose used to garrote her were still wrapped tightly around her neck. Stuffed in her mouth was a yellow paper towel. Later, when they moved the body, the investigators found a gray work glove.

Murder was something far outside Peter Brulotte's experience. No one could remember the village's last killing. Indeed, there were few crimes of any kind that took place in Bernardston, perhaps a burglary now and then, or some kids smoking marijuana, or someone going too fast or driving while drunk or parking too long. That was about it.

Bernardston was a middle- and upper-middle class community of private houses, the residents sleeping there at night, going off during the day to well-paying jobs in Greenfield, Amherst, perhaps even as far as Northampton. They enjoyed the good and secure life in a rural countryside near the Fall and Connecticut rivers, far from the dangers of urban society.

Still, Brulotte knew what was expected of him. He called the medical examiner. He put police tape around the crime scene, sealing it off. He examined the area carefully and thoroughly. The only things he found were the sneaker prints of the eleven-year-old who had come upon the body and the scuffling marks of the boy's dog because the early-morning rain had washed away whatever other marks there might have been.

Returning to his office, Brulotte called the investigative branch of the Massachusetts State Police. And then he made the connection. He had an abandoned car leased to a Connecticut woman in her forties named Joyce Aparo. He had found the body of a woman in her forties who had been murdered about a mile and a half from the abandoned car. He had his dispatcher call the Glastonbury police to tell them the latest news.

That was the end of Brulotte's connection with the case. Investigators from the Massachusetts State Police arrived on the scene soon after his message reached them. He gave them what information he had, and then they took charge. They had experience with this kind of thing and he didn't, and he was just as glad to have them in command. He went back to his normal duties of keeping the peace in his small town.

As the small boy and his dog were stumbling on a body under the Fall River bridge in Bernardston, about seventy miles to the south the Glastonbury police were beginning to take some action of their own. What they knew for certain was that a woman of the town was missing and her car had been found in a brook in another state. Lieutenant Thomas McKee called the Markov house in Rowayton and spoke to Karin Aparo. He told her it would help in the investigation of her missing mother if she would return to Glastonbury as

soon as possible, come directly to police headquarters on
Main Street and not go to the condo. She said she'd be there
as soon as she could find a ride.

An hour later it was no longer a missing person's case.
Now there was a body, and if the growing conviction of
authorities in both Massachusetts and Connecticut was confirmed, that body was Joyce Aparo and the case was murder. The Glastonbury police were certainly more
experienced in dealing with crime, even an occasional violent crime, than Brulotte. The department was considered
one of the best trained, best financed and best staffed in the
state. Its commanders knew precisely what to do. They sent
cops out to the Aparo condo to make sure all the doors and
windows were locked, that the premises were sealed, that
the area was ringed with yellow police tape marking it a
crime scene. Then three cops stationed themselves around
the condo, keeping guard, making sure nobody entered,
while other officers began to canvass the neighborhood to
see if anybody had seen or heard anything out of the ordinary, anything suspicious during the previous night.

Still, murder was not an everyday occurrence in Glastonbury, and there was an immediate understanding that
more experienced help would be needed. The place to turn
was the Connecticut State Police and its major crimes squad.

Detective James Cavanaugh, a large, burly twenty-
one-year veteran of the State Police, seventeen years of
which had been spent investigating murder and other major
felonies, and his partner, Detective Charles Revoir, were
enjoying their day off. They were playing golf, were just
putting out on the fifth hole when Cavanaugh's beeper went
off.

They holed out and then made for the clubhouse. Cavanaugh called in. A woman had been murdered and her
body found in Massachusetts, he was told, and although
positive identification had not yet been made, it was as-

sumed that she was the Connecticut woman who had been reported missing earlier that day. From this moment on the Aparo murder was Cavanaugh's case. Over the next days he would be in Massachusetts for the autopsy, would be traveling around the Northeast, tracking down leads and interviewing the possible witnesses and suspects, while Charlie Revoir would hold down the command post in Glastonbury.

About five-thirty in the afternoon Trooper Dave Kenney of the Massachusetts State Police called Michael Zaccaro. "They wanted a description of Joyce, what she looked like and that kind of thing," he remembers. "I gave it to them. Then they told me they'd found a body that matched the description, and was there any family that could come up and identify the body? I didn't even know then that Joyce had other family in Connecticut. I said the only family that I know of is her daughter, Karin, and she's sixteen. They said that wouldn't do, and they told me I'd have to come up myself and identify the body."

With his partner Ed Giamelli and Phil Murray, the husband of another Athena partner, Ann Marie Murray, Zaccaro set out for Greenfield, where the body had been taken. "We were driving along, and we were in Northampton, about a half hour south of Greenfield. It had been raining, but up ahead it was clear, and the sun had dropped down below the clouds. Now I know this sounds kind of hokey and made up, but honest to God, it really happened. We had a bright sun ahead of us and rain between us and the sun, and all of a sudden there was this huge, beautiful rainbow in the sky. By this time we were positive Joyce was dead. The description I had given matched the body they had perfectly. So we looked at each other, the three of us, and we looked at the rainbow and we said, 'This is for Joyce.' "

The three men reached the hospital in Greenfield a little after eight that night. Zaccaro was led back to the morgue. "It was unpleasant," he says, "which is an understatement, not so much because I didn't recognize her as because she was bloated, disfigured, very beat up. They showed us the body exactly as they found it. Not where it was, of course. It was lying on a slab, but the stocking was still around her neck, her face was bloated, a paper towel was stuck in her mouth with pieces hanging out and she was bloody, black and blue, she was dirty. You could see everything that had happened to Joyce that night.''

Zaccaro made the identification.

Karin Aparo got her ride. Albert Markov drove her up from Rowayton. Though McKee had told her not to stop at the condo, she ignored the request and had Markov drive her there. They arrived about five in the afternoon. There were three cops standing on the lawn outside the condo, and the area was surrounded by yellow tape. Karin and Markov started out of the car, but the cops stopped them. Karin introduced herself and Markov explained that he was her violin teacher. They had stopped, Karin told them, to pick up her ulcer medicine and to see about her cats. The cops said that they couldn't go into the condo, that they were to go directly to police headquarters. One of the cats appeared from somewhere, ran up to Karin, and she picked it up and hugged it. The cops sympathized but said there was nothing they could do. They had to obey orders, and she should, too. Though she later said that one of the main reasons she had driven to the condo was that she thought that there she might hear some news about her mother, she did not ask what the three cops were doing around her home, did not ask if anybody had heard about her mother, and the cops volunteered nothing.

They returned to the car, and Albert Markov drove to police headquarters, where they arrived at about six. He stayed for a few minutes and then drove back to Rowayton, leaving Karin alone.

The initial interview with the Glastonbury cops was a tentative one. Though they were pretty sure the body in

Massachusetts was that of Joyce Aparo, nobody had any desire to tell the victim's daughter that her mother had been murdered. They decided to wait for more positive identification. What Caron, who talked to Karin while a civilian secretary, a blond, heavyset woman in her thirties, Beverly Warga, took notes (she was present as well because of the department's policy that no woman is ever questioned by a male officer without another woman being present), seemed most interested in at that moment was information about Joyce's movements since the last time Karin had heard from her, the night before, and a detailed description of Joyce. Karin filled him in, though, when it came to a description, she later said, "I lied to them about her weight. I thought my mother would be pretty upset if she ever read my statement and saw that I'd told them how much she weighed." When she finished her statement, Karin asked if she could go to the condo. Her ulcers were acting up, she said, and she needed her medication. Lieutenant McKee, who was then the head of the department's detective division, vetoed the request. He didn't want anybody going there, but if she would tell him what kind of medication she needed, he would have a local pharmacy send over the prescription. She told him.

The initial interview over, Caron left the office. One of the things he was going to do was call up to Massachusetts and relay the description Karin had given. Alone with Warga, Karin asked if she could use the phone. Warga motioned to one on a desk three or four feet away and went on typing some notes. Karin made two calls. The first was to her father, Michael Aparo. He and Joyce Aparo had been divorced for more than ten years; he was remarried, living in nearby Hartford and working for the city's Catholic Charities. Karin had not seen much of him over recent years, had, in fact, not even seen him at all since the previous summer; the divorce had not been amicable, and Aparo's second wife, with her own children to raise, was not overly fond of the child of her husband's first, failed marriage.

Nevertheless, Michael Aparo was Karin's closest relative and the one she should naturally have turned to in this crisis.

When Karin told him what had happened, he said he would drive over to Glastonbury to be with her. He arrived at headquarters at about six-thirty.

Karin then phoned Dennis Coleman. It was a short call merely to let him know that she was in town. She told him she was still at the police station, that the police had sealed her apartment, she had no place to stay that night. Could she stay with him, and would he come down to the station to pick her up? He said he would. She said she would let him know when she was finished. "I didn't feel comfortable with my dad," Karin later explained, "and I felt comfortable with Dennis."

Everything changed within minutes of Michael Aparo's arrival at police headquarters. Word reached the Glastonbury police that all the descriptions that had been relayed matched the body; there was no doubt that the victim was Joyce Aparo; the positive identification would be only a necessary formality.

It was then time to tell Karin that her mother was dead, murdered. It could not be delayed any longer. McKee and another officer took Karin aside. It was their job, they realized, to break the news. "I didn't know how a person reacts to this news," McKee recalls, "so we prepared ourselves for any type of reaction." But the one they got they were unprepared for. "Karin's only response," he says, "was one tear. Nothing else."

McKee turned to Michael Aparo, who was standing alone at some distance. He told him his first wife was dead. Aparo's reaction was shock. Still, he made no move toward his daughter. She did not approach him, and he did not approach her, and they neither embraced nor sought any comfort from the other. Evidently even tragedy could not bridge the gulf that separated them. When Karin asked McKee if she could leave for her friend's house, Michael Aparo told McKee it was okay with him. The Colemans—

Dennis, his father, Dennis senior, his brother, Matthew, and his stepmother—were good people and good family friends, he said, though McKee had a feeling that in reality, Aparo barely knew them if he knew them at all. But, McKee says, "it was not my place to question it," so he said sure.

On the way out Karin stopped once more in the office, a small room with a couple of desks and chairs and a bench, where Beverly Warga was working. She asked if she could make another phone call, to her friend Dennis. Though there was a public phone nearby, she ignored it. Warga nodded. Karin picked up the phone, dialed the number. Warga, only a few feet away, was transcribing some notes on the hunt for a cat burglar who had been preying on homes in the town over the past several weeks.

"I'm at the police station," Karin began, and then her voice lowered, dropped to a near whisper. That was enough to make Warga pause, strain a little to catch the next words. Warga's manner, the expressions on her face say that over the years she has seen and heard enough that there is little left that shocks her. But over the next few minutes she was deeply shocked. What she began to pick up in that hushed conversation, at least Karin's side of it, compelled Warga, who attempted to keep her face blank, uninterested, to take out a pad and write down what she heard, as much as she could as fast as she could.

For Karin Aparo said to Dennis Coleman, from the phone in the Glastonbury police station, with a police witness sitting only a few feet away, listening and taking down her words: "Where did you do it? . . . Did you hurt your head? . . . That's okay, you were over at the house the night before we left. . . . Don't worry about it. . . . The police said the house was neat, the bed hadn't been slept in. Did you clean up? Did you make the bed? Do you know if Chris did it? The police don't think it was a cat burglar. . . . Don't worry about it. I'll get you a psychiatrist. Don't forget, I'm going to be a psychiatrist. . . . Think about something else. I'll be there soon to take care of you."

According to Warga's notes, the phrases "Don't worry about it . . . I'll be there soon . . . I'll take care of you" were repeated several times.

Finally the call was over. Karin turned away, went to her father, and together they left police headquarters.

Hardly were they out the door before Beverly Warga accosted Lieutenants McKee and Caron and told them what she had overheard. McKee decided that maybe they ought to have another little talk with Karin Aparo and with this boyfriend, Dennis Coleman. Without waiting for orders, Caron was on his way out the door, only a few minutes behind Michael Aparo and his daughter. By the time he reached the Coleman house, Aparo had already departed. Michael Aparo, showing little concern that his daughter, her mother just murdered, was planning to spend the night at the home of her boyfriend, had simply dropped Karin off and then driven back to Hartford.

Inside the Coleman house Karin and Dennis were off to the side of the living room in intense, hushed conversation when Caron entered. He approached. There were, he said, some questions that had come up as a result of the phone conversation that had been overheard by Beverly Warga. Would Karin and Dennis be willing to return to police headquarters to clear up what might be just a misunderstanding? They agreed.

Over the next four hours the police alternately and separately questioned Karin and Dennis and for much of the time simply left them alone together in the office with Beverly Warga. The two sat together, Karin holding Dennis's hand, as though somehow comforting or consoling him, Warga thought, and they talked, sometimes in whispers, sometimes in more normal voices, sometimes to each other and at times including Warga. Some of what they said was inconsequential, about movies, about Dennis's playing bass in a rock band with some friends, about cars, about other things. "This," Warga remembers, "was just small talk."

But there was more that to Warga was anything but small talk. It seemed so filled with implications, as potentially incriminating and portentous as the phone conversation, that Warga once more took out her pad and surreptitiously noted down words and phrases, some that to her seemed to have particularly crucial meaning, some that were merely enigmatic.

Several times Karin repeated the questions and the phrases she had used during the phone conversation. And there was more.

Dennis was rubbing the back of his head. Karin asked if it was all right. "You banged it on the table at my house when you went in to feed the cats, isn't that right?"

"No," Dennis responded, "I banged it on the stove at work."

When Karin asked the question again, she seemed to have picked up on his explanation.

Karin kept looking at Dennis's hand. "I hope your hand is going to be all right," she said.

"It'll be okay," Dennis said. Then he explained to Warga that one of Karin's cats had bitten it when he had been putting out food over the weekend, though when the subject came up again, he said the cat had scratched it, and yet another time he said he caught his hand in a door.

Karin mentioned something about Dennis's not being able to ski. Warga noted how shocked Dennis seemed, that he turned to her and said that he had been skiing since he was seven.

At one point Karin turned to Warga and said, "I hope the Markovs don't call while we're here. Dennis is very jealous of Alex, you know." Dennis made no comment.

Periodically the police—Caron, McKee, other Glastonbury officers and the first state cops to arrive—took Karin and Dennis off for some separate private conversations.

Those conversations, lasting in spurts until nearly one in the morning, got precisely nowhere. Both Karin and Dennis had ready explanations for everything Warga had overheard, explanations that confirmed what each was saying, explanations that some of the cops on reflection thought sounded rehearsed.

There was, of course, no way she could know anything about her mother's murder, Karin said. After all, she had been far away at the time, in Rowayton.

Dennis, too, insisted that he knew nothing, that he had first learned of Joyce Aparo's disappearance and then her murder from Karin. He had spent the previous evening, he told the police, with some friends, including a guy named Frank Manganaro. He had returned to his own home about eleven-thirty and gone to bed. He had gotten up in the morning at the usual time in order to be at his job at the Tallwoods Country Club by seven. As for the conversation with Karin overheard by Beverly Warga, it was really quite innocent. Yes, he had been in and out of the Aparo condo over the weekend, but that was because both Karin and Joyce had asked him to look after the place and feed their cats while they were away. He had let himself in because he had a key. Karin had made one for him several months before. That was what Karin had meant on the phone when she asked whether he had done it. And he had mentioned to Karin that at some point he had bumped his head and she was inquiring if it was serious and if it was all right. And yes, he had hurt his hand; Karin had two cats, and one of them was constantly disappearing and wasn't all that friendly anyway, and that cat had appeared and bitten him when he was putting out the food over the weekend. That's all there was to it. When the police asked Dennis about Karin's relations with her mother, he said that while they had their disagreements, as did all parents and their children, they had not been serious, and there was no terrible trouble between them.

In her separate interviews Karin told the police just about the same things, sometimes even using the same words and phrases.

The police may have had their suspicions at this point,

but that was all. They had nothing but suspicion to go on. For one thing, they weren't even sure where Joyce Aparo had been murdered. The best guess was that she must have been killed in Glastonbury, strangled in her own bed sometime during the night; the fact that she was wearing only a nightgown when her body was discovered would point to that. But then, again, it was possible that she had been abducted, driven to Bernardston and killed there. If so, the question that loomed was why.

What seemed certain, though, was that at least two people, and two cars, had to be directly involved, certainly if Joyce had been murdered in Glastonbury. Her car had been driven north to the Massachusetts-Vermont-New Hampshire border, where her body had been dragged to its resting place beneath the Fall River bridge, and the car dumped down the slope into the stream a mile and a half away. Unless the killer was from Bernardston itself (but, if so, how had he gotten to Connecticut?), he had somehow had to make his way back south in the middle of the night, and the only way that would have been possible was if there had been somebody else along in a second car to drive him. Karin had a solid alibi. The Markovs could attest to her presence at their home in Rowayton. Dennis seemed to have one, too; it was a long trip from Glastonbury to Bernardston and back, and unless there indeed had been someone else in another car, someone else involved in the murder, there was just no way he could have made that round trip and been at work by seven the next morning.

Anyway, who could suspect these two teenagers, or either one of them, of committing a murder, and a terrible one at that, not a sudden killing in the momentary heat of passion, but a murder by strangulation, a murder that must have taken long, agonizing minutes, during which the victim had to have fought desperately and violently for her life? These two were the kids next door, children of the upwardly mobile middle class, wanting for little.

Tall, slim, red-haired, freckle-faced Dennis Coleman,

son of an old Glastonbury family, was the kind of boy, Connecticut State's Attorney John Bailey said later, that you'd want your daughter to bring home. He was good-looking and personable, a smart boy, with an IQ of 137, a boy who could get by in school without cracking a book, a young man talented in music, something of a prodigy with computers, in love with the outdoors, a skier, a sailor, an expert woodsman who spent long hours carving trails and campsites in forests. He was a child of affluence, his father, Dennis senior, being head of his own prosperous computer consulting firm, where young Dennis worked part-time during the school year and on vacations until after a dispute with his father he had left and found the job at the country club. Though the junior Dennis Coleman had not gone on to college after graduating from high school the year before, had instead initially gone to work as a computer programmer for one of Hartford's ubiquitous insurance companies, he was now planning to go on with his education. In August he was to start at Central Connecticut State University in nearby New Britain. He already had his books and his student ID card. For him, the future seemed limited only by what he would make of it.

And what about Karin Aparo? Except for a little more than a year when she was twelve, she had lived in Glastonbury since the age of five. She was small, only a little over five feet. At the time, beset by the hormonal changes that afflict so many teenagers as they turn from children into adolescents and then into adults, their bodies developing in spurts at no predictable rate, she was a little plump and a little buxom and very concerned about her weight, unaware and unconvinced that before long the baby fat would vanish. She had short dark hair, deep brown eyes, often concealed, or magnified, behind large glasses, and though there was a sharpness about her features, she was, most people agreed, an attractive teenager. And she was bright, brighter than most, people who knew her said; her mind was, at least intellectually, on a par with Dennis's, her IQ 131. If she was a little standoffish, that was perhaps understandable, too, for she was talented, her mother having predicted for years that one day she would make her mark as a concert violinist, and driving her toward that goal. After hearing her play, especially after hearing tapes Joyce said that Karin made, many people agreed. Besides, Karin was hardly more than a child, just entering her junior year at Glastonbury High School. But there was something about her, a sexual aura, that affected men of all ages who came into her orbit. One of the cops who interviewed her that first day and later says, "You spent a couple of hours with that girl and you wanted to jump her bones." Still, she was little more than a child, and she may have been unaware of the effect she had on men.

Perhaps, then, it was all as innocent as they said. It would be incomprehensible to suspect these two not just of murder but of premeditated murder.

At one-thirty in the morning, Joyce Aparo then dead for some twenty-four hours, the questioning of nineteen-year-old Dennis Coleman and sixteen-year-old Karin Aparo, the daughter of the murdered woman, ended. A cop drove them back to the Coleman house. They went to bed together in Dennis's room. Karin later said it was the first time they had slept together in that bed in that house through the night. Over the past year they had made love eighty times. That night they only shared the same bed.

2

Murder didn't happen in Glastonbury. Somewhere else, maybe, in some inner city, some congested urban pressure cooker. But not in Glastonbury. There were crimes, certainly, just as there were everywhere. Indeed, at this very moment in the summer of 1987 the cat burglar Beverly Warga was concerned about was on the loose, preying on unguarded homes in the night. And there was "Benji the Pillow Case Bandit" on his own burglary spree. Both, especially the cat burglar, were the major concerns of the town's police force; extra cars were on patrol every night, cruising the quiet dark streets, stopping and questioning any pedestrian out too late, checking any strange car parked in a residential area. There was, too, as in every city and town across the nation, a drug problem, especially among the young, and there had been a couple of drug busts in recent months, but in Glastonbury most adults were sure drugs were less prevalent than in many another suburb. They were wrong, and the police and the school authorities were aware of it and were dealing directly with the issue with a variety of programs.

But crimes of violence? Murder? Not in Glastonbury, or if in Glastonbury, the crime must have been committed by some outsider who had invaded this safe suburban enclave. Never by a native and certainly not by the protected children of the town.

For Glastonbury was the quintessential, the idealized New England suburb, the dream town of both residents and real estate brokers showing their white clients, those willing and able to pay from $150,000 to $1 million and more for a house, a place to live and bring up their children untouched by the afflictions that beset much of the nation: pervasive drugs, violent crime, racial unrest and so much more. Though Glastonbury was less than a half hour's drive from the center of Hartford, the state capital that, in recent years, had become one of the most poverty-stricken and crime-ridden cities in the Northeast, it was as though the town somehow existed on another planet or in another time.

Its roots were far in the past, its old streets laid out in the seventeenth and early eighteenth centuries. Its oldest homes dated from before the Revolution. Glastonbury had been settled in 1638, only two years after the Reverend Thomas Hooker and 110 members of his congregation had left the Massachusetts Bay Colony, traveled south and established the first permanent settlements on the Connecticut River in what became Hartford, Windsor and Wethersfield. Some of the Wethersfield pioneers, resenting the strict rules of the Hooker congregation and seeing fertile land on the eastern side of the river, broke away and formed their own community on thirty-four parcels they bought from the local Indians. The colonists called their new town Glastonbury, after the place in England where many had been born.

The town prospered, as both an agricultural center and the site of some small industries—a cotton mill, a paper mill, a soap mill, a tannery, a silver firm and, most important in those early days, the Stocking Gunpowder Factory, a major supplier of gunpowder to George Washington's revolutionary army. But industry gradually vanished as the Industrial Revolution took root and factories moved closer to urban centers and the railroads. Glastonbury lapsed into a sleepy agricultural backwater, a place where residents of Hartford, East Hartford and surrounding communities went during the summer to buy local corn, tomatoes, berries and other fresh produce, and cider made from locally grown apples, often crossing the river on the Glastonbury Ferry, which made its first passage in 1655 and continues to run to this day, at least in good weather, and is now the oldest ferry service in continuous operation in the United States.

By the end of the 1950s there were only about eight thousand people in the town, and it had changed little from early days; in 1959, for instance, it was still governed, as it had been since 1692, by the town meeting. But radical change was at hand. Suddenly new highways were laid down, and bridges built across the Connecticut River, bringing Hartford with its insurance companies and other growing communities with their factories within an easy commute. As Glastonbury turned from an agricultural enclave into a bedroom community, home to the growing middle and upper middle classes, the town meeting vanished, replaced by a nonpartisan town manager, appointed by an elected nine-member town council (more often than not with a six to three Republican majority, though registered voters have over the years been about evenly balanced among Republicans, Democrats and independents). Over the next quarter century the population tripled, soaring to more than twenty-four thousand by the mid-1980s, and townspeople predicted that by the turn of the decade they would be joined by another thirty-five hundred people.

But that growth has hardly reflected the demographic

image of America at large. Glastonbury is lily white—in the mid-1980s, 97 percent white, in fact, with a mere 107 blacks, most of them servants, and 365 "others," the others representing an influx of increasingly prosperous Asians. Of the fourteen religious congregations, one is Jewish, two are Catholic, though the Catholic population has grown steadily, and the other eleven are various Protestant denominations.

The median family income in the early 1980s was more than thirty-one thousand dollars; by 1990, according to estimates, it was close to forty thousand dollars. And there is a car not just for every family but for almost every citizen—more than twenty-one thousand cars registered in the mid-1980s.

The town is hardly overbuilt, and if town planners have their way, it never will be; 70 percent of the 468 square miles of land remains undeveloped, much of it heavily wooded parks and state forests where building is forbidden or strictly limited. Multiple dwellings—a scattering of apartments and condominiums, all in the moderately high to high price range—account for a mere 2 percent of the housing, though, in a bow to contemporary pressures, there are now plans for a few residences for senior citizens. The rest are single-family houses, built according to strict zoning regulations that divide the town into three distinct areas: In the most densely populated areas, the rules call for no more than 3.2 families per acre, a second area mandates one house per acre, and the third requires that houses must be built on lots of two acres or more. Where any industry is permitted, it is strictly light, and it is contained in industrial parks on the outskirts.

Glastonbury has from its earliest days prided itself on educational excellence (Noah Webster, creator of Webster's dictionary, began his teaching career in the town, and during the Revolutionary War Yale University relocated its junior and senior classes to Glastonbury). Today the town's budget for schools is one of the highest in the state. The result: About

75 percent of the high school graduates go on to college.

And so for those who settled in this town with all its privileges and all its protective veneer, the idea of murder, deliberate and cold-blooded, was unthinkable.

But it had happened. What was worse, according to rumors that spread quickly in the first days, the murderer was not an outsider but one of those children of affluence.

Early on Thursday morning, the day after the murder, Detective Cavanaugh drove up to the morgue in Springfield, Massachusetts, where Joyce Aparo's body had been moved during the night. He was there to observe the autopsy. It was a thing he had done perhaps eighty times over the years. It was not something in which he took any particular pleasure; it was a job. Besides, most of the other state cops who had moved in on the case during the previous day had been up most of the night while Cavanaugh, the man in charge, had made the assignments and then gone home to bed. He was fresh, the others were not, so he had gone up to the autopsy.

As he stood to one side, watching, the body bag used to move Joyce Aparo was unzipped. He took a photograph. For the next three hours, as the Massachusetts medical examiner, Dr. Peter Adams, painstakingly went over the body, Cavanaugh took more photographs and gathered bits of evidence, including the ragged yellow paper towel that had been stuffed into Joyce Aparo's mouth, and the single gray work glove, now coated with grime and debris, that had been found beneath her body. Then he drove back to Glastonbury, to the command post that had been set up at the Naubuc Elementary School to coordinate the joint investigation by the state and local police, to take charge.

The cops returned to search the Aparo condominium, more thoroughly and carefully this time. Things they had passed over during the previous visits now took on a special meaning. For example, they looked at the rumpled bed shoved away from the wall, with three pillows and a blanket on the floor beside it, another pillow on the bed. The killer must have shoved the bed away from the wall during the struggle, had perhaps used the pillows to smother and stifle his victim's cries. Flung haphazardly across a chair in the bedroom was a nightgown sash that matched the gown Joyce Aparo was wearing when she was found.

As they had noted earlier, in the living room, on top of a coffee table, was a ten-dollar bill and a Texaco gasoline credit card. That nobody had picked up the cash and card seemed to rule out robbery.

On the floor near the bedroom door was an empty box of Glad garbage bags; most of the bags lay on the floor between the living room and kitchen, on either side of a multicolored afghan. Had the killer tried to remove the body in one of those large bags? The forensic laboratory later did a test to see. Perhaps the killer had tried, but if so, he had failed, for the weight of a body ripped open the bottom of the bag. Joyce Aparo's body would have slid right through. Under the sink in the kitchen was an empty roll of paper towels; tests showed that the towel found in Joyce Aparo's mouth had come from that roll, had been the last one on it.

During their search they made only a cursory sweep of Karin's bedroom. But, then, it would have taken hours to search that cluttered room, filled as it was with the treasures of an adolescent. The tops of a high dresser and a bookcase were invisible beneath a menagerie of stuffed animals—teddy bears, pandas, giraffes and more—hats and books and papers. On a low dresser they found a stack of photographs, some of Karin alone, some of Karin with a young man; the young man was not Dennis Coleman. Another photograph of that same young man, Alex Markov, violin nestled beneath his chin, rested against the mirror over that dresser. One bookcase was filled with books and sheets of music, violin scores. The shelves over the desk contained dolls, more stuffed animals and a couple of photographs, most prominent among them a framed one, autographed to Karin, of Archbishop John Whealon, the head of the Hartford archdiocese of the Roman Catholic Church. In a drawer of a bedside table they came upon a couple of books, diaries. Revoir skimmed them. In that quick search, in that cluttered room, they found nothing they thought had any bearing on the case.

If at this point, on the second day, the police had a suspect, they weren't telling anyone. What they were saying was that there were no leads.

Dennis Coleman later said that once they reached his room after their hours at the police station, he and Karin had talked for a long time in the darkness before falling asleep. At that moment he was sure the police had targeted him as a suspect.

Karin Aparo later said that they had gone to sleep almost immediately, had talked not at all.

Dennis was up a little after six and off for his job at the Tallwoods Country Club before seven. Karin, he said, was still asleep when he left the house.

Karin later said that she was up with Dennis, that they had a brief conversation then, that he gave her the keys to his Triumph Spitfire sports car, telling her that she could use it that day and that he would be back after two.

By seven-fifteen Karin had begun making telephone calls. Both Dennis Coleman, Sr., and his wife, Carol, had already left for their own jobs. Only Dennis's younger brother, Matt, was still in the house.

She called her best friend, Shannon Dubois, a girl her own age whom she had known since third grade, a classmate at Glastonbury High School, a tall, pretty girl with short blondish hair who looks like everybody's idea of the girl next door. It was then seven-fifteen in the morning.

Shannon remembers that Karin's voice on the phone was nervous and upset when she said hello. Shannon asked, "What's the matter? What's worrying you?"

Karin said, "My mother was found murdered last night. I need you. I'm at Dennis's. Can you come over right away?"

Shannon said that of course, she would, but somebody would have to pick her up.

Karin said she'd ask Dennis's brother, Matt, whom Shannon had been dating, to drive over and get her. When Shannon told her parents what had happened, they told her that if Karin wanted, she could stay with them until other arrangements had been made.

Next, Karin phoned Archbishop Whealon, at his private number. She had known and been extremely close to him all her life; he had a very special relationship with her and with the Aparo family. She reached him, told him her mother had been murdered and asked if he would conduct the service at the funeral. It was a strange request, for Joyce Aparo was a divorced woman, had almost never attended church, was at odds with the church and had attempted to prevent Karin from practicing her religion. And presiding over funerals was a thing the archbishop no longer did. The last funeral he had conducted was for the late governor of Connecticut, Ella Grasso, in 1981. Nevertheless, Archbishop Whealon agreed to preside at the burial of Joyce Aparo and to do whatever he could to help Karin.

She made two more calls then. One was to Michael Zaccaro, telling him she was at the Colemans' and asking him to drive over because she needed his help. He agreed. The other was to Alex Markov, in Rowayton, to tell him what had happened.

When Shannon arrived at the Coleman house a little later, Karin was waiting for her on the lawn outside. About a hundred yards in front of them they could see the Connecticut River sparkling in the summer morning sunlight, and behind the house stretched a large tract of deep, dense woods. Matt went into the house and up to his room. Karin and Shannon stood outside on the lawn and talked. "I said I couldn't imagine who would have done such a thing," Shannon remembers. "Then I asked her where Alex had been when it happened."

Karin said, "He was with me in Rowayton."

Shannon said, "Who could have done it?"

Karin didn't answer immediately. "She was standing there looking down at the ground, and I had this sudden feeling that she knew who had done it," Shannon says. Karin looked up at the Coleman house. Shannon said, "Do you know?"

Karin said, "Yes, I know. It was Dennis."

According to Shannon, she stared at Karin with disbelief and asked how Dennis had done it. Karin told her that Dennis had strangled her mother with a pair of nylons. "I didn't believe her. I didn't want to believe her."

But Karin offered proof. She led Shannon into the house and upstairs to Dennis's room, opened the closet and pulled out a light-colored duffel bag. Karin opened the bag. Shannon looked inside. She saw what looked to her like black clothes and a black ski mask. And then Karin reached inside and pulled out a bright orange leather purse. Shannon recognized it. "I had seen Mrs. Aparo holding it. I was shocked, and then I saw a wallet inside and I pulled it out, and sure enough, Mrs. Aparo's identification was inside it."

Shannon turned and walked out of the room. Karin put everything back into the duffel bag, put the bag back into the closet, and then she and Shannon went back downstairs and out to the lawn. They stood there waiting for Alex Markov to arrive, and while they waited, they talked more, about the murder and about the past.

A car pulled up outside the house. Alex Markov and a friend name Yura got out and walked up to them. Karin greeted them, and immediately she and Markov went into the house and up to Dennis's room, leaving Shannon and Yura alone on the lawn. After a while Markov and Karin reappeared. In one hand Markov was carrying an envelope. Shannon had seen folders like it before; they usually contained musical scores. Markov and his friend went back to their car and drove off; Markov had told them he had to leave because he had to prepare for a concert.

When they were gone, Karin told Shannon that she and Markov had been talking about their future. If things worked out as they hoped, the twenty-four-year-old Markov would become sixteen-year-old Karin Aparo's guardian. Karin wanted them to live together in the Aparo condominium: Markov wanted Karin to live with him in Rowayton.

Alone again, Karin and Shannon discussed what they would do now. "We talked about how we would have to be quiet about the whole thing." It was, Shannon remembers, something they both agreed was a necessity.

About eleven-thirty Michael Zaccaro arrived. With him were two of his Athena partners, Roland Butler and Ann Marie Murray. They went into the house, and Shannon began to prepare lunch for them. While they waited, Karin and Ann Marie Murray went out for a walk. For about a half hour they roamed through the neighborhood, talking. "Karin," Ann Marie Murray says, "was very concerned about her future and where she would live. She mentioned Mike Zaccaro, but Mike was single then, so that was out. We said we would do whatever we could to provide her with a home, and if necessary, she could come and live with me and my husband. Karin wasn't terribly worried about money, though; she told me that there was about three hundred thousand dollars in insurance."

Back at the Coleman house, lunch was ready, and after they had eaten, Karin, Zaccaro, Butler and Murray left to drive into Hartford to meet with Jeff Sands at his office, to try to make some order of the chaos, to begin to deal with Karin's future. Shannon stayed behind to field phone calls.

For about three hours that afternoon the adults—Sands, Zaccaro, Butler and Ann Marie Murray—and the teenager, Karin, gathered in the conference room at Wiggin & Dana. "Karin was very confused," Sands says, "and she had a lot of questions, and we were there to help answer those questions." It was decided then that Zaccaro would serve as executor and Sands as lawyer for the estate.

There were the unpleasant but necessary topics. There were the funeral arrangements. Karin told them she had already spoken to Archbishop Whealon who had agreed to officiate. A funeral home had to be contacted, and the body had to be brought down from Springfield; Sands took care of those things.

Where, Karin asked, was she going to live, and how was she going to pay for everything that had to be paid for? The obvious answer was her father.

Sands called Michael Aparo. "I asked him whether he wanted to be the executor of the estate instead of Mike Zaccaro. He said he didn't. I asked him what kind of arrangements he was going to make for Karin in the interim. He said, 'I want to do everything I can for Karin. Isn't it awful what happened?' He was very supportive in that first phone conversation. Both Mike and I thought she ought to go and stay with him, though Karin wasn't terribly keen on that idea. But after all, he was her father, and he had responsibilities. Then I got a second call from Michael Aparo, and he said, 'She can't come. Because, well, my wife . . .' It was unbelievable. Her dad's new wife didn't want any part of her. I was dumbfounded by it." Karin would stay with the Duboises for a while, but a more permanent place would have to be found. Karin did not mention her own plan to live with Alex Markov or any other plan she might have had in mind.

"She knew that Joyce had life insurance and a will," Sands says, "but she didn't seem to know how much insurance, and she was under the impression that they were in debt, but she seemed to have no idea how deeply in debt." Karin did not repeat the figure for the insurance she'd offered Ann Marie Murray, and Murray did not bring it up.

What Karin did know was that her mother kept her papers in an expandable file that was either in her closet or in a file cabinet in the basement of the condo. But no one was yet permitted to enter the premises, so, Sands says, "we were at a loss at this point." Any decisions would have to wait until the police allowed them to go in and look through the papers. Sands called the police and asked when they could get into the condo, explaining why it was necessary to do so as soon as possible. He was told that they could go in the next day, that Charlie Revoir would meet them there. Revoir wanted to talk to Karin, anyway, wanted her to look around the condo and see if anything was missing, anything present that had not been there before, if anything was not as she remembered it.

As the conference went on, Karin seemed, Sands thought, increasingly pale, distracted and in some shock, and at one point she broke down and began to cry. They gave her time to recover, which she did rather quickly, and then the discussions went on.

Sometime after five it ended. Zaccaro led her down to his car and drove her back to Glastonbury, to the Duboises' house, where she remained for the next three weeks.

In South Glastonbury that afternoon Shannon Dubois, distraught over what she had been told by her best friend, answered phone calls at the Coleman house and waited, for news, for anything.

At some point, she couldn't remember when, Matt Coleman left, and she was alone. About three Dennis arrived home from work. Shannon went out onto the lawn to greet him, and they stood there for a few minutes, "talking about normal things. Then the phone rang, and I answered it. Dennis went upstairs. He was acting weird."

When she finished the call, she went upstairs after him. He was in his room. He looked at her and said, "Do you know what happened?"

Shannon said, "Yes. Karin told me you killed her mother."

Dennis nodded and then told her how he had done it, told her the details that she had already heard earlier that day from Karin.

About five Shannon went home. Karin arrived a little

later and moved into Shannon's room. Through the evening they tried to act as normally as they could, as normally as possible for two teenagers caught in the middle of a murder. But later that night, in Shannon's room, Karin asked, "Did you talk to Dennis today?"

"Yes, and he told me everything." Slowly Shannon repeated the story Dennis had told her.

"Oh," Karin said, "that's what he told me last night."

For a while they talked about what might happen. "There was," Shannon says, "a kind of understanding that we weren't going to say anything to anybody." It was the kind of compact teenagers are forever making, an essential part of that eternal conflict between the generations. Usually, those secrets are of little interest to anybody else, so it matters little when they are held close. This, of course, was a secret of a different kind, a dangerous one with far-reaching consequences, not just for Shannon and Karin but for many others. Still, for Shannon at that moment and probably for Karin, too, there was something unreal about the whole thing. "I couldn't believe it had really happened," Shannon said later. "I didn't want to believe it."

Then Karin went to the phone and called Dennis. "She was consoling him and telling him not to worry," Shannon remembers.

later and moved the exhausted groom. Or, more aggravating, they tried to act as carefully as they could to be as gentle as possible for the least offensive sight in the stadium, a sorry

3

Joyce Aparo had been dead for two days before Karin went home for the first time. A little after ten in the morning Friday, August 7, Susan Dubois dropped her off outside the condo, watched as Karin went up the walk, unlocked the door and went inside. Then she drove away. For fifteen or twenty minutes Karin was alone.

About ten-thirty Jeff Sands arrived, and a few minutes later, Mike Zaccaro and Roland Butler showed up. Over the next half hour they roamed through the apartment and went down to the basement to search the file cabinet Joyce kept there, a cabinet containing mainly a mass of personal letters. It was a filing cabinet the police were never aware existed; they were not told of it, and they did not then or later ever investigate the basement. Back upstairs Karin led

37

Sands, Zaccaro and Butler to a closet in Joyce's bedroom
and pointed to a small valise filled with papers—insurance
policies, will, title for the condominium, mortgage papers
and more. In a dresser drawer in that room, they came upon
an American Express card and a number of bills, including
an American Express bill that contained a notation about
payments for American Express life insurance. Sands and
Zaccaro took all those papers, sat on the bed and began to
go through them. "Up to that moment," Sands said, "we
thought that what with the debts there wouldn't be much of
an estate." Now they discovered that there was indeed an
estate, and it was not small. There was a group insurance
policy on Joyce's life taken out by Athena and valued at
about $50,000 and the American Express life insurance
worth another $55,000, and both were increased by indem-
nity clauses in case of accidental death. Perhaps most important of all, among the papers they found a credit life
insurance policy that paid off the mortgage on the condo,
leaving the title free and clear. Mike Zaccaro did some
figuring. Joyce Aparo's estate, he estimated, was worth
between $350,000 and $375,000, and even after deduction
of the outstanding debts, which came to about $46,000,
Karin, as the main beneficiary under the will would net
something over $300,000. Sands and Zaccaro explained all
this to Karin. "She seemed quite happy about it," Sands
says.

At some point during all this paper work Karin walked
out of her mother's bedroom and into her own room. The
doorbell rang. Sands went to answer it. Revoir and Beth
Libby, a female officer, were outside. He let them in, and
they all went into the living room. Karin came out of her
room. In one hand she was holding two pieces of paper,
folded twice. Revoir, who had not seen Karin before, asked
her to take a tour of the apartment with him. They wandered
about. Karin looked around. She said that her mother's
purse and wallet, with some cash and credit cards, were
missing. In her own room she pointed to a pair of sunglasses

on her desk and told Revoir she had never seen them before. Revoir put them in an evidence bag. She opened the drawer in her bedside table, Revoir standing by her. In the drawer were three diaries. "I asked him if he wanted them," Karin says, "and he said no, he had already read them and he had no interest in them."

Back in the living room, Karin sat on the sofa, the folded papers still visible in her hand. Revoir sat on the sofa near her. Zaccaro and Butler sat nearby. Sands was in a chair directly across from her. Over the next hour or so Revoir and Libby questioned Karin about her mother's background. "I was just kind of listening," Sands says, "and I thought, *Gee, they asked that question a couple of minutes ago*. Karin hadn't caught on to that, and the answers she was giving weren't quite the same answers she gave the last time. Close, but not quite. All of a sudden, I'm thinking, *Aha, this is an interrogation*. Why would you ask the same question three different ways unless you wanted to see if there's some kind of inconsistency in the answer? So I said to the officer, 'Wait a second here. Look, is this any kind of interrogation? I want you to tell me right now, is Karin is a suspect?'

"He said, 'Well, no, she's not.'

"I said, 'Fine. To the extent that your questions have to do with mundane matters like who had the key, who gave it to whom, things like that, I'll let it go on. But I want to tell you, I'm not a criminal attorney, but if this thing gets out of hand, it's going to stop there.' It pretty much stopped then."

But Sands had noticed something that everyone else was overlooking. The papers in Karin's hand. Revoir asked no questions about them, did not seem to be aware of them. Sands watched and waited. About halfway through the interview Revoir and Libby took a break, got up and walked out of the room. Karin unfolded the papers and read them. She refolded them, crumpled them in her hand, paused, got up, walked over to an open green Hefty garbage bag and threw them inside. Revoir and Libby were just returning to the room. Karin was in full view of everybody. Nobody commented. Mike Zaccaro noticed but, he says, "I didn't think it was anything unusual." Jeff Sands watched but said and did nothing. Nobody else seemed to pay any attention.

The questioning resumed, went on for a little time more, and then Revoir and Libby left. As soon as they were out the door, Sands looked at Karin. "Karin," he said, "I saw you take those pieces of paper and throw them away. If they have anything to do with your mother's death, we have to talk about it."

Karin rose from the sofa and went to the garbage bag, reached in, retrieved the papers and handed them to Sands. He read the first page, looked up at her, then read the second page. "Who wrote this?" he asked.

"Dennis," she said.

"Where did you find it?"

"Between the sheets of my bed," she said.

Sands reread the note. The first page said:

To My Dreamgirl
I will "do the deed." I PROMISE YOU!!

The second page read:

Monday. 4:15 P.M.

Karin,

Hi dear. How was your trip? *O.K.* I hope. I missed you horribly. Come back soon. Listen, I've got a plan for this week. Almost all the details are set. We must seriously talk. It could work. I hate those pictures on your dresser. (Sorry, I wasn't trying to be nosey.) Had a bizarre dream. Your mother was in it. If your mom goes to work tomorrow either call me at work, or I'll pass by on my way home. I can't wait to talk to you. Do you still love me? (I hope). I love you more than

ever. Please don't ever leave me. I see good times for
us in the near future. We'll have fun. Well, the Dud's
[the cat] been fed, we played for a while. Ring me
tonight *any* time if you can. See you soon? Can't wait.
We'll soon be havin' a party, you and me. I promise.
I'm so in love with you my dear. I will ask you to
marry me someday—the right way. *The* most romantic
and loving way I can. I PROMISE. See you soon.

Love,
Den

P.S. I've been eating more lately,
and haven't felt sick—good?

Sands looked up at her. "Why did you throw this
away?"

Karin said, "I was scared."

Sands turned to Zaccaro and Butler and asked them to
leave the condo for a while because he had to talk to Karin
privately. They left.

When they were alone, Sands told her she had to turn
the note over to the police immediately. The police had
been in and out of the condo since Joyce's murder. They
had searched it thoroughly. They must have found that note
and then put it back between the sheets to see whether she
would try to destroy it or give it to them. If she didn't turn
it over, a lot of suspicion would fall on her. At the very
least, she might be charged with hindering prosecution, a
potentially serious crime. If she had anything to worry
about, he said, he would get her a criminal lawyer.

Karin offered little resistance. She said that she didn't
need a criminal lawyer, that she had nothing to hide, that
she was just upset because the note was from Dennis. Until
then Sands had never heard of Dennis Coleman.

Sands held the note and started for the door. Karin
followed. He drove her to the command post at the Naubuc
Elementary School. When they arrived, Revoir was outside
in the parking lot. Sands walked up to him and said that

Karin had found a note in the apartment from her friend Dennis Coleman, and they thought Revoir ought to have it. Revoir led them inside, took the note and read it, with interest and a little surprise. Sands had been wrong in his surmise. As it happened, the police had not come upon the note. During their searches of the apartment they had barely looked in Karin's room.

Where had she found it? Revoir asked.

Between the sheets of her bed.

What did it mean, the deed and the plan?

Dennis had been having problems with his stomach, she said. They thought perhaps he had an ulcer. She had one, and maybe he did, too. The plan, she explained, was that he was finally going to see a doctor. There was just one thing, she said. She didn't want Dennis angry at her and thinking she was trying to make trouble for him if somebody happened to read the note the wrong way. So, if they asked him about it, would they tell him that they had been in her bedroom with her, that when she sat down on her bed, they all heard paper crinkling and wanted to know what the sound was, so she was forced to reach between the sheets, take out the note and give it to them?

Revoir agreed to pass on that explanation when he talked to Dennis Coleman. He decided not to press her at that moment on whether the note might really have another, more sinister meaning, though he was pretty sure the one she had given was made of whole cloth. Revoir was pretty sure he knew what the note was really about, and the fact that it had been left in Karin's bed indicated to him that she might know a lot more than she was letting on.

Revoir knew the law and knew the limits it placed on him. If he pushed too hard, alarm bells would go off, Jeff Sands would call a criminal lawyer and the possibility of any further cooperation from Karin would come to a sudden end.

Revoir also suspected that Karin might have more to say. The way the note had been found, her open display of it, and her lack of resistance to the idea of turning it in led him to wonder if perhaps she was setting Dennis Coleman up to take a fall.

The thing to do, then, was bring Dennis in, show him the note, tell him Karin's tale of how it had been found, see what he had to say and look for inconsistencies.

Dennis Coleman was a little late getting home from the Tallwoods Country Club that afternoon. He had stopped on the way to take care of an errand that he knew should have been done before, at least a day, if not two days, earlier. The stop had been at the Glastonbury town dump. The errand had been to toss a couple of bulging plastic garbage bags into the compactor.

Soon after he reached his father's house in South Glastonbury, the state cops showed up and asked him if he would accompany them to the command post to answer a few more questions. For three hours that afternoon and on into the evening, they went over the story he had told them two days before. And they found the inconsistencies.

He had an explanation for the note, of course. The "deed" he was writing about meant that he was finally going to get a doctor's appointment to see about his stomach troubles.

As for the "plan," he and Karin were always making plans for what they would do, how they would manage to be together. That's what the note was all about. The plan "was our plan for the future," he said. The thing about marrying the right way meant "She was romantic. She wanted a formal proposal, a formal ring, horse-drawn carriage, down on my knees, that kind of thing. Because the first time I proposed to her, I gave her a paper ring."

He had left the note between the sheets of her bed because it was something he did all the time. They were always writing notes and letters to each other, sometimes three or four in one day, and leaving them in the other's room. This was just another of those notes. He had left this one between the sheets of her bed, which was where he often left notes, either on Sunday, August 2, or Monday, August 3, he couldn't remember which because he was in and out of the apartment, feeding the cats and doing the other things Joyce and Karin had asked him to do while they were away. She had told him she would be home on Tuesday, and he was sure she would find it then.

They let all that hang for the moment. They turned to the night of the murder. He had told them when first questioned that he was with his friend Frank Manganaro. But they had talked to Manganaro, and he had told them that yes, he had seen Dennis that night, but it had been at the home of another friend, Kira Lintner, and Kira's boyfriend and their mutual friend Chris Wheatley had been with them, too. Manganaro said they had spent the evening drinking some beer and watching three horror movies; he remembered one, *Friday the 13th,* but he couldn't remember others. He and Kira had left about midnight, to go out and buy a Garfield mug. Dennis and Chris had remained behind.

That was right, Dennis admitted. He had been so upset about Joyce that he'd gotten things mixed up. Actually Frank was right. What he said was exactly what they had done. The one thing he wasn't certain about, he said, was the chronology. He was sure he'd left Kira's about eleven-thirty and had gone straight home to bed because he had to be up early to be at work at seven in the morning.

It was early evening before the police finished with him. By then Dennis Coleman knew he had become the prime suspect in the murder of Joyce Aparo. Indeed, the cops had asked him directly if he had killed her. He had denied it, but he was sure they didn't believe him. He was badly shaken, and it showed in his face when he walked through the door. His father took one look at him and asked, "Dennis, do you need legal help?"

"Yes."

Dennis Coleman, Sr., asked his son just one more question. "Did you do it?"

Dennis Coleman, Jr., nodded his head yes.

His father turned and went to the phone.

The lawyer Dennis Coleman, Sr., called that night was Maurice Hatcher Norris. In his late thirties, balding, of medium height, Reese Norris is a man with a zest for battle, with a dramatic courtroom style, a man who has realized his childhood dream. "I always wanted to be not just a lawyer," he says, "but a courtroom lawyer, and a criminal lawyer at that." That was what he had become.

This was a dream he worked hard to achieve. A native of New Jersey, graduate of Rutgers, he had gone on to the University of Connecticut Law School. As a student he went to work as an intern in the federal public defender's office, for free when it turned out that the public defender had no funds for interns. By the time he was graduated, Norris had handled briefs and assisted on enough cases to begin creating a reputation. At that point he turned to the other side and became an assistant United States attorney in Connecticut, a job he held until, in 1978, he struck out on his own. In the years since, he has become one of the most successful, and expensive, criminal lawyers in southern New England, a lawyer who has lost only about a half dozen of the hundred or more cases he has handled that have gone to trial, many of his victories coming in cases that seemed at first unwinnable. The result has been that he is able to afford the expensive custom-made Porsche sports car he loves, whose license plate reads "NT-GLTY," and other cars, the large sprawling house on several acres in Glastonbury where he lives with his wife and two children and the good clothes he wears, just about all he wants.

Norris met with Dennis for the first time the following morning. It is not, of course, a defense attorney's job to do the police's work for them or to see that legal justice is served. It doesn't matter whether the client is guilty or innocent, for under the law every person has the right to the best counsel he or she can get. The attorney's job is to defend the client as best as he or she can. Norris listened to his new client, who told the lawyer he had done the deed but told him little else, identified no one else as having been involved in any way.

While they were sitting at the Colemans' dining-room table during this initial conference, the telephone rang. It was for Dennis. He took it, listened, said into the phone, "Mr. Norris is here with me now." When he returned to the table, he told Norris that the caller had been his girl friend, Karin Aparo. She knew he was in trouble, he said, and so she had asked Aldor Dubois, at whose house she was staying, if he knew the names of any criminal lawyers. Dubois had mentioned two, Reese Norris and Hubert Santos, a man in his forties with whom Norris had worked when he was a volunteer intern and Santos was a senior attorney in the federal public defender's office; Santos, now in private practice, is considered one of the state's most prominent and inventive criminal lawyers. Karin was calling to pass on those recommendations. Later, when she needed a lawyer of her own, she turned to Santos.

When the conference was over, Norris began making some preliminary inquiries of his own. As far as he could see, the police might have their suspicions, but they had no solid evidence to back them up. The best strategy at that moment, he decided, was to stonewall.

So on Monday, when the police arrived at the Coleman house, Norris was ready for them. The police wanted to interview Dennis again. Norris said no way. They could sit there as long as they wanted and talk about the weather or the baseball scores or anything they wanted, but not about Joyce Aparo or anything to do with her. They wanted to search Dennis's room. Norris said to go try to get a search warrant, and if they did, he would go to court and argue that they had no probable cause for the issuance of such a warrant.

For the moment the police were stymied. They had a suspect, Dennis Coleman. But that was all. As for putting together a solid, convicting case, all they had was a lot of talk from a lot of people, an overheard phone call and a note that might mean nothing or everything. It was not enough.

4

Karin, Sands, and Zaccaro devoted the early part of Saturday, August 8, to the grim task of making the necessary arrangements for Joyce Aparo's funeral. They had no choice; no one else could do it. Their first stop was a funeral home, to see about shipping Joyce's body from Springfield and to set a time and place for the service and burial, which they did in consultation with Archbishop John Whealon. Then they proceeded into the home's showroom to select a coffin from among the dozen or more on display, standing open both to reveal the texture of the interior and, according to those who know, to calm the fears of the mourners that the boxes they are viewing are not empty. What happened then caused both to begin to suspect that Karin was not as innocent as she proclaimed, that she was somehow involved

48

in the murder of her mother. For they were stunned by her actions, by her lack of emotion.

"She was so cold," Zaccaro remembers, "that it was almost unbelievable. When the undertaker took us around to show us the coffins, she didn't look at the boxes; she looked at the price tags and chose the cheapest one. We finally persuaded her to upgrade at least a little."

Sands was still at this point finding rationalization for Karin's behavior. "She was," he said, "concerned about the cost of the funeral and how she was going to pay for it, and she seemed upset by that."

The undertaker asked about the notice in the paper, whether she wanted one in the Hartford *Courant* and what it should say. Did Joyce have any relatives and, if so, who should be included? Neither Sands nor Zaccaro knew much about Joyce's personal history; she rarely discussed it. They knew that within recent years she had been married to and soon divorced from a man named Ed Murphy, for both knew Murphy and had been involved with Joyce and him during the courtship, marriage and breakup. Now they discovered that not only did she have another former husband, Michael Aparo, about whom they were aware, but that both her mother, Rose Cantone, and her sister, Ina Camblor, lived in nearby South Windsor, and that there was a brother, Thomas Cantone, a construction executive in White Plains, New York. But Karin wanted no mention of any of them in the obituary. "She was so hysterical about it," Sands says, "that we told the funeral director in front of Karin, don't include them. After we'd made all the arrangements, I went back in and said, 'Look, do me a favor. We don't know who these people are. Could you please track down their addresses and phone numbers, because we're going to need them anyhow, and prepare the notices for the *Courant* and the other papers, and include those names? I don't think it's right not to have those people in there. I think they'd be very offended.' "

They were. The funeral home managed to track down

Joyce's sister, Ina Camblor, in South Windsor. "They called her," Sands says, "and told her that Karin didn't want her included in the obituary. The next day I'm out mowing the lawn and I get a call and I come to the phone and it's Ina Camblor, and who I don't know from Adam. And the phone call starts, 'You no good son of a bitch . . .' She was livid. She was screaming and yelling about the idea that she wouldn't be included in the death notice. I calmed her down, and I told her, 'Look, the situation was that Karin was hysterical at the time, and you can understand that. She wasn't thinking straight. The reason you got called at all was because we wanted to make sure you got into the death notice.' After about ten minutes she calmed down, and then she gave me her brother's name and her mother's and everything.

"To me, it was absolutely amazing because Karin had indicated to us that there had been a real estrangement between her mother and her family. Ina Camblor readily admitted that there had been a real freeze between Joyce and her family, for whatever reason, she didn't go into it, but that Karin was her blood, her family, and whenever there was a crisis, her family came together. They would be there for Karin, money, shelter, whatever she needed."

From the funeral home Karin, Sands and Zaccaro went back to the condominium, to choose the clothes in which Joyce would be buried. "We went into her closet," Zaccaro says, "and we went through a lot of things. Then Karin picked out this sleazy green pants outfit. It was about the cheapest thing there. Jeff and I picked out a very nice dress. Karin said no. She said she wanted that dress for herself. Eventually Jeff and I persuaded her to choose at least a dress for Joyce to be buried in."

The undertaker took one look at that dress when they returned and was incensed. It wouldn't do at all, he told Karin. It was just too garish. He demanded that she go back home and pick something more appropriate. She did, but the experience was distressing enough to him that in the time that followed he related it to many of his friends.

* * *

Susan and Shannon Dubois took Karin shopping for an appropriate dress for her to wear the next day. On the way back to the house Karin was alone in the rear seat of the Duboises' car. The sky was dark, rain pouring down. Karin began to cry. She had not shed many tears until then. These were the first that either Shannon or Susan Dubois had witnessed. Shannon reached over the seat and held her hand, tried to say comforting things to console her. She turned to her mother and said she was sure Karin was crying because suddenly she was struck by the thought of Joyce lying out in the rain under the bridge in Bernardston before her body was found.

Joyce's funeral was scheduled for Wednesday, August 12, exactly a week after she was murdered. A few days before the funeral the Markovs appeared at the Dubois house. To everyone's astonishment, Karin announced that she was leaving with them. Alex was giving a concert in Philadelphia, and she intended to be there. She would be back in time for the service. It might not be seemly, but she didn't seem to care. She did ask Jeff Sands what he thought, and Sands told her it was not a bad idea for her to get away for a few days. She went.

As she had said, she was back in Glastonbury in time for the funeral. In the morning Alex Markov rode with Karin in the lead limousine to the funeral chapel and then with her behind the hearse to the cemetery. At the funeral chapel Joyce's closed coffin was in a private room. Karin went into that room with Archbishop Whealon and a few others. To the shock of some who were there, she went to the funeral director and demanded that the coffin be opened and left open. He was reluctant. She insisted. He opened the casket. Karin stood over it, staring down at her mother's body, walked around and looked at the body from every angle. It was the first time she had seen her mother since that morning in Rowayton when Joyce set out on her final errands. "I was in shock," Karin said later, "I didn't know what to do." She saw a dark mark around the neck, where the panty hose had been wrapped and tightened to strangle, saw purple bruises all the way down the chest, saw bruises and blotches on the arms between the wrists and elbows, noted the ring still on her mother's finger and that "her face was distorted, it looked out of shape."

To Jeff Sands, she looked emotionally shaken, leaning against Archbishop Whealon as if for comfort. But others saw something else in that scene. One later said, "Karin acted like she wanted to make sure Joyce was really in there."

There were services first in the funeral chapel. It was packed, all the seats filled, people standing at the back and along the sides. The open coffin rested in front of the altar. Karin and Alex Markov sat in the first row. Ina Camblor, her brother, Thomas Cantone, and their mother, Rose Cantone, sat across the aisle.

One of those people standing was Carol Parkola. She arrived just before the services were to begin. There were no seats, so she stood at the rear of the chapel. She was perhaps Joyce Aparo's oldest continuing friend. They had met while college freshmen and had maintained their friendship through the years. Carol lived in Florida now, but she returned to Connecticut for a two-week visit every August, and during those weeks she and Joyce talked often on the phone, had lunch and dinner together, spent time at each other's homes. This August Carol was making her annual pilgrimage north. "I got in, and I was going to call Joyce," she remembers, "but my sister and I spent the Tuesday on a boat down at the shore and it was late when we got home. So I said, 'Well, I'll call her tomorrow night,' because I couldn't call her during the day because she was at work, 'and we'll get together for dinner.' But something came up, and I didn't call, and then my father and I were listening to the news with half an ear, because the national news was over and I wasn't that interested in the local news. And we both said, 'What did he say? Did he say Aparo? He couldn't have.' Then the newspaper came the next morning, and I just, well, I couldn't believe it. For a long time I felt so guilty, and I kept saying to myself, 'What if I had only called her, would I have had her on the phone and then the person who did it couldn't have and she'd still be alive?' ''

All she could do was go to the funeral. At the funeral chapel "I found Michael [Aparo], who was the only one I really knew, and I spoke to him, and he said, 'Have you spoken to Karin?' I said no, so he took me down to Karin. He wasn't even sitting with her. There was a boy sitting next to her; I found out later it was Alex Markov. I was so upset and I was trying to compose myself and talk to her without breaking up and it was all I could do to tell her how sorry I was, and this kid Karin was sitting there and she was not the least bit broken up or upset. She just kept talking to this guy.

"When the service was over, I was standing at the back of the funeral home while they were taking the coffin out the other way, and she came out past me, and she couldn't have been more than a few feet from me and she was laughing and talking with this guy and she wasn't broken up at all. I said to my mother later, 'I can't understand it, she wasn't upset at all.' Then somebody pointed out the sister to me, and I went over and spoke to her, and she was all, like 'Oh, my poor sister,' she was just all broken up and crying so hard she couldn't speak to me, and her brother was holding her up and helping her out. That day you would have thought they were this close, extremely close; only I knew they hadn't even had anything to do with each other for years and years.''

From the funeral home the procession wound its way to the cemetery. There, as he had in the chapel, Archbishop Whealon conducted the service. When he finished, the prayers for the dead said, the services over at the graveside, just as people were getting ready to leave, Karin rose and went to the funeral director. She told him to start filling in the grave immediately. He was stunned. It shouldn't be done, he said, until after everyone was gone. Karin wanted it done then. She wanted no delays. He finally agreed. But except for a shovelful, to show that he was complying, the grave was not filled until the cemetery cleared.

The mourners filed from the cemetery toward the waiting cars. Karin, with Alex Markov at her side, moved toward the limousine that had been rented for her. As she was about to get into it, Lori DeLucca, who had known Karin since fourth grade and had once been a close friend, remembers distinctly, for it was something she could not forget, Karin's turning to the crowd and saying, "Will everyone clap as I make my grand exit?"

The mourners gathered at the Duboises' that afternoon. There was nowhere else to gather. Though Joyce's mother, sister and brother appeared for the funeral, gathered around Karin and offered her their support, support that increased in the time ahead, they had been estranged from Joyce for years, and Karin had little fondness for them. She would not hear of their receiving those attending the funeral. The proper place was where she was, and that was at the home of the Dubois family.

Soon after she reached the house, Karin went into the kitchen. Lori DeLucca happened to be in the room. Karin picked up the phone and dialed. "I need to talk to you," she said into the mouthpiece. "I'm okay. But, oh, boy." She hung up, turned to Lori and said, "Dennis will be stopping over pretty soon."

Dennis had not seen Karin since the moment he left his home for work the morning after Joyce's murder. Later that day she had settled in with the Duboises. They had spoken briefly on the phone once or twice, including the call in which she had given him the names of Reese Norris and Hubert Santos as criminal lawyers who might be able to help him, but that was all.

It was not long before Dennis Coleman arrived. He had not been at the funeral services. He and Karin greeted each other. Lori DeLucca and several others saw them standing in a hallway, then walk away and disappear into a bathroom.

Out in the living room Jeff Sands looked around and saw that Karin was missing. Somebody said she was in the bathroom with Dennis. He walked that way and spotted them through the open door. It was the first time he had ever seen Dennis Coleman, though over the week since the murder he had heard his name often and had become increasingly suspicious of him, increasingly convinced that Dennis was the murderer of Joyce Aparo. "They seemed to be a little agitated," he remembers. "I stuck my head in and said, 'Is everything all right, Karin?' She said, 'Yeah, no problem.' " Sands walked on.

The door closed. How long they were in that bathroom behind the closed door is a matter of dispute; a few years later it became of critical importance.

Soon after they entered, Alex Markov approached the door, knocked on it, said, in his thick Russian accent, "Karin, I'd like to talk to you."

From behind the door Karin said, "Not right now, Alex."

Markov continued to stand by the door, knocked a couple of times more, repeated the request and was met with the same reply.

What happened in that bathroom, as what happened on other occasions and what was said, depends on who is doing the telling.

Says Dennis Coleman: "She started asking me questions about the murder. They were the same questions she had asked over the phone from the police station. I couldn't understand why she was asking those questions when she already knew all the answers. We were in there about five minutes, that's all."

His estimate of the time, at least, is supported by Lori

DeLucca and a few others who saw them enter and then saw them depart.

Says Karin Aparo: "I wanted to tell him what I had seen on my mother, and I wanted to him to explain it all to me. He did. This was the first time Dennis told me the details of how he had murdered my mother, and it took him more than fifteen minutes to do it."

Jeff Sands agrees with Karin's estimate of the time. He saw her disappear into the bathroom, and then he strolled back to the living room. He says that he next saw her emerging from the area around the bathroom fifteen or twenty minutes later.

However long they were in that bathroom, eventually the door opened and Karin and Dennis emerged. Alex Markov was standing right beside the door. The three of them walked into the living room. There Karin turned to Dennis and said, "Does Denny need a hug?"

Dennis looked at her and said, "From you?"

She nodded and said, "I guess so." Then she put her arms around him and held him close. They moved to the couch and sat next to each other. Karin, says someone who was watching, seemed very warm toward Dennis.

From across the room Jeff Sands was watching carefully. "Karin looked a little funny," Sands says, "and I walked by, and she stands up very casually and says, 'Oh, Jeff, I think I need a breath of fresh air. Would you walk outside with me?' "

Out in the backyard Karin turned to Sands and said, "Jeff, I know something, and I need help."

Sands said, "Anything to do with the murder?"

"Yes."

"Karin," he said, "do you want a criminal attorney?"

"No."

"Okay. What do you want to talk about?"

"Dennis just confessed to me. What should I do?"

Sands said, "You've got to go to the police and tell them. If you don't, you're committing a crime, and the police can charge you with being an accessory or obstructing justice or something. So you have to tell them.''

She offered no argument. They went back into the house to tell Al and Susan Dubois they were leaving, though not why and to find Mike Zaccaro, who was due at a local bank to sign some credit papers on a nursing home Athena was about to open; Sands had promised to drive him to that appointment. Sands took Zaccaro aside and told him that Karin was going with them and that he would explain in the car.

As they were starting out, Shannon Dubois saw them. She went up to Karin and said, "Where are you going?"

Karin said, "I'm going to the police."

And then, Sands remembers, "Shannon made some reference to loyalty and friendship. It stuck in my mind, like, what in the world is she talking about?"

On the way to the bank in Glastonbury Zaccaro learned where Karin was going, and why. "She told us," Zaccaro says, "that Dennis did it because Joyce was preventing them from spending the rest of their lives together. She knew about it afterwards because Dennis told her, but she had nothing to do with it. The way she told it, it was a very plausible story."

Sands dropped Zaccaro off at the bank. Then he and Karin drove around for a few minutes before heading for the command post at the Naubuc school. It was only a few blocks from the bank, and Zaccaro intended to walk there, go in and talk to the police before Karin appeared.

As they drove toward the school, Sands said to Karin, "I'll go in there with you as a friend. But I'm not representing you because I'm not a criminal attorney. Are you at all worried about the statement you're going to make? Is there any way it can incriminate you? Any problem at all? Because if there is, we'll just put you on hold and get somebody in here to represent you."

She shook her head. "No," she said, "there's no prob-

lem. I'll go in and tell the police that Dennis has just confessed this thing to me, and I can't live with this.''

Zaccaro reached the command post just as Sands and
Karin were driving up. They waited while he went in to
prepare the way. Cavanaugh and Revoir were there. ''I told
them,'' says Zaccaro, ''that Karin was coming in to see
them, that she had something she wanted to say. But I said
that Jeff and I were concerned that they might use something she might say against her. If that were the case, if they
had reason to believe that Karin might have had a significant
involvement, then she should have a criminal attorney with
her and it could wait until we got one. Cavanaugh said no,
if what she said was the truth, they wouldn't use it against
her. It wasn't that they didn't have any suspicions, but they
would not use anything she said against her, if it was the
truth.''

So Zaccaro went out and brought Karin and Sands in to
meet with Cavanaugh and Revoir. They were led into an
empty classroom. Revoir took out paper and pencils and
began to set down whatever statement Karin was prepared
to make.

The first thing Karin asked was if she was going to
have to testify in court. Cavanaugh said she would. She
accepted that. Then she gave them what they wanted. She
told them that Dennis Coleman had confessed to her that
afternoon in the Duboises' bathroom that he had murdered
her mother. She told him he had laid it out for her in
explicit and excruciating detail, and she repeated those details for the state cops. Among other things, she said, Dennis told her it had happened at one fifty-six in the morning.
He told her about the yellow paper towel stuffed in Joyce's
mouth. He told her other things that had not been released
to the press, that were not common knowledge, that only
the murderer and the investigators could have known. She
was with Cavanaugh and Revoir for more than three hours;
it took her that long to give her statement in a preliminary
form, then have Revoir write it down in longhand for her to

sign; it ran to fifteen pages. In it she gave the police the missing pieces from the puzzle or at least enough of them so they now had probable cause to move against Dennis Coleman.

"Afterwards," Sands says, "Cavanaugh got up and kissed Karin and said, 'You gave us the murderer, you've given him to us, thank you, this is great.' Cavanaugh was very supportive and talked to Karin about a victim support group and the programs they had to help, because this was going to be a tough time for her."

"I didn't suspect her then," Cavanaugh says. "I didn't want to suspect her then."

Still, there were a few troublesome factors, some of which were immediately apparent, others not quite so evident until sometime later. As they looked back, both Cavanaugh and Revoir were struck by the way Karin was able to recite the details of her mother's murder, details that were horrifying, yet show almost no emotion as she did so. That was one thing. Another was how much she knew; she said that the first time she had ever heard the particulars, all the minutiae of her mother's murder, down to the last detail, even to the precise time, one fifty-six in the morning, that her mother had stopped breathing, was that afternoon in the bathroom.

As the two cops read and reread Karin's statement, both of them realized that she and Dennis must have spent at least fifteen minutes, and probably more, alone behind the closed doors of the bathroom for him to have told that much and for her to have absorbed it so thoroughly. That was how long she said they were alone together. But later not merely Dennis Coleman but several others said that he and Karin had been in that bathroom behind the closed doors for no more than five minutes, hardly time enough for him to have said all she claimed.

Just as Karin and Sands were getting ready to leave, Cavanaugh called Sands to the phone. There was a call from Al Dubois. Dennis, he told Sands, was still at the house. He was just hanging around, and they couldn't get rid of him. He was waiting for Karin, and he seemed to be growing more and more agitated all the time.

One thing was certain then. Nobody was going to let Karin Aparo return to the Dubois house that night, not with Dennis Coleman waiting for her, not after what she'd just done, what she'd just said about him.

"Being the nice guy that I am," Jeff Sands says, "I offered to take Karin home to our house and let her stay overnight. Now my wife was suspicious of Karin from the first moment she heard about Joyce being murdered, especially when she heard about that phone call from the police station to Dennis. So I take Karin home, and my wife, Patty, takes one look, and you can see the reaction in her face. 'Hi, Karin. What are you doing here, guys?'

"I explain the whole situation quickly, which doesn't make Patty feel any better, because now she's worried about Karin. And then she's worried about this Dennis, this killer looking for Karin, and God knows if he'll figure out she's at our house. I say to Patty, 'Dennis wouldn't kill anyone else.' I don't know whether she believed me or not.

"So we get Karin settled, and we order a pizza, and then my wife says, 'Gee, Jeff, I'm having trouble getting the comforter down from the spare bedroom closet. Can you come up here a minute with me?'

"We get upstairs. Now Patty is very demure, and she's very straitlaced and never uses foul language. But we get up to the room, and under her breath she says, 'What the fuck are you doing? How could you bring her here? She's a murderer.'

"I say, 'Patty . . .'

"She says, 'All right, she's associated with a murderer. Dennis could be looking for her. Anything could happen.'

"I say, 'It'll be okay. She can sleep in the spare bedroom. It's separated from the rest of the house.'

"She says, 'It won't be okay. You're staying up all

night. You're not sleeping. You're going to protect us. It's your responsibility.'

"Our house is a colonial, with a guest room on the right on the top of the stairs and our room and the baby's room off to the left. I sat on the bottom of those steps all night while Karin slept in the spare bedroom, even though I never thought our family was in danger from either Dennis or Karin.''

5

At two the next afternoon, August 13, the sun bright, the day warm, too hot, some thought, as Dennis Coleman was leaving his job at the concession stand at the Tallwoods Country Club, the state police arrived. Some golfers were just coming off the eighteenth hole; a few others were strolling from the clubhouse toward their cars in the parking lot. Dennis was on his way toward his car when the cops approached. He knew what was about to happen. He waited. They reached him. They told him he was under arrest for the murder of Joyce Aparo and for conspiracy to murder her, they read him his rights and then they hustled him into a police car. There handcuffs were put on him for the first time. In the months and years ahead they were to become as familiar to his wrists as the other clothes he wore.

If convicted, he faced up to sixty years in prison on the first charge and twenty years on the second, and those terms would have to be served consecutively, not concurrently. This meant that Dennis Coleman faced the bleak prospect of spending the next eighty years in state prison.

As he was booked, there was about him a deadness, a sense of something missing, something empty inside. It was not just a lack of emotion; there was not even that wash of relief that the waiting was over, that the inevitable had finally occurred. It was as though somehow he were removed, as though none of this were really touching him.

He got a hint of what the future held immediately. He spent that weekend in jail, though a local one, not the dreaded state penitentiary in Somers, until his father managed to raise, in property and other assets, the $150,000 bond that was set.

But it was not over with the arrest of Dennis Coleman. There were still too many unanswered questions, and he was answering none of them. There was the nagging and basic one: how he had managed to get Joyce Aparo and her car from Glastonbury to Bernardston, dump both of them there and get back home in time to be at work at his regular time.

Once Dennis was charged, Reese Norris had no more grounds to object to a search warrant of the Coleman house or Dennis's car. Had it been served a few days before, absolute convicting evidence would have been discovered both in Dennis's closet and in the trunk of his sports car. But the previous Friday that evidence had disappeared into the compactor at the town's garbage dump. The police, though, did find enough in Dennis's room to give them pause and force them to take a new and different look at Karin Aparo.

Entering his bedroom, they were brought up short. Three walls were covered from floor to ceiling with photographs and memorabilia of Karin Aparo. There were portraits; there were snapshots, some enlarged, some small; there were casual pictures and formal posed ones. "There wasn't a pinup among them," Cavanaugh says, "not even one of her in a bathing suit. The most revealing picture was one where she had her shirt knotted so you could see a bit of her stomach. When we walked in there, it was like we had walked into a shrine dedicated to Karin Aparo." Indeed, Dennis called it his Karin Wall.

And there was more. In Dennis's desk, in drawers, the cops discovered stacks of letters, a hundred and more; there were letters from at least six different girls to Dennis, but the bulk of that correspondence was from Karin to Dennis and, to the puzzlement of the searchers, from Dennis to Karin.

The content of many of those letters was enough to turn Karin Aparo from bereaved daughter of a murder victim and willing witness and ally for the police into not merely a major subject, but an active and willing participant in murder. Some suggested she might even be the motivating force behind a plot that had begun long before. Perhaps there was an innocent explanation for what was written, but the authorities couldn't see one. Neither could Dennis Coleman's attorney, Reese Norris.

When confronted with the letters, Dennis still would not help them, would not even help his own lawyer. Norris, of course, knew that Dennis was the murderer. He, like the police, knew Dennis could not have done the murder alone. And he, like the police, suspected that Karin Aparo had played a role. But his client refused to confirm Norris's suspicions, in fact insisted to Norris that he had done it all by himself, that Karin had played no role in his deed and knew nothing about it. Nothing Norris said could make Dennis open up; nothing could thaw the ice that Norris sensed encased the very essence of his client.

Among all those letters found in Dennis's room not only were the ones to and from Karin fascinating to Cavanaugh, Revoir and others, but there was another letter that seemed to point not merely to a long-standing plot between Dennis and Karin but to knowledge of that plot by someone else, someone else whom Cavanaugh already suspected. It was from Christopher Wheatley to Dennis Coleman, and it indicated that Wheatley had been aware of a plot to kill Joyce Aparo for a very long time. "So, Dude," a paragraph in that letter read, "how's your woman? Is her mother still alive?"

Ever since Chris Wheatley's name had first come up, Cavanaugh had been determined to talk with nineteen-year-old Wheatley, a premed student at Syracuse University, and to his girl friend, sixteen-year-old Kira Lintner, about to enter her junior year at Glastonbury High School, the friends, along with Frank Manganaro, with whom Dennis Coleman had said he had spent the evening of August 4, just before the murder. He was convinced that Wheatley and Lintner were crucial figures in the case. They both were interviewed briefly during the first days by the Glastonbury police and a couple of detectives from the state police major crimes unit, but those interviews had led nowhere.

Now, after the discoveries during the search of Dennis Coleman's room, Cavanaugh was determined to have a little interview with Wheatley. For he had something else that linked Wheatley to the crime.

The night of the murder the Glastonbury police had been out in force, cruising the town's streets for the cat burglar on the loose. When Cavanaugh went over the reports of the town's officers for that night, one stopped him. At about one-thirty in the morning a 1984 white Renault Encore had been spotted parked within a block of the Aparo condo. Within the next fifteen minutes cops saw that Renault drive past the condo twice, and other cops saw it several more times in the area. The license plates of the Renault were noted and checked. The car was registered to a Frank Bollard of Glastonbury. Frank Bollard was Christopher Wheatley's stepfather.

Cavanaugh went looking for Wheatley and his girl

friend. But in the days after the murder it seemed that they had disappeared. Cavanaugh tracked them to a vacation retreat Kira Lintner's mother owned at Lake George in northern New York. He made the trip up there on August 12, the day of Joyce Aparo's funeral, and met with them in the late morning. Cavanaugh's initial impression of Wheatley was that he was a smart, arrogant kid, too smart and too arrogant. When the Connecticut detective told him that he had some questions he wanted answered, Wheatley said, affecting an air of boredom, "Is all this really necessary?"

"You could have heard my roar all the way to Canada," Cavanaugh says. What Wheatley and Kira Lintner had to say was a repeat of what they already said, and what the cops had already heard. They had spent the evening together at Kira's house with Manganaro and Dennis and had watched a couple of movies; Dennis left to go home, and Wheatley, Kira and Manganaro went over to Manganaro's house for a while. Then he and Kira drove back to the Lintner house, where he and Kira spent the rest of the night together.

"Have you ever been inside the Aparo residence?" Cavanaugh asked. He did not mention that he knew Wheatley's car had been parked less than a block away on the crucial night.

"Never," Wheatley replied.

"Have you ever been in or around Mrs. Aparo's Volkswagen Jetta?"

"Never," Wheatley answered.

Cavanaugh heard that, and he didn't believe it. He went back to Glastonbury, where he arrived in time to hear Karin Aparo's revelation that Dennis Coleman had confessed. But he was not about to give up his intuition that Wheatley and Lintner were involved, deeply involved. By Saturday, August 15, three days later, he knew of the "So, Dude," letter Wheatley had written Dennis Coleman a year before; it seemed to confirm his suspicions. He took those suspicions to the state's attorney and the court and got a search and seizure warrant against Wheatley personally, his residence and his car. Handed the warrant, Wheatley was no longer quite so arrogant or quite so sure of himself. He told Cavanaugh that while he was still insisting that he had never been in the Aparo condo or anywhere near the Volkswagen Jetta, he did have some information that he was willing to share. But first he wanted to talk to an attorney his father was going to get for him. Cavanaugh had little choice but to wait.

On Monday, August 17, Cavanaugh got what he needed to prove that Wheatley had been lying to the Glastonbury police, to the state police and to him since the moment of his first interview. The latent fingerprints lifted from both the outside and the inside of the abandoned Volkswagen Jetta had now been identified and matched. They belonged to Christopher Wheatley.

The next day both Wheatley and Lintner were arrested and charged with accessory to murder and conspiracy to murder Joyce Aparo. Like Dennis Coleman, they were facing up to eighty years in prison if convicted. Wheatley had been the driver of the second car on the way to Bernardston, had obviously helped Dennis dump it into the brook at the bottom of the slope next to Chief Brulotte's house and then had driven Dennis back home; Kira Lintner had evidently been with them the whole way.

There was still one more to go. After the search of the Coleman house and the discovery of Dennis's Karin Wall and all that correspondence between Dennis and Karin, correspondence dating back more than a year, the state police obtained another search and seizure warrant, this one on the condo, for letters between Karin and Dennis. Search they did, but they found little, except some letters, which Revoir seized, and the three diaries he had already read; he took one, the most recent, dealing with events of the month of July 1987, leaving the other two behind, though he did take some loose pages that on first glance seemed to be more letters but that turned out to be pages from the diaries dating from the year before.

On August 27 Shannon Dubois, accompanied by her parents and a lawyer, went to see Cavanaugh and Revoir. Her conscience, her sense of morality finally had won out over loyalty to her friend. She could no longer keep secret the things that Karin Aparo had told her. In the weeks since the murder she had been interviewed by the police several times. "I didn't say anything because Karin was at my house and I still couldn't believe the whole thing."

Then Karin was gone for a day. "I was all by myself for the first time, and it all came out." Shannon went to her parents and told them what she knew. "They couldn't believe I knew all that, and they called a lawyer for advice."

They did something else, too. Al and Susan Dubois told Karin Aparo that she was no longer welcome in their home, that she would have to find someplace else to live. Karin immediately called Archbishop Whealon, who arranged for her to stay first with some nuns and then with a Catholic family in Glastonbury. By then Karin also was aware that even greater trouble was looming. But she was prepared. She had already put herself, and her future, in the hands of criminal defense attorney Hubert Santos.

The lawyer the Duboises went to, Richard Brown, called John Bailey, and told the state's attorney for Hartford that his client Shannon Dubois had very important information about the murder of Joyce Aparo and would tell the authorities what she knew if she were granted immunity from prosecution. She was not directly involved, he said; it was just that she had known these things and had not revealed them, so could be charged with hindering prosecution.

If that was all it was, Bailey said, he would have no hesitation in granting immunity.

On August 27 Shannon Dubois met Charlie Revoir and recited to him all the confidences that Karin Aparo had told her that Wednesday morning three weeks before and all that she had imparted in the days and weeks since.

The next day, August 28, an arrest warrant was secured against Karin Aparo, charging that she had played a role in the murder of her mother.

Late that afternoon Charlie Revoir arrived at the home in Glastonbury where Karin was then staying, told her why he had come, recited her rights under the Constitution and then drove her to the police station. The word of her arrest was already out, and a crowd of reporters and the curious had gathered outside. The car pulled up; the door opened. Karin Aparo stepped out and was led inside. If the spectators expected a teenager of remarkable beauty and magnetism or a frightened child distraught by what had befallen her, that was not what they got. What they got was a slightly overweight, buxom sixteen-year-old with sharp features, large glasses and short dark hair, wearing too-tight jeans and an open leather jacket beneath which was a tight shirt that emphasized her bust. But the thing that was most noted, most commented upon and, for many, most disturbing was the arrogant expression on her face and the way she held herself; arrogance seemed to exude from every pore in her body. That moment—that look—would be remembered by all who saw it. It took nearly three years for it to be even partially replaced by another, softer, more guileless image.

Before that first day was out, she was on her way to the women's prison in Niantic. There she spent a night behind bars before a hundred-thousand-dollar bond could be arranged. When she emerged, she was to tell friends that she would never spend another night in a cell, that she would kill herself before that happened.

The possibility that she might, indeed, have to spend another night and more in a cell was about to grow stronger, though. Since his arrest Dennis Coleman had adamantly refused to implicate Karin in the murder, and so long as he continued in that refusal and continued to take all the blame himself, while the state's case against him

might be overwhelming, its case against her was on very
tenuous grounds.

In early September, however, Reese Norris met with
Jimmy Cavanaugh. Norris was searching desperately for a
way to defend his client. At that moment, despite his own
deep suspicions and intuitions, he had nothing, not even a
chip with which to bargain with the state for a sentence of
less than eighty years. Cavanaugh, by now convinced of
Karin's involvement, was sure that the only way she could
be gotten was with Dennis's cooperation. Perhaps he and
Norris together could find a solution to their dilemmas.

They found one. Cavanaugh showed Norris the letters
between Karin and Dennis that had been found in Dennis's
room, showed him Karin's diary that had been found in her
room and told him just how suspicion had first fallen on
Dennis and how the police had learned that he was the murderer. For the first time Norris saw hope for Dennis, not to
keep him out of prison but at least to reduce the portion of his
life he'd spend there. He and Cavanaugh met with Dennis.

For the first time Dennis was told that it was Karin who
had turned over to the police the "I will 'do the deed' "
note, that it was Karin who had gone to the police and
recited his confession with all its details. Then he was
handed Karin's diary. He read it slowly. When he finished,
he stared at Norris and Cavanaugh and began to talk.

In the town of Glastonbury there was shock and horror
and disbelief. The worst fears, the nightmares of the residents had come true. "This just doesn't happen to people
like us," said one native, words, conviction, that echoed up
and down Main Street and along all the small streets of the
town. But it had happened.

A friend of Dennis Coleman and Karin Aparo, of
Christopher Wheatley and Kira Lintner remembers those
days. "I couldn't really believe it," he says. "Dennis is the
last one I would have thought would have done something
like that. Karin, yeah. But not Dennis. Never."

It was a sentiment shared by the vast majority of the people in the town. For reasons only vaguely understood, the town, and soon much of central Connecticut, came to view Dennis Coleman not as a cold-blooded murderer but as a victim, came to view Karin Aparo as evil incarnate, a girl who had wanted her mother dead and had used and manipulated a love-obsessed young man to accomplish that end.

"If this was a couple of hundred years ago and a hundred miles north of here," one resident said, "they would have burned her with all the rest of the witches in Salem."

It was glib, but it reflected the sense of the town, reflected, perhaps, a sense that if one believed it, the whole thing could be explained away. It could not, at least not that easily. If the question of who, of the several whos, seemed to have been answered, the answer was just superficial, and it truly satisfied no one. For there remained a bedeviling group of questions: How had the murder come about? When did they begin planning for it? How could it possibly have remained a secret for so long? How had it been committed? How did these children expect to get away with it? And, finally, what did they hope to gain from it?

And there was the deeper and ultimately more disturbing question of why these teenagers, with everything open to them, would plan and commit murder? There were no easy answers; they lay, perhaps, in some dark places, somewhere in the lives not just of those who had been drawn to do the deed but in the life of the victim herself.

PART TWO

—————— •◦• ——————

WHY THE DEED
WAS DONE

6

The facts were stark, frightening and on the front page. Joyce Aparo was dead. Four teenagers—her daughter, her daughter's boyfriend and two close friends—were under arrest, charged with her murder. The evidence against them appeared overwhelming. The question that bedeviled everyone was why. The answer, many believed, had to lie as much in the victim as in the children.

Joyce Aparo. Those who knew her, who came in contact with her over the years, those who worked with her, who thought of themselves as her friends—though there were few of these, for she was a woman who kept most people at a distance and did not let them look into her private interior world—those who were her neighbors all saw a different woman. She wore a mask, a dozen masks, maybe more, and no one ever completely stripped the disguises from her; perhaps she herself never looked beneath them.

To those who worked with her, in her chosen field of social work and the care of the elderly in nursing homes, she was a brilliant woman, an extraordinary administrator, incorruptible, imaginative, a perfectionist, intolerant of anything less than total dedication from those around her, caring and concerned about those who depended on her. When she opened a door to her personal life, what was revealed was her daughter and her pride in that daughter's gifts.

To friends, the very few who thought themselves close to her, she was also a brilliant woman, lively, fun to be with, knowledgeable about just about everything, perhaps opinionated, expert at anything she put her hand to, a perfectionist who insisted on only the best for herself, a good listener and sounding board for friends' problems though rarely revealing her own inner feelings or deepest concerns, except her pride in her daughter.

To neighbors, she was cold and forbidding, a woman who erected an unbreachable wall around her home and kept the world at a distance, who considered herself and her daughter superior to the common herd, those inferiors not worth associating with. In the glimpses they caught of her, she was cruel and abusive, to them, to everyone and especially to her daughter. They likened her to the Wicked Witch of the West and, indeed, said that she had told them she was a witch, and many believed it.

To her husbands and the men in her life, she was bright and domineering, taking orders from no one, giving orders to everyone, manipulating them and the world to her whims and desires, abusive and scathing in word and deed, rigid, impossible to live with.

To her daughter, she was the mother who taught her to sew and crochet and knit, to cook and bake, to make strawberry jam. She was the mother who shared her dreams and fantasies. She was the mother who put in her hands the violin, the instrument that became the center of her life, and who sacrificed so that she could learn to play. But she was also the mother who rarely, if ever, showed affection, let alone love, the mother who abused her physically and emotionally from the time she was a baby, the mother who manipulated her without end to her bidding. At home as much as at the office, Joyce was a mother who was intolerant of any mistakes, real or imagined, a mother who filled her daughter with tales that left her uncertain about herself, left her in terror. Joyce isolated Karin from much of the world, trapped her in a home and a life that was unendurable and from which there seemed no escape.

And there was something else, something many did not fully realize until after her death. She was an inveterate liar. Her second husband, Michael Aparo, later called her pathological, a woman who invented so many stories it was often impossible to ferret out the truth, and perhaps it came to a point where she herself did not know where the truth lay.

She was born Joyce Cantone in 1939, the youngest child of a lower-middle-class Italian family, several years between her and her brothers and sisters, some adults by the time she was born. She grew up in a cramped second-floor tenement apartment in the Italian south end of Hartford. It was not a happy home. Her father, she told a college friend, was a day laborer and a heavy drinker, a man who more often than not arrived home drunk and, when drunk, vented his fury and frustration on everyone, beating her mother and then turning on her brothers, sisters and herself. The situation was intolerable and did not change for the better as the years passed. She kept trying to persuade her mother to leave her father, she said, but they were practicing and deeply devout Catholics, and that was something that just wasn't done.

Then her mother met a man. They fell in love, and he promised to marry her if somehow she could free herself from her husband. "Joyce said her mother went to see a priest," her friend Carol Parkola remembers, "and then the priest came over to the apartment with an altar boy and spread incense all around and explained that he was going to cleanse the apartment, and all this would get rid of the evil spirits and all the evil that was involved with leaving her husband. Well, Joyce said she got so mad she opened the door and she took the priest's hat and she threw it down the stairs and told him to go chase it. She just didn't take to the church telling her what to do or how to do things." Her father, she said, later died as a result of his alcoholism.

That was one story. There were others. Her father, Joyce later was to tell other acquaintances, as well as repeat often to her daughter, had been a brilliant and sensitive man, a man with outstanding musical talent, a superb pianist who should have been destined for the concert stage. His dream had been to become a conductor, and as a young man he had shown considerable promise with the baton. But her mother would have none of his dreams. In front of the children she constantly derided him, sneered at him, berated him for spending his time and money on useless things while she was forced to struggle just to keep a roof over their heads and food on the table. Her wrath, though, was not limited to words and gestures; on a number of occasions she turned on him with her fists, with frying pans, with whatever was available. He never struck back. Finally, Joyce said, thoroughly beaten, all his hope and dreams gone, he committed suicide.

There is nothing in the local newspapers to support Joyce's tale, but, then, a poor man's suicide was rarely noted or reported, and suicides in Catholic families were often hidden, the death attributed to other more natural causes.

Her brothers and sisters, she later told a friend, were older so that she had little to do with them. She rarely saw any of them after they left, saw them not at all during the last decade of her life.

To another friend she confided that her brothers and sisters had made her life miserable. Just like her mother. They picked on her constantly, ridiculed her because she was too smart, because she was stubborn and had a mind of her own, because she was a rebel in a home where conformity and traditional values were not merely the norm and expected but demanded and because she was attractive, never without beaux flocking to her. She prided herself on her intelligence, her talents and her ambitions. But she was not quite so confident about her beauty. Her large dark eyes were all right, one of her best features, and her dark hair was thick and soft. But she hated her nose, thought it too large, too Italian. A long time later, in the early 1980s, she finally did something about it. She had it bobbed. A friend remembers meeting her in the Gallery restaurant in Glastonbury shortly afterward. "Joyce came in, and she was grinning. She always had this big grin whenever I saw her. And she was just preening. She said, 'How do you like my new nose? I finally had something done to it.' You know, I didn't even notice it at first. I guess they did a good job because it fitted her face."

Very early she announced that she had no intention of following the accepted path laid out for the youngest daughter in a poor Italian family. She would not find a husband as soon as possible, marry without finishing school and then spend the rest of her life cooking, cleaning and raising a large family, modeling herself after her mother and sisters. She was going to finish school, go on to college and then carve out her own career in the professional world. She would make her mark. If a husband came along at some time, all well and good, but she was not going to go out looking for one and holding her breath until she found him. Her pronouncement, she said, served only to exacerbate an already oppressive situation.

That's not the way her sister Ina saw it. Joyce, she said, was the pampered youngest child, catered to by everyone in the family, including her sisters and brothers,

given things that were denied them. While they were made
to toe the mark, follow all the rules and do what was expected of them, and woe if they didn't, Joyce was allowed
to do pretty much what she wanted and, even when she
broke the rules, was rarely punished severely. "Joyce," she
said, "was showered with a lot of attention as she was
growing up since she had the advantage of older sisters and
older brothers and a myriad of cousins. She was also for-
tunate in that economic times were better and my parents
were able to give her dancing lessons, art lessons and a
college education. Joyce was a very intelligent girl but also
a very manipulative person."

She was also a lonely child. Even her mother, Rose
Cantone, who now lives with daughter Ina, says that Joyce
"grew up more or less alone." Because, people who knew
her say, she acted as though she were better than and superior to everyone else, she had few friends and no real
confidantes. Alone and friendless, then, thrown on her own
resources, she retreated often into a world of fantasy, of
make-believe, and expressed those fantasies as though they
were real. Someone who knew her when she was a teenager
remembers a day when they ran into each other on the
sidewalk and Joyce held out her hand. "See my new ring,"
she said. "The queen gave it to me when we were in England." The Cantones made no trips abroad. Others remember that she always had a story, about trips, about
meeting and becoming close to famous people, and that she
always told them with such absolute conviction that many
believed what she said.

That she was very intelligent is indisputable. She invariably scored high marks all the way through school and
graduated near the top of her high school class. She had, a
friend says, a photographic memory. "I was a little intimidated by her. She knew Latin, Italian, French—three or
four languages. I had to work like crazy, study all the time
just to get by, and she could pick up a book and just glance

at a page, her eyes just darting over it, and that was it. She knew it all.''

Her education did not end with high school. When she was graduated, she enrolled as a business major at Hillyer College in Hartford, now the University of Hartford. According to what Joyce told friends, her decision to go on to college, rather than being supported by her family, was bitterly opposed. She fought constantly with her mother. They agreed about nothing. Finally, she said in one version, her mother threw her out when she was sixteen, and from that day on she made her own way. Like so many other things she said, then and throughout her life, that just didn't happen to be true. All through college she lived at home with her mother and commuted to school, though a bed and a roof were about all the support she got. She paid for her college education with scholarships and by holding a job as an assistant to an insurance agent named Gino Dinatto at the Aetna Life and Casualty Insurance Company from her freshman year right through graduation in 1961.

With a degree in her hands, she had a kind of real independence she had never possessed before; she had credentials; she had education. One thing she knew for certain was that now she could cut all but the most casual ties with the home where she had felt trapped, where she was sure nobody had understood or sympathized with her and her ambitions. The opportunity to do just that was there for the taking: Robert I. White. Over the years of college their friendship turned into a kind of romance. When he proposed, she accepted, and within days of graduation they were married. It was a small ceremony, attended by only a few friends and some family, so small and casual, in fact, that one person who was there cannot remember who else attended, cannot even remember if it was a religious ceremony. When it was over, Joyce had cut the ties; rarely after that did she see her mother, brothers or sisters.

Hardly had the vows been taken before Robert and

Joyce Cantone White were gone. They moved to New Haven, where he had found a job as a beginning executive with Good Humor, the ice-cream company. Joyce continued her education. In New Haven she spent her days taking graduate courses in sociology at Yale, eventually, her résumé noted, earning master's degrees in social work and education.

The marriage lasted less than five years. White will not discuss the marriage at all. He will say only that it was a relief to him when it finally ended. Some who saw them occasionally say that the marriage was doomed from the start. Whatever expectations White had, Joyce did not share. He wanted children. Children were the last thing she wanted. She had decided on a career, and children could only interfere with that. That was only one problem with the marriage. Another was that White expected to be the head of his home. Joyce unfortunately took orders from nobody. Eventually they divorced.

Joyce left New Haven, took an apartment on her own in East Hartford and quickly found a job with the state of Connecticut, as a social worker with the Department of Child and Youth Services. She did not discuss the failed marriage or Bob White at all—not with family, friends or even members of the wedding. If asked, she said only that it hadn't worked out.

With strangers and new acquaintances she had a different story, one that she was to repeat to everyone over the years. White had not understood her at all. The marriage had been a disaster from the beginning. After a few years it was falling apart, and there was little hope of putting the pieces back together. In fact, she had no desire to keep the marriage alive, so she told White that she was going to leave him and get a divorce. White became more and more despondent. Then one day, when she arrived home, she found the house strangely quiet. She walked into the kitchen; White was slumped over the table. He had taken a .45 caliber revolver and shot himself in the head. The wallpaper in the kitchen was splattered with his blood and brains. That, she said, was why she never had wallpaper in her house; it reminded her too much of that awful moment.

She told the story of White's suicide to nearly everyone she met through the years, and everyone believed it. There seemed no reason to doubt it. Who would make up such a wild story if it weren't true? It was only in the summer of 1990 that the truth finally came out; Robert White, by then white-haired and paunchy, looking older than his years, appeared in a courtroom in Hartford and pronounced himself alive. "I couldn't believe it," said a friend of Joyce's who had heard the story often for more than two decades. "It blew my mind when he showed up."

She invented that story of suicide, perhaps, because on her return to Hartford she met another man. She always had men around her, at least that was what she said, but this man was special. His name was Michael Aparo. He was a deeply religious Catholic, a close friend of the head of the Hartford archdiocese, Archbishop John Whealon. He had studied for the priesthood, leaving the seminary to become a social worker for the city's Catholic Charities about the time he met Joyce Cantone White in 1966. He fell in love with her. There are those who speculate that she came up with the tale of White's suicide because there was just no way that the devout Aparo would have married a divorced woman. A widow was something else. In any event he proposed and she accepted. They were married on July 30, 1966, and moved into an apartment in East Hartford. She was twenty-six; he was a year older.

Through her new husband, she came to know Archbishop Whealon, and a close friendship soon developed, the Aparos meeting socially often with the archbishop. By 1967 Joyce was not only seeing Archbishop Whealon but writing him long letters, filled with the events of her life, problems she faced, personal matters, and Whealon was responding. She kept all that correspondence in a filing cabinet in her basement.

As time passed, though, Joyce began to invent, embellish and whisper other stories about her meeting with Aparo, their courtship and marriage. But, then, she always seemed to have other stories about everything.

In one version she and Aparo met while he was home from Rome, where he was studying for the priesthood and was about to take his vows. He fell in love with her, so deeply that his dedication to serving the church as a priest vanished as completely as a puff of smoke caught by the wind. They went to his friend and mentor Archbishop Whealon and discussed the situation. Whealon gave them his blessing and then sent them both back to Rome, where Aparo was given dispensation and permission to leave the seminary. Then they married.

As far as anyone knows, Michael Aparo and Joyce never made a voyage across the Atlantic, never went to Rome.

As time passed, she began to tell yet another story, this one more disturbing to those who heard it because of its import. She had met, she would say, Archbishop Whealon right after her return from New Haven. Just how she never said, for she was not a churchgoing or even a believing Catholic, her devotion to the church having vanished years before. There had been an instantaneous and uncontrollable attraction between them, a passion that transcended his priestly vows of celibacy, to say nothing of his position as head of the church in Hartford. They had begun an affair, one they were to maintain through the rest of her life. To cover that affair, Whealon tapped his protégé Michael Aparo, persuaded him to leave his studies for the priesthood, become Whealon's cuckold and marry the woman who was Whealon's mistress. To make the arrangement at least partly palatable, Whealon made Aparo a deacon in the church, a position open to married men for whom the priesthood was no longer possible.

* * *

The marriage of Michael and Joyce Aparo lasted ten years. Aparo worked for Catholic Charities, Joyce for Connecticut's Department of Youth and Child Services. Those who knew her and worked with her then say that she displayed a very real and intense desire to help the abused, neglected, needy and even delinquent children whose cases landed on her desk, was totally dedicated, worked long hours, often took unusual and imaginative actions and did an extraordinary job. She once told a friend that in order to find out what some of her kids were really going through, she spent a week, day and night, in one of the children's detention centers, experiencing what those kids experienced, listening to what they had to say. It was invaluable; it made a lot of difference in her work, in the way she approached those kids, she said.

The devout Aparo, apparently never completely reconciled to having given up the priesthood, spent most of his spare time on religious devotions in church, even erecting in a room in their home a small private chapel to which he often retreated for prayer.

Joyce had her own life apart from her husband, and some of that life was in sharp contrast with his. A woman always with an inquiring mind, anxious to learn all she could about anything that might interest her or that she might use, she explored a variety of esoteric diversions. For a time, in company with a friend, she spent Sundays on Park Street in Hartford, in a house where a spiritualist congregation held its meetings and séances. There were services; there was a medium who would go into a trance and then, in the voice of someone from the beyond, communicate messages from the beyond, from the departed, to one or another of the waiting congregation, revealing secrets about the past, hopes for the future.

"Joyce," says the friend, "really liked it. She was fascinated. I don't know how she found out about it, but she did. I think she just wanted to learn what it was all about.

And then after a while it just sort of petered out." But not completely, never totally. Throughout her life she kept packs of tarot cards in her desk drawer and now and then used them to read fortunes. In the spring of 1987 she once read Dennis Coleman's future. What she saw was a long life and great success and happiness.

There was something, though, that fascinated her even more than spiritualism. She devoted what spare hours she had to an increasingly important and lucrative sideline. Jewelry and precious and semiprecious stones had dazzled her for years. She began collecting stones of all kinds, working with them, making her own jewelry, and was soon selling it to a growing number of customers. Carol Parkola remembers visiting the apartment in East Hartford in those days. "She had this thing on the kitchen table, and there were rocks in it, and she told me you had to keep turning them to smooth and polish them down before you could begin to work with them. Later, when she was in the condo in Glastonbury, she had all these machines down in the cellar for transforming plain little rocks you'd pick up and go 'ugh' and throw away, for cleaning and polishing and cutting them and turning those stones into good jewelry. When she finished, those stones were just gorgeous. She used to go up to the quarries in Vermont and other places and look for semiprecious stones, and she could pick them out from stuff anyone else would think was just junk. I remember later she said she was taking a second mortgage out on her house so she could have the money to go to Australia and look for stones and buy an opal mine. She was crazy about opals. She was going into partnership in that mine, she said, with some military man, an older man, who was going on the trip with her."

Going to Australia and buying into an opal mine, with or without a military man as a partner, though, were just other embellishments, another of Joyce's stories.

Nancy Polydys, Carol Parkola's sister and a friend of Joyce's, remembers a time on Cape Cod "when we went into Provincetown, and we walked by Thunder Rock, which is not the jewelry store it used to be. I remember Joyce walking down the stairs and seeing this fiery opal and she fell in love with this fiery opal, and it was two hundred sixty-eight dollars. She just had to buy this fiery opal, and she did. When she saw something and she liked it, she bought it.''

Indeed, she did. All through her life. But only the best. She was very fond of good things and disparaging of the second-rate. Says Carol Parkola: ''She would save her money to buy one good thing. She'd never shop at K Mart or Bradley's or a place like that. She'd die before she'd walk into one of those stores. She would save her money so she could buy one nice blouse instead of going into a store and buying a couple that didn't look as nice. She would say to me, 'Carol, save your money. Even if it takes all year, do it and then buy one good piece of jewelry.' Joyce had crystal and silver and china, all good things. She never bought anything that she didn't think was the best; she wouldn't have anything that wasn't the best in her house.''

She had cats, too, two Siamese in the mid to late 1960s. Those cats went everywhere with her. Carol Parkola's mother and father had a summer house on Cape Cod. Joyce was a frequent visitor, sometimes with Michael Aparo, more often without, but never without her Siamese cats. Carol Parkola recalls, ''One time she was up there and one of those cats—I hate Siamese cats—climbed up on the breakfast table and put its foot in my orange juice. I yelled, 'That's it! Get that cat out of here!' She got so upset about that because those cats were her babies. Really. She treated them just like they were her children, maybe better.''

Indeed. For while she may have empathized with the children who came under her protection at work, she seemed to have little patience with children outside, had her own ideas about how they should be raised, standards that nobody else could meet. Again Carol Parkola: ''When my daughter was just a couple of years old—this was sometime in the late 1960s—Joyce was over one night for dinner. Now, my daughter wasn't one of those children who ate with their fingers and threw food all over the place. My sister and I weren't brought up that way, and my children weren't brought up that way. Anyway, Bonnie dropped something out of the high chair and somebody picked it up off the floor, and Joyce said, 'You're going to let her get away with that? If I ever have children, they're going to behave the way they're supposed to behave.' ''

But children were definitely not part of Joyce Aparo's plans for the future. Michael Aparo might want them, might talk to her about having a child, might try to persuade her, but she was having none of it. She had her own life and her own career, and that was what was important. Children would only sidetrack her.

Though he was a deeply convinced Catholic, who believed firmly in the church's teachings and dictates, his wife practiced birth control. Much as he might resent it, there was nothing he could do about it. He was, everyone who knew him was certain, a weak man totally dominated by a strong wife. ''You'd have to say that Michael was really a wimp,'' says a friend of long standing. ''If Joyce ever raised her voice to him, he'd just back away and kind of cower. I really think he was afraid of her.'' She ruled their house, and she made the rules. As she told a friend, ''There's no way the church is going to tell me what to do about birth control. It's none of their business whether I have children or don't have them.'' Besides, she told that friend, she probably couldn't have children anyway. She had had several operations, she said, her insides filled with stitches, and the doctors told her she should not even consider having a child.

Further, the marriage was turning out to be something less than idyllic. Aparo's devotion to his religion, his obsession with it, his constant praying and churchgoing infuriated her. She derided him and sneered at him.

"Throughout our married life," he says, "I was a victim of her abuse. It was practically always verbal, psychological. Joyce had the capacity of talking circles around anyone. Unfortunately, I think, her great intelligence ended up serving the purpose of her cruelty."

Then, in the middle of 1970, Joyce Aparo learned that she was pregnant.

7

She was furious. The child was not planned, and she did not want it. She blamed Michael Aparo; somehow he had tricked her. She was not going to have the baby. She was going to get an abortion.

"I was in pain," Aparo says. "I was feeling that I was being totally rejected because of this pregnancy. And this was my child. I was devastated." He sought help from a psychiatrist. Joyce went with him for one session. It didn't seem to help. Then "I don't know why," Aparo says, "but she changed her mind."

Though she had changed her mind about giving birth, she had yet to change her mind about being a full-time mother to a baby. In January 1971 she saw her brother Tom, the White Plains construction executive, for the first time

90

after a long separation. She told him how she felt about having a baby. "I told her," he says, "have the child and I will adopt it." Without discussing the offer with Aparo, who learned about it only years later, she said she would consider it.

The baby, a girl weighing five pounds four and a half ounces, was born just before four o'clock in the afternoon of February 12, 1971, at Hartford Hospital. She was christened Karin Elizabeth Aparo. Her godfather, she would be told by her mother, as would everyone else, was Archbishop John Whealon.

The pregnancy had been a trying time. Joyce later told Karin that she had been ill through much of it, had spent a lot of it in bed. Hard as the pregnancy had been, the delivery was even worse. She told Karin that she had suffered terrible agony, had been in constant pain and had nearly died during labor and had been seriously ill for weeks afterward.

Good husband and father that he was, Michael Aparo notified his wife's family. Sister Ina went to the hospital to visit Joyce and her new niece. Joyce, she says, was anything but the proud mother. Rather, she was bitter. She had not wanted the baby in the first place, she said, and now that it was here, she still didn't want it and was thinking about putting it up for adoption.

Brother Thomas arrived for a visit after the baby had been taken home. What he saw distressed him greatly. Joyce ignored the child, ordered Aparo to change the baby's diapers, feed her, put her to bed, take care of her. Joyce seemed to have no interest at all in her infant daughter. It was, Tom Cantone thought, time to renew his offer. "I wanted to adopt my niece to get her out of the environment she was living in," he says. "I told my sister I would take my niece, raise her as my daughter—with the stipulation that my sister would not have any claim or any contact with the child."

The offer couched in those terms, with those conditions, was something Joyce was not willing to accept. She might be willing to turn the infant Karin over to her brother, but only on condition that she have unlimited rights to visit her, that Karin be told that Joyce was her mother and that Joyce have the ultimate say in her upbringing. Tom Cantone would not agree. He dropped his proposal.

A year later, during another upsetting visit, he repeated it once more when he learned that Joyce had not yet accepted her role as mother and seemed determined to rid herself of this burden. The offer was made with the same conditions. Joyce spurned it. She might not want to raise the child herself, but she was determined to lay down the rules under which she would be raised no matter who did the raising.

So after all, she would raise her daughter or at least have her daughter in the same house. She hired a woman, Jill Smith, to take care of Karin during the day, and she let Michael Aparo do the tending at night. Michael Aparo might think, with all the baby care he was doing, that he was being both mother and father to his child while Joyce was ignoring her, and him, and going back to work, this time in a more important job at the state's Department of Mental Health. But Michael Aparo was dominated by his wife, she was the strength in their house and that was obvious to anyone who came through their doors.

By the time Karin was two, Joyce finally began to take an interest. Karin was talking by then; Karin was showing signs of absorbing information; Karin was revealing an intelligence beyond the usual; Karin was beginning to function as something other than what Joyce considered a totally dependent creature whose only responses were instinctual and who was only an onerous burden for a smart, ambitious woman. Now Joyce began to see her as a kind of empty slate ready to receive whatever Joyce cared to write on it, an unformed stone waiting to be carved into whatever shape Joyce wanted to carve. She would issue the orders, and the child would follow them to the letter with no deviations.

She would lay down the rules, and her child would obey them completely.

Ina Camblor remembers a visit when Karin was about three. By then, she says, Karin was a very quiet child who never laughed, never played and displayed little emotion. She picked the child up, talked to her and tickled her, trying to get her to laugh. Joyce, she says, ordered her to put Karin down. "That," Joyce said, "is not the way I'm raising my child."

Ina Camblor said, "Babies need love. I'm a mother, and I know how to raise children. They need love. Until they're ten, they're still babies."

"Don't tell me how to raise my daughter," Joyce said.

On another visit she watched as Joyce slapped Karin hard across the face. "Don't do that in my house," Ina ordered.

Joyce ignored her, turned to Karin and said, "Don't you dare cry." Karin didn't.

"If you want to slap her on the bottom," Ina said, "that's okay. Any parent does that. But to slap her across the face—that's not right."

"Mind your own business," Joyce said. Then she gathered Karin and stormed out of the house. Ina never saw her sister again, did not see her niece again until the day of Joyce's funeral.

Those slaps across the face in Ina's house were not isolated incidents. Her earliest memory, Karin says, is of her mother slapping her. She was about four then, and "there were people over to the house. They were in the living room with my mother and father, and my father was offering them drinks. My mother asked me, 'What are those people doing with Daddy?' I said, 'They're drinking,' She slapped me across the face and pushed me out of the room."

It was something Karin grew used to. She says Joyce slapped her across the face almost every day of her life until she was about twelve. They were not simple cuffs; according to Karin and to some who witnessed them, the slaps were hard, were invariably first a backhand across one side of the face and then the palm across the other, and they sent Karin reeling across the room.

Joyce might, then, show little affection, might explode and strike out for little or no reason, might make demands beyond any hope that they could be met, might inflict punishment far beyond any cause, yet she was proud of her daughter, had grandiose dreams for her, perhaps saw a way of reliving her own life and realizing all her unfulfilled dreams through her. Karin was bright and quick and eager to learn. And so, when Karin was just past three, Joyce enrolled her in a Montessori school, where open classrooms replete with a variety of materials available make it possible for a child to progress at his or her own rate.

For the first few months all went well. "Karin," says her teacher then, Janet Stachelek, "was very bright, and she did very well, and she was a typical happy-go-lucky three-year-old." There was, though, one disturbing element even then. Karin always came to school immaculately dressed, inappropriately so, the teacher thought, for the kinds of trips the kids took and for the outdoor play and other physical activities that fill so much of the kids' time in such a pre-school environment. She sent notes home to Joyce, even called, asking that Karin be dressed more appropriately. Joyce ignored them.

Then Joyce began to appear, demanding to know why Karin wasn't reading yet, why she wasn't doing math, why she wasn't doing other advanced work. Stachelek attempted to explain that at a Montessori school the children set their own pace, do things when they are ready for them. That wasn't answer enough for Joyce Aparo. If she couldn't force the school to push Karin, she would do it herself.

"Karin," Stachelek remembers, "would come in and say, 'My mother says I have to do this today,' instead of

'I'd like to do this today.' " Stachelek got in touch with Joyce and asked her to ease up on the pressure, just to let Karin play and enjoy herself.

Joyce responded, Stachelek says, by declaring that she had an IQ of more than 140 and Karin took after her, and so her teacher ought to be doing something to use those brains and abilities and push her ahead. Stachelek dismissed those demands because Karin was doing very well on her own.

But the demands kept coming, and the pressure on Karin kept mounting. "One day in Montessori," Stachelek says, "Karin and I were playing a rhyming game. We were just making simple words that rhyme. And she wrote two sentences that rhymed. I wrote them down on paper for her. To me, it was just a fun thing. But to Joyce it was that Karin had composed poetry, so Karin was forced to bring in a new poem every day. I could just picture the kind of thing she had to go through at night at home."

There wasn't much Stachelek could do to make Joyce back off and ease up on the pressures. But there were some things she couldn't dismiss or ignore, some things that convinced her she had to take some action. The children spend a long day in a Montessori school, often from seven-thirty in the morning until about five in the afternoon, when their mothers arrive to pick them up. One afternoon when Karin was four, Joyce appeared to retrieve her. "She obviously had not had a good day at work," Stachelek remembers. "But Karin also had had a very long day, she was whiny, hungry, tired, and she wanted to go home. She wasn't getting her jacket on quickly enough, and before I could even realize what was happening, Mrs. Aparo had backhanded her across the face so hard she flew into the water fountain and cracked her head. I immediately stepped between them and told Mrs. Aparo that her behavior was totally unnecessary. I bent down and put Karin's jacket on for her. What surprised me was Karin's response. She didn't cry at all. She just stood there. A little four-year-old girl with her eyes sparkling with tears but refusing to cry. I asked her, 'Does your head hurt, honey?' She shook her head no. Then Mrs. Aparo was immediately contrite. 'Oh, I don't know what came over me. I've had such a bad day.'

"But the next day when Karin came into school, she had a large bump on the back of her head, and I asked her, 'Honey, does your head hurt?' She said, 'No, my head doesn't hurt. That didn't hurt as much as a real spanking.' "

That was enough for Stachelek. She decided to take some action. She put in a call to the Department of Child and Youth Services. Stachelek made that call anonymously. "I knew she would pull Karin out of my classroom or out of the school completely if she knew I had done anything, and I didn't want that to happen." Stachelek told the DCYS what had happened, said that she suspected that Karin was being terribly abused, both physically and emotionally, probably more psychologically than physically, and someone ought to go into the Aparo home and investigate.

Somebody did. And Joyce Aparo, well versed in the vocabulary of child abuse, of the department where she had once worked, managed to explain it all away. But she was furious. She suspected somebody at the Montessori school of having made the report. She confronted Stachelek. "She was livid that somebody would have the nerve to suspect her of child abuse. I can clearly remember her telling me that it was just ridiculous. Karin, she said, was on a first-name basis with Archbishop Whealon, and she herself was beyond reproach, and she couldn't believe that anybody would suspect her of this."

By then her marriage to Michael Aparo was falling apart. They had moved from their apartment and bought a small house on Wesleyan Street in Glastonbury, near the border with East Hartford. Karin was five then, in her last year at Montessori before entering the first grade in the Glastonbury public school system. What she remembers of those days, before the move and after, are constant battles and arguments between Joyce and Michael Aparo.

According to Aparo, many of those fights were over his objections to Joyce's treatment of their daughter, though "most of her cruelty at that time was directed toward me. And then there was a time, I think it was November 1976, Armistice Day, Veterans Day, and we were both home on vacation. Karin was holding a small bowl with strawberries, and she stumbled and spilled some of the juice on her T-shirt. Joyce began to act as if the kid had committed murder and really began viciously hitting her. I intervened and pushed her away. And she stumbled and fell and accused me of battering her. And within a matter of days I was served with divorce papers. I have to say I was happy to leave. I would never have initiated the divorce because of my religious convictions. But once she initiated it, I was happy to leave."

The precipitating cause of the divorce, according to what Joyce told friends, had nothing to do with Karin; it had everything to do with Michael Aparo and his dedication to, she called it obsession with, his religion. "I went over to her house," a friend recalls, "and Joyce and I were talking, and she said, 'This is why I'm not with Michael. I can't take it any longer. And I'll show you why.' She took me upstairs, and she showed me a bedroom, and she said, 'This is why.' In the bedroom was a prayer stool and an altar and a lot more, what she called his prayer room. 'He spends so much time up here,' she told me; 'he can't leave it; he hasn't been able to split from it. There's just too much religion.' "

For Karin, then five years old, Joyce had a mixture of explanations for the departure of Aparo. "She said my father used to hit her, and once he tried to throw her over the balcony." There were others. Her father had always regretted his decision not to become a priest, she was told, and the church was still holding him, would not let him loose; he was religion-obsessed and had no time for them, only for his religion. There was yet more. Joyce often told her that the real reason for the divorce was Karin herself, that if it hadn't been for a child, Aparo might have been able to realize his dream of becoming a priest.

So, five-year-old Karin believed her mother's lies and had that burden to carry. She carried as well the burden of her mother's grandiose, outsize expectations, even obsessions. Unwittingly Stachelek opened a door, and Karin passed through into a new world that was to dominate her life and her mother's fantasies from that time on.

Karin had not been in first grade in Glastonbury's Naubuc Elementary School for more than a few weeks before Joyce called Stachelek. "She said that the first-grade teacher was hopelessly miserable and that the principal couldn't seem to understand that Karin was gifted. That's what she called her, gifted. She asked would I come to the school with her for a meeting and explain to them what Karin had been doing in Montessori. I agreed. It turned into a disaster, with Joyce ranting and raving and screaming at the principal and accusing the teacher of having a blue-collar mentality that she couldn't deal with. She didn't want her daughter subjected to this. I tried to get her to ease up a little, but she just wouldn't have any of it."

But Stachelek had a suggestion that she hoped might help both mother and child. If Karin was so bored in school, why not find her an outside interest that would challenge her? Music is an integral part of a Montessori school, and Stachelek had noticed that while Karin was in her class, she came sharply awake and was captivated whenever classical music filled the room. She mentioned this to Joyce and mildly suggested that it might be good for Karin to take music lessons, the piano perhaps.

A few weeks later Joyce called to say that she had followed that suggestion. But it wasn't piano lessons that Karin would be taking. Her daughter, she said, wanted to play the violin, so Joyce had enrolled her in a class at the Julius Hartt School of Music in Hartford, perhaps the most prominent music school in the area, where she would learn through the Suzuki method.

A month later Stachelek got another call. Karin, Joyce said, was a true prodigy. After only four lessons she was playing brilliantly. Stachelek ought to come and hear her. "Mrs. Aparo ordered Karin to play 'Twinkle, Twinkle, Little Star.' She played and she missed a few notes, which was understandable since she'd only had a few lessons, but the song was certainly recognizable. When she finished, I clapped. But Mrs. Aparo began screaming at me, 'How could you possibly applaud when Karin was playing so many wrong notes and her teacher says she's come so far?' She made Karin play that song again and again, at least four times, and Karin was near tears. Finally she played it perfectly. Joyce was the only one of us who was smiling. And then she sent Karin into the family room to practice the scales."

Joyce's battle to conquer the school system intensified as she discovered that Karin had begun playing hooky. At six Karin was a latchkey kid. Joyce went to work early and came home late, and Karin was expected to wait alone in the morning at the school bus stop, then take the bus home at the end of the day, let herself into the house and wait alone until Joyce appeared. But neighbors noticed that all too often Karin started out in the morning, then, before reaching the school bus stop, turned and went back home, let herself in and did not reappear all day. The reason, Joyce maintained, must be both boredom and hatred of teachers who neither understood nor appreciated her. The solution was to put Karin in second grade immediately. She called Stachelek and asked for her support. If Stachelek spent a day observing Karin at home, Joyce said, she would see the truth of Joyce's claims.

Stachelek, indeed, learned a lot that day, but not necessarily what Joyce expected. She learned, for instance, that

every morning before she left for work, Joyce posted on the
refrigerator door a list of chores Karin was required to do
when she got home from school and before Joyce returned
about six, including feeding the cats, vacuuming the living
room, general cleaning around the house and setting the
table for dinner. If they weren't done to Joyce's rigid standards or if they weren't finished, she made Karin do them
again. What Karin didn't tell Stachelek then, though later
she did tell friends, was that if Joyce wasn't satisfied, she
hit her across the face, backhand, then forehand, before that
second round of housework could start.

Stachelek learned that if the phone rang while Karin
was home alone, she was not to answer it unless it was
Joyce giving a special signal: two rings and a hang-up, then
one ring and a hang-up, followed immediately by another
ring. On weekends and vacations Karin was again left home
alone while Joyce went to work; she was not permitted to go
outside or play with friends or answer the phone; she was to
stay in the house and do what was required of her.

That day Stachelek followed Karin about as she did her
chores, watched a little television and made her own lunch.
But there was something particularly chilling. Karin spent
much time in the closet in her room. She had turned that
closet into a fort and filled it with her stuffed animals. It was
there that she found comfort and protection. Being alone in
the house after dark frightened her, so she went into the
closet, into her fort with her stuffed animals; it was the one
place where she felt safe.

"I tried to talk to Karin about all this, about why she
didn't go to school and all the rest. She said she didn't want
to go to school because she wasn't allowed to play with any
of the children. Her mother had told her that she couldn't
make any friends because she didn't want Karin associating
with children who were not on her intellectual level. That
was the real reason Karin was skipping school."

Joyce didn't believe it. Joyce couldn't be wrong. Joyce
was determined to battle the school to get her way, threat-

ening lawsuits, threatening publicity, threatening more. Joyce won the battle. Karin was moved to the second grade.

The victory was short-lived. From the very start it was apparent to the second-grade teacher, Sharon Rickard, that the idea had been a dreadful mistake. "Karin was a sweet, shy kid," she remembers, "but she didn't interact socially with the other children. How could she? She was very much a six-year-old, and the others were seven and eight, and at that age there's a big difference."

There was the day when she came out of the classroom at the end of school and found Karin leaning against the wall, crying. She asked why.

"I missed my bus," Karin said.

"That's okay. It happens. I'll call your mommy, and she'll come and get you."

Panic filled Karin's face, and she begged Rickard not to make that call. She seemed so terrified that Rickard complied and said instead she would give Karin a ride home herself.

"Mommy's not home," Karin said.

Then she'd drop her off with a neighbor, Rickard said.

"You can't do that," Karin said. She had to go straight home, and then she would let herself in. She had a key.

That was something Rickard didn't like. A six-year-old kid with a key going into an empty house just didn't seem right. "If something happened," she asked, "what would you do?"

Karin said she'd call a neighbor. Rickard wasn't quite so sure she would. Nevertheless, she drove Karin home and watched as she unlocked the door and let herself in. The incident left a bad taste.

About the only time Rickard saw Karin animated and excited was the day she arrived at school and told the teacher she was about to have her first communion. "Uncle John," she said, "is going to do it for me. He's my godfather, you know." Who was "Uncle John"? He was, Karin explained, Archbishop John Whealon.

After a couple of months Rickard and others at the school knew that they had to move Karin back into the first grade. The situation was impossible for her. Pamela Merwin, another first-grade teacher, went to the principal. "Listen, no one is thinking of Karin. I want that child in my classroom," she said.

Karin was moved. "I'll never forget the first day. The guidance counselor brought her into my class. She had big brown eyes with dark circles under them. She was perfectly dressed. The first thing she said to me was 'My name is Karin, with an *i*.' "

As the days passed, Merwin became increasingly concerned about her new charge. "She was always somber, always very depressed, always dressed perfectly. It was almost as if all the outward appearances were of a perfect child and of a perfect family. The way I run my classroom, I try to have a very trusting and open atmosphere so that the children could come and talk to me. They knew I was there for them. There were days when Karin was definitely upset, and you could tell she had been crying even before coming to school. One day I said, 'Karin, what's the matter?' She said 'Mrs. Merwin, I was so excited about going to see my daddy, and I told my mother, and she flushed my tropical fish down the toilet.'

"This little girl was terribly abused emotionally. I really watched for signs of actual physical abuse, but I never saw any although Karin shared with me specific instances where she was terribly punished and slapped. There was a distinct pattern. On weekends when she went to see her father, she did not come back to school until maybe Wednesday. I suspected it was because Mrs. Aparo kept her home so that the signs of abuse did not show."

Perhaps. Or perhaps some of that physical abuse had more to do with the fact that neither Karin nor the school was living up to Joyce's expectations. "Karin's mother came to me in a parent conference with a wealth of papers that we do in first grade," Merwin says. "Part of my program is to use positive reinforcement. Even if there was a mistake, I would say, 'Good, keep trying.' She came to me with all these papers and threw them at me and was questioning my ability as a teacher. What was wrong with me? How could I accept that kind of work? She would make Karin correct them. One example I'll never forget. It was for initial consonants. And the picture was of a camel, and Karin had put the *c* for the beginning sound and the *l* for the ending sound. Mrs. Aparo shoved that paper in my face and said something about the number of humps it had and it was supposed to be a dromedary. This was the kind of expectation she had for Karin.

"I was worried about Karin taking her own life at some time, if she continued under this pressure."

That extreme dissatisfaction with what the school was teaching and Karin was learning, expressed to both school and child, never let up. Later, when Karin was learning cursive handwriting, she showed her work to Joyce. Joyce looked at it, raged that the handwriting was awful, made her practice the cursive lettering again and again for hours and threatened to go to the school and force it to send Karin back a grade unless she improved.

It was not just Merwin and others at school who were taking notice that all was not well in the Aparo house. Concerned neighbors had been watching Joyce and Karin for some time and wondering what to do. One neighbor remembers when Karin broke the rules and brought her daughter into the house to play dress-up. The two children played until Joyce suddenly and unexpectedly arrived home. Terrified, Karin hustled the other child down to the basement and hid her until when Joyce was otherwise occupied, she could sneak her out the cellar door.

Another neighbor decided to take some action on her own and called the Department of Child and Youth Services to report that Karin was being left alone after school and into the evening. But she made that call anonymously and was told that because she wouldn't give her name, the DCYS could do nothing.

Finally, in early June 1978, when Karin was seven, an event occurred that was so blatant it could no longer be ignored. One morning a neighbor, watching her own child heading for school, saw Karin turn away from the school bus stop and return home, unlock the door and disappear into the house. She did not reappear all day. That night the woman told her husband, Richard LaCroix, a Hartford insurance company executive, when he got home. He walked across the street and rang the Aparos' bell. Joyce, who had just returned from work, opened the door. He told her what his wife had seen. Joyce was furious, railed at him, told him Karin would never do such a thing and slammed the door.

About a half hour later his doorbell rang. Joyce was standing on the stoop, gripping Karin's arm tightly. "I owe you an apology," she said.

"I'm not concerned about apologies," he said, "What I'm concerned about is Karin being left alone. She's just a little kid."

"I can assure you it won't happen again," Joyce said. She turned on Karin and hit her in the side of the face with a closed fist, then dragged her down the steps and across the street, punching her all the way home.

LaCroix followed across the street. "I couldn't take what was happening," he said. He rang the bell. Joyce answered. "I told her that what she was doing was totally inappropriate, and it was no way to treat a child."

Joyce glared at him. "I'll show you what this kid did to me today," she snapped, and then smashed Karin in the face with her closed fist again, knocking her to the floor. Then she slammed the door in LaCroix's face.

As it happened, LaCroix once had been both a member of the DCYS board and its chairman. When he got back home, he picked up the phone, made a call and filed a formal complaint of child abuse against Joyce Aparo.

So began a three-month investigation by the DCYS. The initial report of the department reads:

On 6/3/78, a referral was received via the Care Line. Caller reported that Karin was left alone, unsupervised, between 3:00 P.M. and 7:00 P.M. Caller was not sure if this happened everyday [*sic*]. A neighbor witnessed mother punch Karin in the face with her fist because she did not go to school. Another neighbor said Karin was hit in the mouth and it was bleeding. Caller alleged that mother practices witchcraft.

Contacted Joyce Aparo at her place of employment. Immediately upon [my] telling her of the referral, Mrs. Aparo became very defensive. It took a considerable amount of talking to persuade Mrs. Aparo to discuss the allegations. She initially referred me to her lawyer but did open up and converse more freely later on. She confirmed that Karin had missed school one day. Apparently Karin had decided she did not feel like going to school and stayed home that day. No one had called in to say that Karin was absent and the school did not contact the mother to find out what was wrong. This upset Mrs. Aparo very much. When she returned home, a neighbor informed Mrs. Aparo that Karin had stayed home. In the neighbor's presence, Mrs. Aparo spanked Karin quite hard which resulted in leaving a bruised area. She denied ever hitting Karin in the face with her fist. She raised a valid point in saying that the school social worker or teacher would have noticed some marks on the child's face if she was punched. She said Karin was not bleeding at all. She accused the caller of being an outright liar. Mother also thought the accusation of her practicing witchcraft was ridiculous.

Mrs. Aparo does admit that her child is left alone every day from 3:30 to 5:00 P.M. because she works. The child is left with several phone numbers in case of emergency. One of the numbers is that of a neighbor about 1 mile down the road. She also mentioned that her daughter is not a "normal" seven year old in that she had an IQ of 145 and is very mature for her age. It was explained that despite her high IQ, this was really an unsuitable arrangement for her child's care. Mrs. Aparo said she had tried various alternatives. She did have a live-in person for a period of time but it "did not work out." She had a 12 yr. old babysitter but Mrs. Aparo felt that the capacity of this person was hardly much more than her own intelligent daughter. She also was going to try day care but this would involve leaving work to transport her child which she was unable to do. Other attempts to hire a babysitter have failed also due to transportation problems and people not willing to sit for 1½ hrs.

Mrs. Aparo mentioned that the lack of supervision of Karin will no longer be a problem in about 1 week. She is enrolled as a full-time student for the Montessori School in Rocky Hill for the entire summer. It was explained to Mrs. Aparo that this does solve the immediate problem for the time being but more suitable arrangements will have to be made upon resumption of the school year. She said she would continue trying to find an appropriate alternative. . . .

Conclusion: Abuse has not been confirmed but neglect has been substantiated. This neglect is in the form of lack of supervision of a 7 year old child for 1½ hrs. every day. This immediate problem appears to be temporarily solved. . . . It was suggested that she contact this agency for suggestions should she have difficulty [in making arrangements once the new school year started]. It was also explained that should we receive another referral of a similar nature at that time, we will become involved (whether we are requested or not) in making more suitable arrangements with potential of the case transferred to treatment.

Over the next several weeks attempts by the agency to interview Joyce Aparo face-to-face rather than by phone were unavailing, Joyce explaining over the phone that her heavy work schedule made such a meeting impossible. The agency did not press.

On September 5 the whole matter was dropped. The DCYS notified Joyce: "I have not received any further inquiry from you regarding the protective services referral of June 5, 1978. Since you have not contacted me, I will assume that you have no further questions. Therefore, I will be closing your case. I apologize for any inconvenience caused by the involvement of this agency."

A long time later an executive with the agency said, "Look, nobody could have predicted what was going to happen in nine or ten years." The agency is flooded with calls and complaints, has a limited budget and a small staff. It has to set priorities. At the top of the list are cases involving the major problems that cannot be ignored, such as sexual abuse, patently battered kids and delinquency. Obviously, with Joyce and Karin Aparo, those problems did not seem to exist to the agency. And there was something else. Joyce Aparo was intelligent and motivated, and most important, she knew the special language of the social worker; she had all the right answers, so had a ready explanation for everything. "I don't want to offer this as an excuse," the agency executive says, "but if things were as bad as people say, why didn't the father intervene? Why didn't some other member of the family? Why didn't Archbishop Whealon, who was supposed to be so close to Karin, to Joyce, to the family, why didn't he step in and do something? They all should have been a lot more knowledgeable about the situation than we were."

Nobody, of course, did anything, then or later. Joyce's explanations were accepted. And the accusations that she practiced witchcraft were just as easily dismissed when she contemptuously denied them. Yet, neighbors say, she openly told them when she first moved into the house on Wesleyan

Street that she was a witch, though she gave no details. Perhaps it was just a way of keeping at a distance neighbors she wanted nothing to do with because she considered them as much beneath her as she thought their children were beneath her daughter.

But the boast was there, and some gave it credence; if they were not adults, then at least other children believed it. Lori DeLucca, a friend of Karin's until the fourth grade and an acquaintance thereafter, remembers that when they were friends, Karin told her and Shannon Dubois about her closet, about sitting there and meditating for hours, told them that if they sat outside in the dark and stared at the moon, they would be able to leave their bodies. Lori went home and told her mother, who said, ''Stay away from that girl. There's something not right about her.'' Lori obeyed, and the friendship died.

8

In any person's life there are seminal events, essential in the formation of later attitudes and actions. On the surface they may seem trivial, of little lasting significance at least to the outsider. But in the psyche they are unforgettable and take on a crucial aspect. For Karin Aparo her seventh birthday, on February 12, 1978, was such an event.

Years later she wrote about it to Dennis Coleman, during a critical phase in their relationship. It was in early August 1986, and she had watched from her window as he walked out of his house and got into his car. She had turned away to put on some clothes, meaning to go out and speak to him. But by the time she got dressed, he had driven away without looking in her direction or speaking to her.

As she watched him leave, she suddenly remembered

her father's doing precisely the same thing on that seventh birthday. It was to have been a special day. She had never before had a birthday party for friends, and now Joyce was about to give her one. A rum cake had been ordered, made specially for her, and Joyce had purchased candy and other treats, party favors, napkins and plates and all the rest to make this a gala occasion.

Karin was just returning with her father from a weekend together. Those weekends were special, for they were the only times she saw him, and during those days he treated her like a princess. As they drove up to the house, he suddenly proposed that she go upstairs, change, and then he would take her to visit her grandmother—his mother—and other relatives, who all had presents for her, and they would spend her birthday together.

She was ecstatic. She raced into the house. Joyce was busy cleaning and getting everything ready. As she tore up the stairs, Karin announced her plans. Joyce was furious. She picked up the phone and began calling the kids who had been invited; there would be no party. Michael Aparo appeared. He and Joyce had a bitter argument. Karin, upstairs, frantically trying to change her clothes, heard them. Then she heard the front door close. "My dad left. He got into his little yellow Volkswagen bug & sped away in the opposite direction. He didn't even say goodbye."

A few minutes later Karin descended the stairs. She asked where her father was. Joyce told her he had run out on them as usual. Karin began to cry. Joyce told her to stop because she had brought the situation on herself. Through her tears Karin asked if they could call her friends and tell them that the party was really on and that the first call had been a mistake. Joyce refused. She ordered Karin to throw out all the party favors, the plates, napkins and the rest, to put the candy away and leave the rum cake in the refrigerator. Then she ordered Karin to go back upstairs, unpack her weekend suitcase, return and finish all the housework.

Karin got no presents that birthday. The party that

never was, as she later called it, was supposed to be the present from Joyce. From her father, she thinks she got a card, though she can't remember it. The cake remained untouched in the refrigerator, bringing tears until Joyce eventually threw it out.

"Well," she wrote to Dennis, "instead of 'little yellow Volkswagen bug' put in 'little yellow Triumph Spitfire' then maybe you'll get the idea of how hurt I was." The one difference was that this time she didn't cry. But, she wrote, she had begun to wonder if perhaps she should never get dressed again. When she did, something bad inevitably happened. Her father had once been, and now Dennis was, her only escape from her mother. They both gave Karin time away from Joyce. They both endeared themselves to her, gave her nice things, made her forget her troubles and problems. But they both deserted her in a time of desperate need, and they both "didn't even say goodbye."

Michael Aparo barely remembers that event. But it convinced Karin that she could never depend on him in time of need. He became a figure of increasingly less importance or influence in her life. Though she continued to see him now and then, the meetings became fewer and fewer as time passed, and the distance between them grew ever wider.

Her father had disappointed her, but she could escape him. Her mother, who did worse than disappoint her, she could never escape. And the agony of living at home with her grew worse as the years passed. There would be the times, many of them, repeated often, she says, when Joyce "made me stand in the middle of the floor while she was in bed, and then she would go over me critically from head to toe, making remarks. 'Look at your hair. It's always in your eyes. You look like a dog. Hold your face up or you'll get a double chin. You're getting fat. I don't know why you don't listen to me. You're an intelligent girl.' "

And there was the day "I was standing with my mother and she was ironing and she was yelling about something I had done and she held up the iron and said, 'Come here. I want to burn your face.' '' Fortunately Karin didn't move, and the cord wasn't long enough to reach her, though Joyce kept stretching it and screaming at Karin to come to her and get burned. Suddenly the washing machine in the other room started making noises, spinning out of balance. Joyce glared in that direction, then at Karin and ordered her to go and fix it.

But there were things to fill the emptiness, to blunt the terror. There was the violin. Karin and Joyce, in reality and fantasy, shared it, and in the sharing they forged whatever bond existed between them. Among the earliest memories of neighbors and friends is the picture of a small, sad-faced child with big dark eyes, soon concealed behind large glasses like those her mother wore, and dark hair, always with a violin case in her hand. Among other memories are those of a grown woman talking constantly, pridefully of her daughter and her daughter's future with that violin.

Karin picked up the violin for the first time just before her sixth birthday, in January 1977, and it remained in her hands, central and crucial to her existence and to her relationship with her mother, for the next ten and a half years. Karin later told a psychiatrist that the violin was the only thing in her life that belonged to her alone. Her mother might tell her how much she loved music, might share that love with Karin, but the violin was "my thing," the one thing that took her away from her mother, the thing that became the focus of her identity.

Joyce brought her to Constance Sattler, a teacher at the Julius Hartt School of Music, a practitioner of the Suzuki violin method, based on the idea of constant cooperation and interplay among teacher, student and parent, in which the parent attends the lessons, an individual one and a group one with other children every week, observes, gets some instruction herself and then, at home, is able to help the child during practice sessions.

Sattler remembers clearly that first meeting. Mother and daughter arrived. She looked at Joyce, and her immediate thought was that she must have gone through some terrible tragedy; her hair was snow white. "Then I saw her a couple of weeks later, and her hair was a different color, and over the next several years, it changed color again and again."

Karin took lessons with Sattler at Hartt for the next four years. At first Joyce was always there, sitting off in a corner, observing and embroidering something in satin with ornate gold and silver thread. When Sattler casually asked what she was doing, Joyce told her she was making a headdress for an archbishop.

"Her moods," Sattler recalls, "were very changeable and unpredictable. She could overflow with love and approval one minute or one time and the next be icy with disapproval, all for no apparent reason." No matter what Joyce's moods were, Karin never seemed to react.

There were other things about Joyce that Sattler noticed. As Karin got older, Joyce, at the teacher's urging, showed up less often. Michael Aparo sometimes, or a variety of other men, for Joyce invariably had men around her, dropped Karin off for her lessons and then picked her up when the lessons were over. Once, when Sattler expressed concern for Karin to Aparo over the way she was being treated by her mother, Aparo had no comment, acted, the teacher thought, as though he were helpless to do anything.

Through the years Sattler heard a variety of stories from Joyce about her plans. "She talked about marriage all the time. She would come in and say, 'I'm getting married next week.' It never happened." And once Joyce told her that she was about to leave on a long business trip to Australia, perhaps the one she had told several friends she was making to hunt for semiprecious stones and buy into an opal mine, and that Karin would be flying out a few days later to join her. But Karin missed only a couple of lessons, and when she was back at the music school, she explained that her mother had returned sooner than expected, so she hadn't made the trip. As it happened, Joyce hadn't made the trip either.

Joyce's expectations for Karin as a violinist were out-size and far beyond the child's ability or talent, as were her expectations about everything. "Karin," Sattler says, "was not as good as I first thought she would be. There was something blocking her talent and development. She was an average student, and she should have been a very good one. She started off with a bang and then dropped off."

But Joyce had convinced herself that Karin was the best, and she demanded perfection. Once when seven-year-old Karin was playing in a music school recital as part of a group of twelve children, her bowing suddenly went out of sync with the others. In front of an audience of about seventy-five people, Joyce leaped from her seat, rushed onto the stage, dragged Karin off into the wings and began to scream at her.

A year later Karin was slated to play a solo at another recital, but Sattler wasn't satisfied that she was quite ready to perform this difficult piece and gave it to another child. After the performance, in the midst of the crowd of parents and friends, Joyce grabbed hold of Karin, and shouted, "Listen, everybody. Karin can play that solo as well as anybody. Listen while she plays the piece." She forced Karin to play, to Karin's mortification and the embarrass-ment of everybody else. When Karin finished, Joyce looked around with obvious satisfaction and pride and proclaimed, "There, didn't she do it better than the other one?" It didn't end there. Joyce advanced on the other child, snarled at him, "See, Karin could have played it better than you." Then she began to curse at him and his parents.

"I never saw anything like it before or after," Sattler says.

Joyce was a woman with an obsession, a woman driven to achieve all her dreams through her daughter. Karin would

be Joyce's star. Karin would be famous and rich and celebrated. Karin would be all that Joyce had ever wanted to be.
Joyce preached that idea constantly. She filled Karin with
stories about her own father, the musical genius, the conductor of enormous promise who had been derided at home
and driven to suicide, and stories about herself as a musical
prodigy on the piano who had been blocked by that same
family opposition. Karin had obviously inherited their talent
and would do what they had been stopped from doing.

Karin had talent, yes, but, as her teacher said, not as
great as Joyce assumed, or dreamed or fantasized, and demanded.

But Joyce was convinced that the talent was there and
that Karin towered over all her contemporaries. Joyce also
used the violin as a weapon to maintain control, to keep
Karin subjugated. She bought better and more expensive
violins and then threatened to take them away if Karin didn't
maintain the standards Joyce set. She made Karin practice
in front of her for at least an hour every day, and no matter
how well Karin played, Joyce never seemed satisfied. On
the way to lessons, she forced Karin to play for her what she
was going to play in class, and if she didn't do it to Joyce's
satisfaction, Joyce turned the car around and drove back
home, refused to let Karin go to her lesson. There were
times, too, when dissatisfied with the way Karin was playing, she would grab the violin out of her hands and beat her
across the back with it. After recitals she never let Karin
share in refreshments that had been laid out. Instead she
dragged her away and told her that Karin had embarrassed
her mother by playing some wrong notes. "I felt like standing up in the middle of your piece and walking out and
letting you find your own way home," she said more than
once. But that was merely talk, that was merely the attempt
to force perfection. The dream did not die. Later she enrolled Karin at the Manhattan School of Music and for
several years drove her down to New York every week for
lessons.

She might say to Karin that she was a disappointment, was not fulfilling her promise, but when Karin wasn't around, Joyce constantly boasted of Karin's great progress, of her growing expertise, and related fantasies as though they were true, as though they had really happened.

To one friend she told a story of how she and Karin had gone on vacation to Bermuda. "Joyce said that Karin took her violin with her because she didn't want to miss any practice time. And somebody heard her playing and asked her to play in the restaurant and she did, and everybody gave her money." The only thing was, Joyce and Karin never went to Bermuda.

To other friends she told how Karin had been invited to the Soviet Union over a Thanksgiving vacation to play a concert. Only Karin and Joyce did not go to Russia; Karin was never invited to play there.

There were stories that Joyce told about Karin's playing with the New York Philharmonic, about Karin's going to Scotland to play a concert there. They were inventions.

Jeff Sands remembers Joyce's telling him that Karin was going to England to play a concert. "Joyce brought in a tape that she told everybody was Karin's rehearsal with the New York Philharmonic. I asked Joyce if I could listen to it. I put it in the tape deck of my car and listened to it on the way to work one morning. It was a stunning tape. The pieces were beautifully played, and the violin was the featured instrument. Then I gave it back to Joyce, and she was so excited about this and the trip and everything. Later on I mentioned it to Karin, and she said it wasn't her; she said it was a tape of Alex Markov playing with the New York Philharmonic."

"That woman was insane, she was a dangerous personality," Constance Sattler says, "and I thought so from the time I first met her." Years later, when Sattler heard on the radio that Joyce had been murdered, she says her first reaction was "If anyone ever deserved it, she did."

9

—————

And there wasArchbishop John Whealon, for more than two decades head of the Hartford Roman Catholic archdiocese, the twelfth-largest in the United States. He became and remained perhaps *the* most important figure in the fantasies and realities of both mother and daughter.

For Karin, he was a father figure, supplanting Michael Aparo even before Aparo had faded from her life. For Joyce, who had nothing to do with her religion, who was contemptuous of it and its practitioners, who later did not permit Karin to be confirmed or even to attend church, Whealon inhabited a very special place in her mind, her fantasies, her delusions.

From the time Karin was small, barely able to remember, she visited him at St. Mary's Home, where he maintained his apartments, and for years she made his bed, cleaned his room, tended his garden and did other chores for him. She wrote him letters, first in a childish scrawl corrected and recopied by her mother, later in a more accomplished manner. They were filled with the events of her life and of her dreams, the kinds of letters one writes not to a stranger but to someone close, someone in whom it is possible to confide. They were filled not only with her thoughts and feelings but with those of her mother as well, for, she says, when she was young, her mother used to write many of those letters as though they were from Karin, some of them by hand, some on a typewriter, and then have Karin sign them. To most he responded in an affectionate, caring manner, not the kinds of letters one would expect from a priest to just an ordinary member of his congregation.

Kept in a filing cabinet in the basement of the condo on Butternut Drive, the correspondence fills thick file folders, letters from Whealon to Joyce Aparo dating from 1967 until shortly before her death and from Whealon to Karin from 1974 until mid-1990, along with copies of some of the letters they wrote to him.

"We saw your picture in the paper," begins one dated March 17, 1979, just after Karin's eighth birthday, a letter that Karin later said was actually written by Joyce although Karin signed it. She had cut out that picture and added it to a growing collection she had of him in her room, so many that Joyce kept coming across ones she hadn't seen before.

Karin had a gray and white cat named Franklin Roosevelt Cat that often misbehaved, she wrote Whealon. She had made more progress with the violin, was now playing *Judas Maccabeus* by Handel and would like to play it for him, though he never seemed to have the time to listen. "I know you are busy," she wrote, "but you should take a little rest and see friends."

She and her mother often drove by St. Mary's Home and his church, but Joyce always refused to stop. Karin wished the two of them, Joyce and Whealon, could be friends again, since Joyce always said she liked Whealon even though she wanted nothing to do with anybody else in the church. Perhaps, though, it might be possible for Karin and the archbishop somehow to get together during the summer.

She was sure the archbishop would be interested in all she had been doing, so she wrote about a trip to Florida where she had seen an aunt and some cousins and had gone to Disney World, ridden the Space Mountain roller coaster, which she loved but which made Joyce's stitches, from an operation, act up and which made Joyce throw up as well. But Karin wanted another ride on the Space Mountain, and some nice strangers had obliged. And, she wrote Whealon, they had stopped in Washington on the way home, gone to the zoo and seen the pandas. She had a camera and was taking lots of pictures with it. She had taken one of the name on the exhibit, Lesser Panda, but before she could shoot the animal itself, she had run out of film.

More seriously, she and Joyce were in an automobile accident right after they got back to Glastonbury. They had been shopping for groceries when the car crashed. Joyce broke her glasses, and Karin hurt her elbow, the right side of the car was a complete wreck, the groceries were destroyed and the backseat and floor of the car were a mess, littered with broken bottles, smashed cartons and all the rest.

Now that they were home, they were doing spring-cleaning, Joyce scouring and polishing everything and impatient to finish so she'd have time when the weather got warmer to go out, hunt for and then cut her rocks.

Karin asked the archbishop when he had last worn his miter, apparently one that Joyce had made for him. She wrote that she had never seen him in it. Also, she noted, Whealon had promised to give her a chair from the church, and she hadn't received it yet. She hoped that he wasn't doing the same thorough spring-cleaning that Joyce was and in the process had thrown it out.

"Be good," she wrote, "and try not to get into trouble and I'll do the same." Maybe they would get to see each other on a Saturday, the day she was with her father, because Joyce was proclaiming that she never wanted to see Whealon again. Of course, Whealon could always drive out to Glastonbury and visit them, and if he did, Joyce would have to act her best. What bothered her was that "nobody will tell me why you guys are mad at each other."

As on all her other letters to Whealon, she signed this one "Love, Karin."

In another letter, which Karin says was also composed by Joyce for her, written three years later, on March 24, 1982, Karin wrote that she and Joyce, in celebration of spring, had driven out to the cemetery to visit the grave of Sister Mary Thomas, apparently a special nun close to Karin and Whealon, on which they had laid a wreath of pinecones. While there, they tasted some maple sap, and "best of all, I left a message at the edge of your vegetable garden. The message said, 'I LOVE YOU, KARIN.' "

It bothered her that the garden seemed overgrown and untended, and, she wrote, she really wanted to work on it with him, cleaning it up and getting it ready for planting. She might have added more to the message she left, but she didn't know whether he had already planted something; besides, if it rained, the message would be washed away.

"I miss you a lot," she wrote. "It is time for us to take a little walk and have a little talk. I could use that. I am growing up. I told you I would—just wait for me a little more."

Indeed, she was growing so rapidly, she wrote, her arms lengthening, that Joyce had purchased a two-hundred-year-old French-made violin for her, and she was playing it both in the Glastonbury school orchestra, in which she was first violin, and in the University of Hartford children's intermediate orchestra, in which she was second violin. What she really wanted was to play it for him.

Life at home, she told him, was fine. Joyce was wonderful; she was everything good and bright. Joyce was going to a ball, apparently for Catholic Charities at which Whealon was to be present and the host, and Karin wanted very much to go, but Joyce said that she was too young, that when she was eighteen, it would be time enough. Didn't Whealon think sixteen was old enough? A lot of Joyce's friends, she said, were going to be at that ball, people Joyce knew from her jewelry making and from her work with nursing homes. Especially important was a Mr. Murphy, whom, the letter said, Karin really liked and who kept telling Karin he wanted to marry Joyce.

"Maybe you could save a dance in your heart for me," she wrote. "Actually, I want them all. . . . Try to steal away 15 minutes for a little walk and talk with me. I love you, Karin."

Though Karin does not remember when she first met him and began calling him Uncle John, she does have two early recollections of Archbishop Whealon. "I was three or four, and my parents were still married," she says. "They dressed me up to take me to mass, and he was going to officiate. At the end of the mass he led the procession down the aisle, and my parents moved me to the end of the row, and he picked me up and carried me against his chest out of the church."

She remembers, too, that Archbishop Whealon administered her first communion and that she did not have to prepare for it. "My mother had a letter from Archbishop Whealon, and we worked it out," she says.

But there was a dark secret that in the years to come became not quite so secret. Joyce told it to her from the time she was small and kept repeating it all her life so that Karin came to believe it without question. Later Joyce told it to so many others that after her death it was just about the first piece of information imparted to questioners by those who knew her.

It was the kind of secret that even if true should never have been revealed. It was the kind of secret that could only do irreparable damage to everyone: the person who told it, the person who heard it, the person it was about. It was, without doubt, the deadliest of all the poisons Joyce fed her daughter, the cruelest of afflictions laid upon her.

Archbishop John Whealon, Joyce told her daughter over and over, was her godfather, yes. But he was more than her godfather. He was her natural father.

Joyce said that she had had an affair with a young priest; Karin had been conceived out of that affair. The affair had not ended then, she said, but had continued over the years with few interruptions. Just before her death she maintained that the affair was still going on. That young priest, she said, had risen high in the church, had become an archbishop, and his name was John Whealon.

When she was about twelve, Karin remembers, Joyce gave her a present, a pink dress that had been hers. But, she warned, "never wear it when you go to visit Archbishop Whealon, because it may remind him of a summer night long ago."

There were the days when she would come home from a visit with the archbishop and Joyce "would ask me if the nuns at St. Mary's had said anything about the remarkable resemblance between me and the archbishop. She said they were always commenting on that resemblance." Karin would go to her room then, take the autographed photograph of Whealon she kept on a shelf, hold it beside her face and look into the mirror, trying to see the resemblance, wondering if indeed there was a connection. She did it alone, and she did it in the presence of her friend Shannon Dubois, asking if Shannon, who had been told the story of the presumed parentage, noticed a resemblance.

Sandra Yerks, who knew Joyce and Karin later, remembers evenings, not one but several, during which, with Karin in a chair across from them, she sat on a sofa with Joyce in the living room. "Joyce," she recalls, "said that

Archbishop Whealon was Karin's father and that he was Karin's godfather, and that she knew how to satisfy him, and that Karin would learn how.''

That secret, that "revelation" by her mother, ate at Karin like a malignancy. She was, after all, a Catholic and a believing one. She believed that when a priest took his vows, pledged himself to a life of celibacy, those vows were not taken lightly, were never broken. Sex was outside the life of a priest; he was father to his congregation, not natural father to any member of it. For a priest to have sex, to father a child, was a mortal and unforgivable sin, and the child of his union must necessarily be steeped in that sin, must be beyond redemption. It was a belief Karin was forced to live with until her mother's death and beyond, until a day more than a year after that death when she went to Archbishop Whealon and finally asked him directly if he was her father. He told her he was not. She believed him.

But the damage had been done. It was irreparable.

10

There was another side to Joyce Aparo, another world, one in which she was admired and respected and in which she accomplished much that was good. Through the 1970s she became an increasingly important and powerful figure in the state's welfare bureaucracy, rising to ever-higher positions in the departments of Human Resources, Mental Health, Social Services and Welfare. By the end of the decade she had become a health planner for the State Health Coordinating Council, with wide powers over the nursing home industry.

Jeff Sands, only a couple of years out of law school and working as an associate lawyer at Wiggin & Dana in Hartford, specializing in the law dealing with nursing homes and other special care facilities, met Joyce Aparo for the first time in 1981, and they quickly developed a close professional relationship. "Health care is one of those regulated industries where you can't sneeze without going to a regulator and getting approval. Now Joyce was in the planning department of the Health Department, which was charged with coming up with the rules and the methodology that would be used by the state for approving projects, and she was really incensed that Connecticut for a long time had systems in place that discouraged people from building or developing new and innovative programs for the elderly or for people with special injuries who needed long-term care. She tried to do something about it because she cared a lot about those people. She really authored a lot of the systems that we still use today, coming up with how and when and where nursing homes and other long-term facilities should be approved."

In the process she became Connecticut's leading authority on demographics and found herself able to predict what the future would hold, what would be required in the years to come. Both people who worked with her and outsiders say that she saw, before almost anyone else, the explosion in the elderly population and the spiraling need for facilities to take care of many in that aging group, and she set in motion means to deal with it.

"I thought she was very dedicated," Sands says. "She was always willing to take your phone call, always wanted to discuss an issue. She was very encouraging. Almost any developer who came into Connecticut—and there are an awful lot of big developers in the long-term health care field—would call Joyce. Every inquiry went in one way or another through her office. But she would not talk to anyone until she got references. She would call me, she would call other people she knew and trusted and she would talk to someone only if the references checked out and she thought these people were going to be okay for the state. It was a personal task for her. If you were okay for the state, then she would give you the secrets of the need methodology and the secrets of the regulatory process and tell you who you should hire as your attorney. There were two or three of us that she trusted and put on her good list. And she would tell you who you should hire as your accountant and what towns you should go to and who you should talk to in those towns. She had a wealth of information, but she didn't want to be affiliated, even by a phone call, with some schleppy developer who would come in and ruin what she was trying to accomplish. I always had a high regard for her in that position. It was kind of neat to see that somebody in the state government had those kind of personal ethics.''

And those ethics, that rigid moral sense, at least in her professional life, were essential. For they brought her power, and she gloried in the power to manipulate people and events. It meant more to her than money. "If you think about this whole thing of one person trying to design the health care planning process in the state of Connecticut,'' Sands says, "you realize that there's a lot of money involved, and it's very lucrative for some people. Here these people are going to spend all that money on the preparatory development of nursing home facilities, and here's Joyce handpicking who comes in and does it, and then handpicking who their representatives are, and then always being in there, kind of in the background, when the projects get built or developed. But everybody knows that it was her hand that put the players in place and made it all happen. She loved it, to kind of manipulate the scene. But then when it was done, there was this nice thing built and the elderly were being cared for, so it was all for a good purpose, and never for her own personal gain, certainly not financially.''

What she had was power, power enough so that those whom she favored, who gained her ear and earned her confidence and support, profited handsomely. "If she was your friend, she'd do anything for you,'' Sands says. "From time to time, she'd call me and say, 'Jeff, what are you working on? What projects? How can I help you?'

"I'd say, 'Well, I'm having a hard time with zoning down in X or Y town.'

"She'd say, 'I think that's a good project. I happen to know the first selectman down there. I'll give him a call, see if I can talk to him, tell him I think it's a good idea.' "

There was, though, something about the way she dealt personally, face-to-face that intrigued and even bothered Sands and others who met with her. "She was very nice," he says, "but she was always a little strange. She didn't ever talk directly to you. She would even refer to herself in the third person. She was one of those people who talk a little to the side. And she would talk in riddles. Sometimes she'd call and she'd say, 'Here's an idea I have. What do you think about it? Do you think it will work in practice? Let's sit down and talk about it.' But it was never that easy; it would never be that kind of question. It would always be kind of 'Well, if one were to do this and think about that and do this and do that, how would you react?'

"I'd say, 'Are you asking me how do I react to it or what? Do you want to do this?'

"She'd say, 'Well, I don't know exactly about doing it. I'm hypothesizing.'

"It was always this kind of funny communication. Nice enough. Always got to the bottom line eventually but got to it circuitously."

It was during these years, at the beginning of the 1980s, in her position of power and influence, that she met two men who were to play crucial roles in her life and the life of her daughter in the years ahead. One was Michael Zaccaro, about fifteen years younger than she. The other was Ed Murphy, about fifteen years older.

Zaccaro, then in his mid-twenties, was running the Connecticut operations of New Medical Associates, known as NewMediCo, a New England health care management and development firm. It was only natural that he and Joyce Aparo would come into contact, she the regulator and he the developer. That contact blossomed into close association and friendship. Zaccaro had much that she could use. "Mike," says a friend, "is one of the best people with numbers I've ever seen. He can do things quicker in his head than you can do them on your calculator. So Joyce leaned heavily on him to test her different formulas, to see what was possible. When you look at the needs in the health care field, it finally comes down to population samples. You take a thousand people sixty-five and over, how many are going to need nursing home beds in any given year? It's really statistical analysis, and Mike was brilliant at it."

Joyce used him extensively. A deep friendship developed. Zaccaro was not married then, did not marry until shortly after Joyce's death, and there were rumors that what they had was more than just friendship. Zaccaro denies it, as do many who know him and knew her. Their relationship, says Jeff Sands, who was close professionally and personally to both, "was something like mother-son. It certainly didn't extend to a romance." Nevertheless, New-MediCo was a major beneficiary of her powers, and when Zaccaro and several others left NewMediCo and formed Athena Health Care Associates, the new company became one of her pets.

Her relationship with Ed Murphy was something else. A man with an appetite for strong drink and good times, he was a nursing home administrator in Darien. He and she met at some business affair in 1981. Both had been married before. They were soon seeing each other socially. Taken with her, Murphy proposed. Joyce accepted, then backed out. Murphy proposed again. The pattern was repeated several times, Joyce accepting and rejecting, perhaps wondering whether a new marriage would be any better than the two previous ones.

Her relationship with Michael Aparo was still full of friction. He remembers one weekend when Karin was with him and he received news that his father had suddenly been taken ill and taken to the hospital. He and Karin rushed there, to be with his mother while they waited to learn his father's condition. Joyce called the hospital, got Aparo and ordered him to return Karin to her immediately or she would call the police and file charges against him for kidnapping. "I felt helpless," he says, "and I left my mother alone in the emergency room in order not to create a scene by the police coming to arrest me for kidnapping."

Later, in April 1982, as Joyce was in the midst of her internal debate over whether to marry Murphy or not, Aparo's father died. He collected Karin and prepared to take her to the funeral home. As they were about to leave, Joyce called and "told me that 'unless you bring Karin home immediately, I will send the police to the funeral home.' I left my mother alone—I'm ashamed to say it because I probably should have let the police come—but I left her and my own father's funeral to bring my daughter back home to avoid that scene."

But then Joyce's fury with Michael Aparo had eaten away at her since before their divorce. Maybe, she reasoned, she would have better luck with Ed Murphy, and she finally accepted his proposal. In the spring of 1982 they married, and Joyce and Karin left Glastonbury and moved into Murphy's house on the grounds of the nursing home in Darien.

It was not, despite what Karin or Joyce wrote to Archbishop Whealon during the courtship, something that made Karin happy. She was eleven, and she was being taken away from the home in which she had lived much of her life. Bad as that homelife may have been, there was nothing to assure her that the change would make much difference. She was also being taken away from her school and her friends to a place where she knew nobody. She was being forced to give up her violin lessons with Constance Sattler at Hartt, though Joyce told her that it was time, anyway, to move on, that she was too good, that she needed really professional instruction and Joyce would find her a new and expert teacher. Worse was the situation in the small house Murphy occupied. "He had adopted four or five kids who were older than Karin and more grown-up, in their late teens and early twenties," says Zaccaro. "They were kind of rowdy. They didn't like the fact that Joyce and Ed got married, and then Joyce and Karin moved in, and they sort of made life close to living hell for them down in Darien."

The wedding of Joyce Aparo and Ed Murphy took place in the home of Sandra Yerks, a friend of Murphy's and a colleague in the nursing home. It was a small ceremony, a handful of friends and associates of Murphy and Joyce in attendance. Yerks remembers Karin arriving for the wedding, "wearing a white dress, like a woman of twenty-five, not a child, never smiling, prim and proper, not at all part of what was going on." Yerks suggested that Karin go upstairs to be with her children. Joyce vetoed that, telling Karin to stay right where she was.

"That night we left to go to a party," Yerks remembers. "No one cared where Karin was going to stay. My husband and I made sure she stayed at our house with our children. When we got home, it was very late. The kids were still up and taking advantage of the fact that their parents were out. They were jumping on the bed and doing all sorts of things they shouldn't have been doing. The minute she saw me, all Karin kept saying was, 'Please don't tell my mother. Please don't tell my mother.'

"I said, 'Oh, for heaven's sake, Karin don't worry about it. I'm not going to tell.' And I yelled at her as I did at my four children.

"The next morning, when Joyce and Ed arrived back at the house, the woman walked in and took one look at Karin. It was May, and she had on a pair of slacks and a shirt. Joyce insisted that she go and change immediately because she was not appropriately dressed."

For Karin, then, little had changed. The dress code, always to look like a lady, now in clothes that were often identical to those that Joyce wore, if in smaller sizes, was rigidly enforced. So was the rule that other children were not her equals, that all contact with them was to be avoided. So was the rule that a multitude of household chores was to be done as soon as school was over, that there was to be no dallying on the way home. The other kids in school in Darien, seeing her for the first time, made fun of her. It was childish cruelty but affecting enough that Karin often called Sandra Yerks and asked her to take her home from school because she was not feeling good, had a stomachache, had a headache, had some other ailment. Yet when she got home, she was constantly tormented by the Murphy sons. There was nowhere to flee.

Yerks remembers that one day Karin arrived at her office carrying a book of raffle tickets for a school charity. "What do I do with these?" she asked.

Yerks told her, "Honey, I'll tell you. It's not a problem. Walk up Brookside Road. Ring the doorbells, and ask the people if they'd like to buy a raffle ticket for the school. Then cross the street and go down the other side. I'll bet you can sell something."

Karin, Yerks says, grew excited by the idea. She went out, went up and down the street, rang the bells and within a half hour had sold all the tickets. She went back to Yerks and told her.

"As she was explaining to me what she did," Yerks says, "Joyce walked into my office and asked what was going on. We said, 'Look, Joyce, look what happened,' and we told her. Well, she chastised that child to the point of humiliation. She asked Karin to leave the room, and then she laced into me because I was making her daughter common by having her go out and sell raffle tickets."

Still, in Karin's isolation there was always music to fill the empty hours, music into which to escape, music she could play knowing this was something that won her mother's approval. Ed Murphy watched with dismay. He couldn't understand it. "There were the violin lessons and the piano lessons and the bloody French horn lessons and

the tennis lessons,'' he complained. ''Finally, I said,
'Knock it off. She can play the violin if she chooses. But
everything else stops.' ''

Joyce paid no more attention to that order than she
did to anything else Murphy said. Above all, though, it
was the violin that was the thing, that was essential. She
found Karin a new teacher, one she was sure would be the
right one to train her for a career on the concert stage. His
name was Albert Markov. He lived in nearby Rowayton,
an enclave in Norwalk on Long Island Sound, with his
wife, Marina, and his son, Alexander. All three had left
the Soviet Union in 1976 and emigrated to the United
States. All three were violinists of considerable note. Marina played with the New York City Opera Orchestra.
Alex had captured a number of prizes in violin competi-
tions beginning at the age of nine, when he began performing publicly in Russia. In 1982, when he was
nineteen, he won the Gold Medal at the Paganini International Violin Competition in Genoa, Italy, an award that
carried with it a European concert tour, including a performance on Paganini's own violin in Genoa. A year later
he made his New York debut at Carnegie Hall, playing
unaccompanied solo violin as well as violin trios with his
mother and father; *The New York Times* critic John Rock-
well said of Alex that his playing was ''inspired'' and that
''a talent he most surely is.''

Albert also played frequent concerts around the country, as he had done in his native Russia, to considerable
acclaim. Albert Markov was not only a concert soloist but
a teacher with a growing reputation. He had taught his son,
had been, in fact, Alex's only teacher, and since arriving in
the United States, he had been teaching others at the Manhattan School of Music, where he was attempting to prop-
agate his own methods. In contrast with the traditional
teaching that stressed hand positions and fingering, he was
concerned with giving his students a more direct sense of
where on the strings the tone lies.

Now Karin Aparo joined the ranks of Albert Markov's students, journeying to New York with Joyce to take lessons at the Manhattan School and making the shorter trip from Darien to the Markov home in Rowayton for private lessons there.

Before long the formal relationship of teacher to student and teacher to student's mother had turned into one of friendship. Joyce discovered that Albert Markov shared her passion for long hikes on rocky slopes searching for rare and semiprecious stones, and soon they began to go off for a day now and again on rock climbing and hunting expeditions.

Until Joyce's death, Albert Markov remained not only Karin's teacher but also another father, a man she could look up to, admire and respect, a man who was not slow with his advice to her.

All was not well with the newly wedded Murphys. Hardly had the marriage been consummated before trouble erupted. It was as though Joyce, once she had won, once she had captured Murphy, had abandoned all her feminine poses and turned once more into a virago. "I knew on the second day," Murphy says, "that I was in trouble."

He had no idea how much trouble. Murphy, who liked to lift a glass with friends, overimbibed on occasion, perhaps on too many occasions for his new wife. Indeed, once was one time too many for Joyce. More than once was intolerable. He found himself under attack, assailed as an incorrigible alcoholic.

Joyce soon added another charge. Says Yerks, it was not long after the wedding before Joyce began to charge Murphy with being not merely a drunk but a homosexual as well, a charge she repeated again and again, in front of Karin, in front of Murphy, in front of everyone. Murphy just sat there and took it, without response. She had, Joyce claimed, walked in on Murphy having sex with another man on their living-room sofa.

Yerks remembers vividly a night when she received a panicky call from Joyce at the Murphy house. Joyce was in an uncontrollable rage. Yerks sped to the home, was greeted by a terrified Karin. She put her arms around the girl to comfort her. Joyce raced out of the living room and attempted to drag Karin away, screaming that Murphy had come home drunk and was in the bedroom at that moment. She was going to force Karin into that bedroom and "uncover Murphy and let Karin see what was going on." Yerks stopped her.

About nine o'clock on a Sunday evening some months later Yerks and her husband had just settled in to watch a movie on television when the phone rang. A soft, calm voice said, "Sandy, this is Joyce."

Yerks said, "Hi, Joyce. How are you?"

"I thought I would call to tell you that I am going to run the Mercedes off a bridge." With that the line went dead.

Yerks was frantic. She knew that Murphy had just flown off to Texas, that Joyce was home with Karin and Murphy's adopted sons. She knew, too, that there had been considerable and mounting friction in the house between Joyce and Karin on one side and the boys on the other. This time that antagonism must have boiled over. She ran to her husband and shouted, "We'd better get to the Murphys'."

It took them only minutes to drive to the house, but during those minutes Joyce had called the police, and they had arrived. There were several patrol cars parked outside and cops in the living room. They had taken one of the Murphy sons into custody on Joyce's complaint, were holding him and trying to calm Joyce down and restore the peace. The Yerkses rushed into the house. Karin ran up to Sandy Yerks and put her arms around her. Joyce glared at Karin and ordered her away. Karin walked over to the corner and stood there.

One of the cops approached Sandy Yerks. "Can you help us calm this lady down?" he asked. "If you can, we'll release this kid in your custody and you can take him home.''

Yerks tried. ''But,'' she says, ''Joyce was off the wall; she was just out of her skull.'' She ran into the bedroom, and Yerks and Karin followed. Joyce was yelling, screaming and threatening everyone. She picked up the phone and started to dial. Yerks said something calming. Joyce turned and threw the phone at her. She kept screaming, ''They tried to kill me.''

Then she turned on Karin, ordered her to go pack her belongings, pack Joyce's things, too, and load them in the car. ''We're leaving this minute,'' she shouted.

Karin obeyed, packed and loaded the car. When the car was ready, Joyce ordered her to unpack it, she'd changed her mind. Karin did as she was told. Once the car was unloaded and the luggage back in the house, Joyce demanded that Karin pack it again. ''Five times that night,'' Yerks says, ''from ten-thirty at night until five-thirty in the morning, she made Karin pack and take the bags out to the car and load it and then unload it, then reload it and unload it again and again.''

Joyce and Karin did not leave that night.

By the summer of 1983 the Murphy household was a bomb, fuse lit and burning inexorably, ready to explode. Joyce and Ed Murphy had been married little more than a year, and Murphy was regretting every moment more and more. The woman he had courted was not the woman who was his wife. The woman he had courted had been all smiles and warmth, understanding and helpful, sharing his profession and his interests; the woman to whom he was married was scowls and ice, scathing and demeaning, bitter and in a constant rage, demanding subservience, sharing nothing. Joyce hated her stepsons, who returned that hatred. They vented their wrath not only on Joyce but on Karin, tormenting her, brutalizing her. Murphy had come to adore his stepdaughter, but there was little he could do to help her; she was cowed and dominated by her mother, fearful of doing anything that would incur her mother's fury; when Joyce was around, he says, "it was like shutting off the TV, blank." And she was terrified of the adopted sons.

Joyce's rage mounted, at everything and everyone. She was gone often on business, commuting frequently to her office in Hartford with the health planning agency, going around the state checking on new nursing homes. Her days were long; the pressures on her to oversee a burgeoning industry, to make sure that it hewed to the regulations, to ensure that only the best developers got into the field, to visit every new home as it opened and to make repeated visits to existing homes to check on them, were demanding. She was on the edge, teetering, trying to do her job, trying to do what she thought best to raise her daughter, trying to manage a house distant from her job, a house that contained youths she despised and a man for whom she had contempt. It was an impossible situation. By the time she got back to Darien at the end of the day, she was exhausted, and that exhaustion only seemed to magnify any failing, real or imagined, of others, served only to send her off into paroxysms, send her lashing out in word and deed at Murphy, at his sons, at Karin, at the world. Finally she decided she needed a place of her own, so that she would not have to make that trip every night. With three thousand dollars advanced by Murphy to help with the down payment, she bought a condo on Butternut Drive in Glastonbury, where she spent several nights a week.

But when she was in Darien, any peace that existed in the Murphy house during her absence, though there wasn't much of that for Karin, with the Murphy boys always there, always at her, vanished. Her orders and demands to Karin became sterner, and the punishments harsher. Her tongue lashed Murphy, and sometimes her fists as well, and she began to talk divorce.

Then the bomb exploded. It was inevitable.

11

Late in the afternoon of August 10, 1983, the phone in Sandra Yerks's office rang. Ed Murphy was on the line. "Sandy," he said, "would you get up to Norwalk Hospital right away? Karin tried to commit suicide."

There were those, Jeff Sands and Michael Zaccaro among them, who, when they heard about the suicide attempt, were sure the reason was the Murphy boys. "Everybody," Sands says, "who knew the situation assumed it was just because of the unbelievable torture she was getting from those kids. I had just constantly heard these stories about Ed and the drinking and the kids and one of Ed's sons threatening Karin with a knife. It was just an awful, awful situation that was going on."

Zaccaro agrees. "Being aware of that situation and

knowing what was going on, I'd be willing to bet anything that the attempted suicide was not because of abuse by Joyce as much as that Karin hated, absolutely hated what was happening to her down there, with those kids of Ed's.''

They, and the others who thought that way, were wrong.

Earlier on that Wednesday afternoon Karin, alone in the house, had canceled a dentist appointment. Joyce called a little later to find out what the dentist had said and done. When Karin told her she hadn't gone, Joyce railed at her, screamed over the phone, threatened dire punishment when she got home. Terrified, Karin went into the bathroom, opened the medicine cabinet, took out a bottle of Tranxene, an antidepressant Joyce sometimes took for anxiety attacks, and swallowed four tablets. If it was not enough to kill her, it was certainly a cry for help, perhaps the first she had uttered in her life.

A few minutes after taking the pills, she called a friend who lived nearby and told her what she had done. The friend's mother called Poison Control and then got in touch with Ed Murphy to tell him. An emergency medical service ambulance sped to the Murphy home and rushed Karin to the Norwalk Hospital emergency room, where she was treated with ipecac. It was not long before Karin had been calmed, her system cleared. The hospital proceeded to call Murphy, Joyce and Michael Aparo.

Sandy Yerks arrived a few minutes later, while Karin was still in the emergency room. Karin was, naturally, pale and shaken. Yerks went to her and held her. Karin held on tightly, kept saying over and over, ''Please don't leave me, please don't leave me. Mom's on her way. If she comes, please don't leave me.'' She was, Yerks says, ''scared to death.''

Soon Murphy, then Aparo and finally Joyce arrived. ''You could hear her through the door,'' Yerks says. ''She was coming down the hall, and she was an absolute maniac, screaming and yelling. She was going off at me, at the doctors, at everyone. If she could have gotten her hands on that child, she would have done bodily harm to her. They had to hold her back so she couldn't get at Karin.'' Sandy Yerks did not exaggerate.

Once in the room Joyce started toward Karin. "Her hands were out," Karin says, "like she would grab me by the neck and strangle me.'' Aparo tried to restrain Joyce. She began shouting at him. He grabbed her right arm and tried to pull her away, out of the room. She struggled, and as she broke free from his grip, she fell against a counter in the hospital corridor and bruised her forearm. She screamed in pain, accused him of hitting her deliberately, of breaking her arm, and demanded that her arm be X-rayed. It was. Only bruises and a small contusion were found.

The hospital staff was watching the whole thing, watching Joyce and Aparo, watching Karin and her reactions. What they saw they noted on their reports.

"Had occasion," reads the first report filed later that evening, "to witness Mrs. Aparo interacting with her daughter in the E.D. [Emergency Department]. She appeared vindictive, aggressive, hostile and totally domineering of her daughter. Prior to the arrival of the mother, Karin was animated and conversant; she is an intelligent and responsive young lady in the absence of her mother. After her mother arrived, she became quiet and withdrawn. She appeared to be very intimidated and afraid of her mother."

The hospital psychiatrist added that Karin was "an anxious, compulsive 12 year old who was intimidated by her mother's anger. . . . child is at risk of emotional abuse/ neglect. Verbal abuse is reportedly severe." Joyce was described as "a rigid, angry, paranoid personality under stress. . . . close to falling apart."

It was enough that the hospital decided to follow up, to refer the matter to Child and Youth Services and let it look into it and talk further with Karin, with Joyce, with both Ed Murphy and Michael Aparo. Although Karin attempted to make light of the episode, telling an agency interviewer that her relationship with her mother was generally good and that what she had done was stupid, there was a feeling that she might well be covering up for her mother. The agency dug deeper.

A DCYS report, written a few months later and based on that digging and interviews and other investigations, reads in part:

8/11/83: . . . Mother called the floor early this morning, sounded bitter, refuses to see Karin until she straightens up her act. Karin's relationship [sic] with father and stepfather are good. Karin says mother and stepfather are on verge of a divorce.

. . . She is a petite, pert 12 yr. old, who appears quite sophisticated. She did not seem at all depressed. She wants to go home, said things are OK between her and mother, she has called twice today. Karin explained what led to her attempted suicide. Her mother was angry with her on Tuesday 8/9 because she had not bought Kitty [L]itter and taken books back to the library. On Wednesday mother was upset because Karin misunderstood instructions and changed her dental appointment. She called her annoying and irresponsible, said she never listens. Karin was afraid mother would yell at her when she got home. Mother does not hit her, only did so once this summer at the beach. Karin views her relationship with mother as good, better than average. She did not express any negative feelings about her. She did say mother does not yell at her when stepfather is around. Karin expressed understanding that mother is under stress and very tired when she gets home, as she works in Hartford. Sometimes mother stays in Glastonbury where they own a condo. When mother is home, she makes dinner, they eat and then mother falls asleep, so Karin said she really does not see her a lot. Karin is not sure why she took the pills, said she has never done anything like that before and will never do so again. Karin said she is not eating in the hospital and "that's good, I'll lose weight." She is not at all overweight.

I told Karin that DCYS would remain involved with her and mother for a while because we are concerned. I mentioned counseling, but she is not sure what that would accomplish.

8/12/83: . . . Mother tried to call Kay [hospital social worker] yesterday about 4:30 P.M. and was very agitated when she was unable to reach her. Kay offered to call her at home about 9:00 P.M., but mother said no, she'd be exhausted and asleep. However, she complained to the Social Services Department this morning that Kay did not call her at home. Mother also complained that the hospital staff told everyone in her office about Karin's suicide attempt. . . .

P.C. [phone call] from mother. She talked in circles, I had difficulty following the conversation. Much of what she said concerned herself, not Karin, about whom she expressed little concern. Mother identified herself as "Joyce Aparo." She is making arrangement for her and Karin to move to Glastonbury within a few days, which will bring stability to their lives, something they have not had for 1½ years (the length of the marriage). Her attorney is making arrangements with Mr. Murphy re: the move. She is filing for divorce, which was "on hold" because he keeps changing his mind. Mother described herself as a "raving tired lady," said both she and Karin were drained, used up emotionally, with no resources to build on. She said Karin deserves more than a mother who is tired all the time and that the move to Glastonbury will cut her commuting time down considerably. . . .

Hospital is preparing to discharge Karin. Dr. Cuello saw her, said she is well put-together, not suicidal. She is, however, afraid of her mother's anger.

Psychotherapy is being recommended for mother and Karin, to which both agreed. They also know DCYS will follow-up. Dr. Cuello described mother as "at the ragged edge." She recommends using softest touch possible with her. Kay met with mother, step-father this afternoon. The couple has decided to have a gradual divorce, to be finalized in 3–6 months, rather than a sudden move. The mother does not want the marriage to end, is using Karin as a pawn as step-father is very fond of her. He describes Karin as "pure gold, a solid rock." Throughout Kay's interview, Karin looked at step-father, not mother, and was somewhat seductive with him. He told Kay mother's verbal abuse of Karin is as sharp as a knife and he is a buffer between them. Karin was guarded during the interview.

Mother admitted to Kay she is close to falling apart. She has a demanding job at the State Health Department in charge of distribution of health funds for the elderly and disabled. For four years she was director of the State Department of Mental Health. Mother's first husband killed himself when she was 22, then her elderly father committed suicide.

Step-father wants a divorce and at the end of the interview asked mother when she would be moving out.

Kay talked to Karin alone. She is aware that the next few years will be anxious ones, but after that she believes she will manage very nicely. Both Kay and I are unsettled by the level of her maturity. She is obviously a very bright child. She is delighted that they are not moving to Glastonbury right away. . . .

8/16/83: . . . Step-father called Kay yesterday, wished to share some information. He said mother is a pathological liar. . . . She is "diabolical," fakes injuries and fainting. She once wrote a letter to a mortgage holder that Mr. Murphy had died and he did not know of this letter for months. He is "scared to death" for Karin because of mother's mood swings. She is either euphoric or depressed, there is no middle ground. She is using Karin to prolong the marriage. By taking the pills, Karin brought everything to a head and he is hopeful that things will change. . . . Mother claimed that father used to abuse her and Karin. However, Mr. Murphy does not believe that and suspects she may have assaulted the child herself.

Step-father said Karin is a terrific kid with lots of potential. He thinks sending her to a boarding school would be a good idea.

Step-father has told mother to be out of the house by 11/16/83, exactly three months from now.

Kay called mother today. She was very sweet and appreciative. She indicated they had a wonderful weekend with Karin home and noted what a compatible family they are. Mr. Murphy's children were there and helped move some of her things out of the house already.

The agency recommended, indeed insisted, that both Joyce and Karin see a psychiatrist for therapy. For a few months they saw one on a few occasions and then simply stopped.

Those sessions did nothing to reconcile Joyce and Ed Murphy. The divisions, the disagreements, the incompatibility were simply too great for anything to help. So the marriage came to an end. In November 1983 Joyce and Karin left the Murphy house in Darien for the last time and returned to Glastonbury. "I did the best I could," Murphy says. "I hung in there longer than I should have. Finally I told her, 'You're out of here.' I put her stuff in a truck and drove it up to Glastonbury and dropped it off and told her, 'You're not coming back.' I felt sorry for Karin, but I had no choice."

Much later Murphy was asked how long he had been

married to Joyce Aparo. "I can't remember," he said, "and I don't want to remember."

They were married for a year and a half.

Joyce, of course, had another story about the reasons for the split. Murphy hadn't thrown her out, as he claimed. She couldn't stand what she saw as his weaknesses and his attempts to tell her how to bring up her daughter. And she couldn't stand his kids a minute longer. So she told him it was over, and she and Karin left.

As least they were back in the town where Karin had spent most of her life, where she had friends. There was that. But she could not forget what her mother had said to her when she left the hospital and what she repeated time and again thereafter: "The next time you'd better take the whole bottle or I'll shove it down your throat myself."

12

Plus ça change, plus c'est la même chose.

They were back in Glastonbury, in the two-bedroom condo on Butternut Drive that Joyce had bought and furnished with its blue carpeting and off-white walls, crystal chandeliers and sheer full-length white draperies.

Karin started school, now in seventh grade at the Gideon Welles Junior High, and renewed old acquaintances. There was, especially, Shannon Dubois, who was again her best friend. In many ways Shannon was a role model. "My daughter," Susan Dubois says, "was not a gifted child; my daughter was not affluent enough for Joyce; she was not in an influential enough family; we probably weren't up to Joyce's standards." Perhaps she was right, but Shannon was something of an idealist who saw good in

145

everyone. Shannon was a sympathetic listener. Above all, Shannon had the kind of family Karin dreamed of having, and Shannon was the kind of person Karin deeply wanted to be, and could not.

There was a new friend, too, with whom she forged a bond. Her name was Kira Lintner, and she was the antithesis of Shannon Dubois. "She was a good kid until she got into the sixth grade," says an old-time resident of Glastonbury, an editor for the local paper for whom Kira worked for a time. That was the year that Kira's father arrived home one afternoon, gathered her and her two younger siblings around him, looked at them and announced, "Good-bye, you little bastards, this is the last time you'll ever see me." He turned and walked out of the house, and that was, indeed, the last time they ever saw him. "It was downhill all the way from that day on." Kira grew into a tall girl, taller than Karin by several inches, a little chubby, her brown hair cropped close. There was a hardness about her, the blue eyes icy and devoid of emotion, something of a sneer perpetually painted on the snub-nosed face that might have been pretty had there been a softer look. By the time she was in her teens, she was given to wearing leather jackets, clinging T-shirts, and tight jeans and later took to riding a big motorcycle. "She's wacko" seemed to be the general consensus among the kids who knew her in school. "A lot of people were afraid of her in high school," says a fellow student at the time. "One second she'd be this calm, very polite kid, and the next she'd be talking about beating the shit out of somebody. She was a strange, strange girl." And she became close to Karin.

Joyce now made an easy fifteen- or twenty-minute commute to her office in Hartford, the hour-and-a-half drive each way to Darien a thing of the past, though she still spent days touring the state, watching over the new and the old nursing homes.

There were changes, of course, but the more things

changed, the more they remained the same. The slaps across the face might be gone, ended with the abortive suicide in the summer, but the emotional torment remained, grew even worse. For Karin was about to turn thirteen, about to become a teenager, so about to have new interests, about to be filled with the natural desire of all teenagers, to break free and begin to live and make a kind of life of her own. Joyce, like generations of mothers before her, was determined to retain control, to keep Karin subservient, to mold Karin into the image she wanted.

Joyce had many weapons; Karin had few. But she began to use the few she had. One was illness. Within weeks of her arrival at junior high school she reported to Maria Bonaiuto, the school nurse, complaining of a headache. She had headaches all the time, she told the nurse, sometimes so bad it was hard for her to function. Bonaiuto called Joyce. The only explanation Joyce had was that Karin was subject to a lot of stress, what with the divorce from Murphy, the move back to Glastonbury and all the rest.

A few weeks later Karin was back in the nurse's office. She'd had an accident, had bumped her head. Bonaiuto examined her. The bump seemed minor, and Karin appeared no worse for it. Still, a head injury is not something to make light of. The nurse, who tried unsuccessfully to reach Joyce, finally put Karin on the school bus for home at the end of the day. That evening, just to make sure everything was all right, she called the Aparo house. Joyce answered and immediately began to scream at her. "What did you people do to my child? She looks unconscious. She's lying there, just a heap on the couch."

"It was just a bump," Bonaiuto said. "I didn't think it was that serious. But look, why don't you take her to the doctor and have him check if you're worried?"

A couple of days later Karin was back in school. When the nurse asked if she was all right, Karin shrugged it off. It had been nothing at all, really, she said, just a stress reaction, the kind of thing she had often.

But a pattern developed. Three or four times a month for the next four years Karin dropped by Bonaiuto's office. There was always a medical reason. She had a headache, a backache, was suffering from nausea, something else relatively minor. The real reason was that she wanted to talk, and she had found in Bonaiuto someone who would listen and sympathize, even empathize. She told the nurse of her problems at home.

"Mom went out the other night, and she didn't tell me where she was going, and I worried the whole night, practically didn't get any sleep." Bonaiuto heard about that several times.

"I wanted to be with my friends, and my mother made me stay home and do the housework." Bonaiuto heard that many times.

"My mom's always telling me that I'm fat and ugly. She says I look like a two-ton heifer. She's always making me diet and exercise, and then, after I eat, she makes me go to the bathroom and throw up. And then you know what she does? She goes out and she buys éclairs and keeps them in the front of the refrigerator, and then she tells me I have to eat them." This tale, Bonaiuto says, was repeated every couple of months.

"My mom and I fight all the time about the violin and my lessons. She never thinks I'm good enough no matter how hard I practice."

When the nurse heard from a friend of Karin's that Joyce had beaten her with the violin after one of those fights, she called Karin in to ask, "Is that true what I heard about your mother hitting you with the violin?"

Karin shrugged. "Well," she said, "nothing hurt, so everything's okay. Only please don't call my mother."

"Please don't call my mother. She'll be mad at me, and it'll be a lot worse if you call her." That was a litany Karin recited after every tale. She was perfecting the technique that her mother had practiced for so long, that of manipulating people, and she was doing it better than Joyce ever had. There was always something effortful about Joyce; she tried too hard, and though she succeeded, there were many she used who realized, if not at the time, then later, that they were being used. Not Karin. She told her stories with absolute guilelessness. If at times they were exaggerated, there was always some truth in them, so those she told them to believed them implicitly, had no sense that she might be using them for her purposes. That she, if few others, had an understanding of what she was doing emerged later, when she told Bonaiuto that she was very worried that she was becoming too much like her mother. It was a nice touch, guaranteed to gain more sympathy and assurances that she was different.

They were, of course, different, and one of the ways in which they were different was in their attitude toward their religion. They were Catholics, but while Karin was deeply believing, Joyce had fallen away and had no use for the religion of her birth and rearing or for any of its practitioners, save, perhaps, her idealized Archbishop Whealon. The difference in attitude inevitably led to a clash.

It came when Karin was about to prepare for the rite of confirmation. Karin's friends, especially Shannon Dubois, were studying in anticipation of the event that would mark their turning fifteen. But when Karin told her mother she wanted to prepare, Joyce was adamant. There was no way she was going to let Karin go through that; she was not even going to let Karin go to church. All of Karin's pleading could not alter that decision.

Karin turned for help to the only source she thought might have power to sway Joyce. She wrote to Archbishop Whealon.

He wrote back in his own hand, not on a typewriter. He told her he was pleased that she had written to him about her problems with her mother over religion, particularly over Joyce's refusal to allow her to practice Catholicism.

He offered her advice. Rather than feel isolated and alone, misunderstood and not loved, she should write to him when she had questions, and he would try to answer them. She ought to realize that many kids, children of broken homes and not close to their parents, were in similar situations. But they should not resent or blame their parents and begin to withdraw and become depressed. "Self-pity," he wrote, "is the worst of attitudes." It was important to remain outgoing, active, interested in everything and to keep a sense of humor. She shouldn't forget that other people had worse problems than she.

No matter what, he said, she should obey her mother, remain loving and respectful to her and help her. If Joyce told her not to go to church, then she shouldn't go. It wouldn't be her doing or her fault.

She had to remember that as far as God was concerned, it was the intention that counted, and hers was to practice her faith if she could. Someday she would be able to do that, and she ought to wait until that day came.

She also must remember, he wrote, that it was not necessary to be confirmed in order to marry or enter the convent. Baptism was essential, or course, but she had been baptized. And later, when she was old enough and so able to resume practicing her religion, that would be time enough to be confirmed.

He told her that even though Joyce was preventing her from going to mass on Sundays or holy days, there were other things Karin could do. She could read the Scripture lessons for that particular day in the Vatican II Sunday missal, or she could watch him perform the mass on television, as he did once a month.

She should set aside a few minutes every day for prayer or devotions and should try to get to confession a couple of times a year while she was on vacation and away from her mother.

It was hardly the kind of help she had wanted. Whealon had let her down, as Michael Aparo and others had done before, and as others would do, she was sure, in the future. She could not, when she needed him most, depend on Whealon, any more than she could depend on her father or any man. But, then, her mother always told her that men will always disappoint you in the end.

The only one who was always there and upon whom she could rely, then, was her mother. And they were linked not only because they were mother and daughter and shared the same house but because of the violin. It might be Karin's only escape, but it was ever more intensely the focus of Joyce's dreams. Karin would be a star, and the credit would belong as much to Joyce as to Karin.

So, on Friday nights after work, Joyce drove Karin down to Rowayton for an evening with the Markovs, during which Karin had a lesson. Sometimes they stayed over, and when they didn't, they drove back to Glastonbury, and then, early Saturday morning, Joyce drove Karin the hundred miles to New York for another lesson with Albert Markov at the Manhattan School. She took Karin to concerts, made sure she played in the school orchestra and in Hartford's children's symphony, tried to get her solos wherever and whenever she could and made her practice hours every day, demanding perfection all the while.

It was, of course, a fantasy. "She was okay," a teacher at the Manhattan School says of Karin. "She knew how to bow, and she had pretty good technique. It would have been pretty strange if she hadn't. She'd been studying how long? She was, what, fourteen, fifteen then? So maybe she'd been playing ten years. You can tell by then; hell, you can tell sooner. She sounded just like any other fairly talented kid that age. What I mean is, you couldn't pick her out from the rest. You know, you hear somebody really good, the one in ten thousand, and you know it right away, as soon as you hear the first notes, maybe even the minute the kid tucks the fiddle under his chin and picks up the bow, the way he does it. There's just something there. It shines out. But not Karin, not most kids. There was nothing particularly distinctive about her playing, nothing spontaneous or idiosyncratic, and not much emotion. She was accomplished, and she played well in a technical sense, but that's about it. A career? Not really. If she got lucky, maybe in some small city, maybe a fill-in when somebody needed a violinist. But not first chair. Soloist? No way.'' What he remembered best was Joyce, the omnipresent and overbearing mother.

Nobody ever told Joyce this evaluation of Karin's talent or even suggested it. It would have done no good anyway. She would not have believed it. Holding on to the illusion was essential. It had been her dream for a decade, and she could not give it up. Had she been forced to abandon it, her world might have collapsed. If Karin realized that, understood her limitations, she could never have breathed it to her mother. As long as she played the violin, as long as she took lessons, as long as she practiced those hours, there was a chance for harmony at home, and it was possible to win her mother's approval and acceptance. Besides, realizing it was her road to freedom, she held to that same dream. One day she might accept the harsh judgment and find some way to deal with the inevitable cataclysmic repercussions. But not then, not when she was thirteen or fourteen. That day would surely come, but it would have to wait until she considered and was ready to act on the alternatives. At that moment, for both mother and daughter, the dream was vital to survival.

Another dream, or fantasy, began to surface now. Karin, a teenager, growing into a young woman, in Joyce's mind always older and more mature than her chronological age, constantly thrown into the world of adults and expected to behave like one, would meet a man, older, established, successful, and marry well. Though Joyce was forever telling people she herself was about to get married, for some unexplained reasons those marriage plans never came to fruition. And nobody ever seemed to meet the men she was going to marry. In the past, as Karin was growing, Joyce occasionally took her to the openings of new nursing homes, to other parties and celebrations. But now she became Joyce's constant companion, Joyce certain she was ready to be part of adult gatherings, to participate as an adult. Karin might be out of her depth there, but she went without complaint, went and stood to the side listening without comment as her mother paraded before the others Karin's accomplishments, Karin's promise, Karin's glittering future, as Joyce boasted and invented stories to back those boasts.

There Karin came to know the men in Joyce's orbit, particularly Michael Zaccaro. Joyce saw him as a man on the move. Running the state's program to regulate nursing homes, an industry in which Zaccaro was emerging as a major force, she was in a position to help him achieve his ambitions. Since Zaccaro's reputation was above reproach, she didn't have to bend any rules to help him—he fitted precisely the standards she set. Further, he was such a font of knowledge about the business that she could, and did, turn to him for expert advice. She could even bounce her own ideas off him.

Their business association quickly turned into personal friendship. Joyce made it a point to be at any nursing home affair when she was certain that Zaccaro would be there as well. Often they wended their way from those occasions to dinner together, and she began to invite him to her home for a meal, for an evening when they played Trivial Pursuit, Monopoly, and other games, listened to music, listened to Karin play the violin. Sometimes she went with him to wrestling matches, a spectator sport he particularly enjoyed. Inevitably Karin went along.

It was a relationship in which there were potential dividends for everyone. The state Health Coordinating Council, the planning agency on which Joyce sat as a major bureaucrat, was part of Connecticut's Health Department. But it was funded by block grants from the federal government, and the Reagan administration, with a disdain for social programs, was cutting back on those grants with the aim of eliminating them altogether. The states, with their limited resources, would not be able to fill the gap, so agencies like the Health Coordinating Council were doomed. When that day came, Joyce Aparo would need a job. With her knowledge, expertise, and contacts, she would not want for one, she would be deluged with offers; the company that won her would gain an invaluable asset. Zaccaro was determined to be the winner. So he set out to woo and win her.

What Zaccaro had only a faint sense of was that Joyce saw him as a fitting consort for her daughter, though he was twice her age, nearing thirty while Karin was fourteen. "When I got engaged in 1987," he says, "I didn't really talk to Joyce about it because I had gotten the feeling that she was hoping I'd wait around for her daughter to grow up."

That was, indeed, precisely what Joyce was hoping. Karin was caught in the middle, thrown constantly in Zaccaro's way, her every talent and every attribute praised to him. While Zaccaro was fond of her, he was more the kindly uncle than the lover.

Still, Joyce was constantly telling her that Zaccaro had expressed deep feeling for her, that he had told Joyce that he wanted to marry her when she grew up, and when she did, he would court her in a proper fashion, with presents, dinners and much more. Zaccaro did give Karin small gifts, a bottle of perfume, a gold watch and some other things, all of which she proudly displayed to her best friend, Shannon Dubois. "Karin," Shannon later said, "told me she liked Michael Zaccaro very much romantically."

That, of course, was not the way Michael Zaccaro liked her. Karin gradually came to realize it, and the dream of Zaccaro faded. Perhaps Joyce saw it, too, though she never totally relinquished the vision of her daughter and her friend united. Had she been younger, or he older, she might have set out to capture him for herself. But romance never blossomed, though the friendship grew ever closer.

As the romantic vision of Zaccaro receded, it was replaced by another one that Joyce saw as even more fitting. The man in this fantasy was Alasdair Neal. He was in his mid-twenties. He was handsome and courtly. He was exotic, born in Scotland, still speaking with a burr. Best of all, he was talented in a way Joyce admired. He was a conductor, so he embodied the true picture that she had of her daughter's future. Neal would conduct the orchestra while Karin played. It was a dream they could share, one that united them more fully than ever before.

Karin was just starting ninth grade, was not yet fifteen when she met Neal. He was in residence at Yale and was conducting the symphony group in Hartford in which Karin played. "When I showed up for rehearsals the first day, he was the conductor," she says. Joyce was with her, and after the rehearsals Joyce went to Neal, talked to him, beckoned Karin to join her.

From that moment on Joyce talked about Neal constantly, and Karin, seeing him three times a week at rehearsals, felt herself increasingly drawn to him. She introduced Shannon to him and later told Shannon she thought he was "handsome and cute and a terrific person. I had a crush on him, and my mother said she had a crush on him, too," Karin said.

Indeed, so highly did Joyce approve of Neal that she did everything she could to bring Karin and him together, and so highly did she approve that her attitude toward Karin altered radically. No longer did she complain constantly; no longer did she find fault relentlessly. At last they got along. They drove to New Haven several times to hear concerts Neal was conducting, saw him as often as possible. Joyce appeared ecstatic whenever he was around, whenever his name was mentioned.

New fantasies emerged. Joyce began to tell Zaccaro

and others how close Karin and Neal were, how deep was
their feeling for each other. Then, early in 1986, she announced that she was leaving for Scotland with Karin and
Neal; he was going to conduct an orchestra there, and Karin
was going to play solo. Further, while they were in Scotland, they all were going to stay with Neal's parents, Lord
and Lady Neal.

For a week or more Karin was out of school. Nobody
saw her. The phone at the Aparo home went unanswered.
They had, everyone believed, gone to Scotland on that concert tour. Indeed, Joyce was in Scotland—but not accom-
panying her daughter and Alasdair Neal on a concert tour.
She was on one of her rock-hunting expeditions. Karin remained home, under strict orders not to answer the phone,
not to leave the condo, not to be seen. Everyone was to
think they were in Scotland.

It all had gone beautifully, Joyce proclaimed when she
returned. The concerts had been well received, they had
stayed with Lord and Lady Neal and the noble couple just
loved Karin.

Karin listened in silence as Joyce rhapsodized to
Michael Zaccaro and others. She did not tell them that she
had not been to Scotland, that she had not played the violin
with an orchestra conducted by Alasdair Neal, that she had
never met Neal's parents, who were not, anyway, a lord and
lady. "I just sat there and didn't correct her because I was
fifteen and I knew I couldn't correct my mother."

Then Alasdair Neal was gone. By the spring of 1986
he had other commitments, so it was time to leave Yale,
time to leave Connecticut. He had looked with perhaps
amusement or tolerance on the adolescent infatuation lav-
ished upon him by one of his violinists and on the adulation
of her mother. For him, it had not been a serious thing; it
could not be; the girl, after all, was only a child. He never
realized, nor could he, how important, how crucial he had
been to Karin, to Joyce and to both of them together at that
moment, nor could he have had any sense of how devas-

tating his departure would be to them. Over the next months Karin's diary entries were filled with plaintive "Oh Alasdair, please come back and make things better!" . . . "Miss Alasdair" . . . "Miss Alasdair *terribly*."

For when Alasdair Neal left, the era of good feelings between Karin and Joyce vanished.

With what she saw somehow as Neal's abandonment, Karin looked elsewhere, anywhere for solace. She experimented with sex for the first time, with a boy her age named Jeff. It was not especially satisfying, did nothing to ease the sense of loss. Worse, somehow, perhaps through reading the diaries Karin kept in her bedside drawer, Joyce learned of it or sensed it, and the condo was filled with recriminations and threats. Karin would do what Joyce wanted, or Joyce would spread far and wide the tale of Karin's delinquency, would destroy Karin's reputation.

So Karin, in the late spring of 1986, retreated into herself more and more, her mind churning to discover some way out of what had become once more an intolerable situation.

13

All her life Karin Aparo had been a victim, brutalized physically until she was twelve, and worse, tortured emotionally without end. She was on the verge of being murdered, not physically but emotionally. What had been, what was being done to her was what psychiatrists have come to call soul murder. In his study *Soul Murder: The Effects of Childhood Abuse and Deprivation*,* the analyst and clinical professor of psychiatry at New York University Dr. Leonard Shengold defines soul murder as "my dramatic designation for a certain category of traumatic experiences: instances of repetitive and chronic overstim-

---

* Leonard Shengold, M.D., *Soul Murder: The Effects of Childhood Abuse and Deprivation* (New Haven: Yale University Press, 1989).

ulation, alternating with emotional deprivation, that are deliberately brought about by another individual.'' He writes:

> The capacity to destroy a soul, hinges entirely on having another human being in one's power, and this confrontation of the powerful and the helplessly dependent is inherent in childhood. . . . What happens to the child subjected to soul murder is so terrible, so overwhelming, and usually so recurrent that the child must not feel it and cannot register it, and resorts to massive isolation of feeling, which is manifested by brainwashing (a mixture of confusion, denial, and identifying with the aggressor). . . . In individuals, psychic murder is founded on the relations between hostile, cruel, indifferent, psychotic, or psychopathic parents and the child prisoner in their charge.

Karin Aparo was that prisoner, and Joyce Aparo was the parent in charge, hostile, cruel, indifferent, psychotic, psychopathic. The home in which Karin was kept was nothing so much as a concentration camp. She was a prisoner, at the utter mercy of a mother whose capricious and often wanton cruelty, ladled out with a shovel and interspersed by occasional drops of kindness, made her a combination commandant and guard. Karin was trapped, unable to find any escape, knowing that even if she managed to flee, her mother would find her no matter what it took, return her to captivity and there subject her to even worse. She was only fifteen, and there were three years lying between her and possible escape to freedom, years that seemed like forever.

Joyce Aparo was a very sick woman. This moment, in 1986, should have been for her a time of celebration, a time of fulfillment. She had achieved in her career much that she had sought. As Michael Zaccaro foresaw, those block grants to the states to aid social programs had come to an end, and

the health council on which Joyce sat had been phased out.
Zaccaro had left NewMediCo and, with a group of colleagues, started Athena Health Care Associates, to develop
and operate nursing homes and convalescent facilities.
Joyce Aparo was just what he needed. He made his pitch.
She accepted and now was heading Athena's social services
division, earning about fifty thousand dollars a year. The
drive to Waterbury, where Athena made its headquarters,
was longer than the one to Hartford, but there were plenty
of compensations. The work was what she knew and what
she enjoyed. She was being paid well for that work, was
associating with people she respected. She was doing good
for many.

But it satisfied none of what was eating away inside her
mind. Nothing could. She was a classic compendium of neu-
roses and psychoses. The symptoms were there, had been
spotted long before by many who came into her orbit. They
were growing worse, consuming her and those closest to her.

Her obsession with Archbishop John Whealon, the stories she invented and repeated about her relationship with
him, say psychiatrists who have examined her history, have
all the earmarks of what is called erotomania. DSM-III-R,
the *Diagnostic and Statistical Manual of Mental Disorders*
(*Third Edition Revised*), compiled by the American Psychiatric Association, defines it as ''an erotic delusion . . . that
one is loved by another [and] the person about whom this
conviction is held is usually of a higher status, such as a
famous person.'' The sickness, though, was not isolated in
Joyce alone. While Whealon might dominate her inner life,
she attempted, as well, to infect her daughter with the virus,
trying to convince Karin that she was loved and desired by
Mike Zaccaro, Alasdair Neal, and other men of success and
promise.

Erotomania was only one, and perhaps one of the least,
of the psychiatric ills that afflicted Joyce Aparo. It would be
nearly impossible to look at the relationship of Joyce the
mother with her daughter, of Joyce the wife with her hus-

bands, and not see a pervasive pattern of cruel, demeaning, and aggressive behavior—symptoms of what many psychiatrists call a sadistic personality disorder.

From the time she was a child demanding undivided attention from her parents and siblings, through her teen years, when she was flashing a ring and claiming it was a gift from the queen of England, on to her tales of foreign travels and adventures, to having her nose fixed to enhance her beauty, to her constant berating of Karin, with whom she so closely identified, as too fat or otherwise physically unattractive, Joyce Aparo was forever demanding, in the words of the American Psychiatric Association's diagnostic manual, "reassurance, approval, or praise; [was] inappropriately seductive in appearance or behavior; [was] overly concerned with physical attractiveness; [was] uncomfortable in situations in which she [was] not the center of attention; [displayed] rapidly shifting and shallow expressions of emotions; [was] self-centered; [had] no tolerance for frustration or delayed gratification; [attempted] to control the opposite sex or enter into a dependent relationship. Flights into romantic fantasy [were] common. . . . Interpersonal relationships [were] usually stormy and ungratifying." It all added up to an aberration called histrionic personality disorder.

That was not all. Joyce Aparo neatly fitted the descriptions of at least two other major psychiatric disorders. Her unreasonable demands for perfection in everything, both from herself and from Karin, demands that could not possibly be met and that therefore too often meant that things could never be completed satisfactorily, and her preoccupation with compiling detailed rules, lists, schedules, and more, combined with her insistence that they be followed precisely with no deviation, are clear demonstrations of what the manual calls obsessive compulsive personality disorder.

Her reaction to criticism—the rage, shame, even humiliation she felt when either she or Karin was criticized—

together with her constant exaggerations of her own and Karin's achievements and talents, and her conviction that she and Karin were unique and that only very special people could possibly understand them are manifestations of the manual's narcissistic personality disorder. People with this disturbance, the manual says, are "preoccupied with fantasies of unlimited success, power, brilliance, beauty or ideal love; [and] lack of empathy: inability to recognize and experience how others feel." This was Joyce Aparo indeed.

These illnesses, and more, these disturbances did not exist in isolation, wreaking their havoc on Joyce Aparo alone. They were infectious. Her daughter was as much a victim as she, and the effect was devastating. As Karin grew, Joyce passed along the viruses.

Some years later Dr. John Cigalis, a psychologist specializing in personality disorders, and Dr. Walter Borden, a general and forensic psychiatrist, were asked by Karin's lawyer, Hubert Santos, to examine her and offer their opinions on her mental and emotional state and stability. Cigalis saw her three times in 1988 and once in 1990. Borden saw her about a dozen times between the fall of 1987 and the winter of 1988. Both have testified often in criminal cases, almost always for the defense, so their views perhaps, may be colored, may be biased considering the general purpose of their examinations. But other psychiatrists who have looked at Karin's past, as re-created by her and others, though they did not personally see her, tend to agree at least in part with Cigalis and Borden.

Karin, all agree, suffered from a multitude of personality disorders. It would have been nearly impossible had she not. She was a battered and abused child, both physically and emotionally, from her earliest memories. The result was what has come to be called post-traumatic stress syndrome, a condition that is given popular currency by the delayed reactions of prisoners of war and especially by Vietnam War veterans after they returned to civilian life and that is common among battered children when they reach adolescence. The trauma is devastating, an event or series of events over which the victim has no control and no ability to change: the captivity and brutal punishment of prisoners, the horrors of a senseless war and the constant battering of the small child. The episodes may appear to have no immediate effect and may be borne stoically during their course. Later, though, the impact hits, and when it does, it can be crushing. The victim is beset by recurring memories, waking and sleeping, of the event or events; as much as he or she tries to avoid them, they cannot be shaken off, there is no escape and it is as though the times were being relived. With that come a marked loss of interest in ordinary things, a feeling of isolation and detachment and estrangement from the world, an inability to feel ordinary emotions like love, a sense that the future holds little or nothing, not career or marriage or children or success.

There were frequent episodes, increasing as Karin grew into adolescence, of anorexia nervosa and bulimia nervosa, the starvation and the vomiting after eating, induced by Joyce's constant haranguing that Karin was too fat, that she ate too much, and then filling the refrigerator with éclairs and other sweets and insisting that she eat them and then vomit.

Karin had all that, and more. There was an induced psychotic disorder, which psychiatrists describe as a delusional system that develops in one person because of that individual's intimate relationship with someone who has a psychotic disorder with his or her own delusions. Eventually the two people will at least partly share these delusions. Nowhere was this more clearly evident than in the dreams Joyce maintained, and fed to Karin, about her future on the concert stage. A key element here is that the shared delusion is usually within the realm of possibility. It doesn't matter if one of this pair is healthy, sane, at the beginning of the relationship. If the dominant partner is the one with the delusions, and the relationship is not one that can be easily escaped, then the sane one's fall is almost inevitable.

Karin was fifteen, and inside, she was assailed by conflicting emotions: She hated her mother because of what her mother had done to her, yet she loved her because she was her mother and she had been taught that one loves one's mother without question, no matter what. As a result, when questioned by people in authority, often she denied her mother had done anything out of the ordinary and said they got along well.

Karin craved acceptance by her contemporaries, but she had been drilled to believe that she did not need them, that she was better, that she was special, and they were not worthy of her. She believed it, and she did not believe it.

She wanted to be like her friend Shannon, have a family like Shannon's, but she had been taught, and so believed and disbelieved, that her mother was best for her, her family life the one suited to her.

She wanted love, but with frozen emotions she could not really feel it. She wanted men to come to her aid, to protect and defend her, the role her mother had instructed her was theirs, but men always failed her, always let her down, always abandoned her, as her mother said they would in the end.

She was becoming more like her mother all the time, a thing she wanted and a thing she hated. She had become adept, even better than her mother, at manipulating people to her own use. She was confused, her mind a hornet's nest of forbidden thoughts and desires she wanted to act out and feared.

She needed help, and she knew she needed it, but there was no way she could get it. One time she went to the school nurse, Maria Bonaiuto, and asked if there was any place she could go to get away from home, any way she could get somebody to take custody of her. All that Bonaiuto could suggest was that she go to Youth Services and ask for help with her problems. Karin said that was impossible because that required parental approval, and Joyce would never give her approval. Indeed, when Bonaiuto approached Joyce about the possibility of counseling for Karin, Joyce flatly rejected the idea. Nobody could counsel Karin, she said, because nobody except Joyce understood Karin.

Karin's soul was being murdered, and there seemed no escape from the murderer, no hope. Then she met Dennis Coleman.

PART THREE

HOW THE DEED
WAS DONE

14

In the summer of 1986, in one of the scores of letters Dennis Coleman placed in Karin's secret mailbox, the slot in her bedroom window between the screen and the glass, he sent along a tape he had compiled of seventeen rock songs, "in an attempt to express my appreciation of your love. You may not appreciate modern music as much as other forms, but these songs *are* me. They are my essence. *Listen to the lyrics* and you'll hear my soul, my heart."

On that tape were songs by Julian Lennon, Steve Perry, Dennis De Young, and the rock groups Journey, Led Zeppelin, Chicago, Giuffria, and Styx. The beat was mainly hard, but all the songs were love songs. In another time, with a beat for a different age, they would have been called love ballads, and even in this age that theme filled them:

"Want Your Body," "Patiently," "Open Arms," "Stairway to Heaven," "Faithfully," "Running Alone," "Foolish Heart," "It's Only Love," "You're the Inspiration," "Hard Habit to Break," "I'll Be There," "Desert Moon," "Call to the Heart," "Babe, Don't Let it End," "Come Sail Away," "Lights."

A month or so later he slipped another note into that mailbox. "I'm listening to the first song on your tape, 'Want Your Body,' for the 21st time in a row. I've been listening while writing. I'm lying on the floor . . . crying. I don't know if it's good or bad. Quite literally, *you* are the only thing I've got left."

The soft rock music and the lyrics, by Julian Lennon, had become special to both of them and, particularly to Dennis, the most special of all the songs on that tape he had made. As he wrote, Dennis played it over and over, day after day. It was the song that led the tape, the first among the equals.

They had known each other then for not quite a year, had met, exchanged words for the first time on a mild evening in May 1986. Joyce and Karin Aparo were returning to their Butternut Drive home from a concert at a local school where Karin had played her violin. Joyce pulled into the parking lot, turned off the engine of her Volkswagen and started to roll up the window on the driver's side. Something was wrong with the handle; it was jammed, the window frozen wide open. She was exasperated. She glanced across the parking lot and spotted a tall, red-haired young man working on his car. She turned to her fifteen-year-old daughter, Karin, and said, "Go and ask that person over there if he'll come here and fix the handle on this window."

Still in the dress she had worn for her performance, appearing older, more grown-up, a young lady, not a fifteen-year-old adolescent, Karin Aparo walked across the lot and approached Dennis Coleman for the first time. He looked up from the open hood of his MGB sports car, listened to the request, closed the hood, picked up some tools and followed her across the parking lot. Joyce Aparo, standing beside her Volkswagen, showed him the window, demonstrated her problem. He examined the stuck window critically.

"Do you think you can fix it?" she asked.

"Sure. No trouble."

The idea of leaving a car overnight with its window open, even in a safe suburb like Glastonbury, even in a neighborhood of culs-de-sac, had not been an appealing one. Who knew what could happen to an unprotected car late at night when everyone was asleep? The assurance by Dennis that he could fix the car was what she needed to hear. Relieved, she thanked him, then turned and started for her house. Karin stayed behind and watched as Dennis took out some tools, did a few things and quickly had the window rolling up and down. While he put away his tools, he and Karin began to talk, and for the next fifteen or twenty minutes they stood together in the parking lot by the car. Neither was able later to remember what they talked about. "This and that," Karin said, "nothing major."

So eighteen-year-old Dennis Coleman, within a few weeks of graduating from Glastonbury High School, took notice of fifteen-year-old Karin Aparo, just finishing ninth grade, her freshman year at that school—or, as some later had it, Karin Aparo, fifteen going on thirty, decided at that moment that Dennis Coleman, eighteen going on twelve, was the boy for her.

They had been neighbors on Butternut Drive for about two and a half years, Karin and Joyce at number 3, Dennis, his younger brother, Matt, and his mother, Carol Louise Coleman, at number 8, directly across the parking lot. Dennis's father and stepmother, coincidentally also named Carol Louise, with whom he spent most weekends, lived a few miles away, in South Glastonbury, in an old house, near the river and surrounded by woods, that had been his grandparents'.

Karin later said that she had noticed Dennis at least a year before, his red hair and his sports car impossible to miss or ignore. But she was sure he had never noticed her; there were those three years between them and she was certain Dennis was very popular with the girls his own age. Besides, it was about then that she had begun to be filled with idealized romantic fantasies about Alasdair Neal.

Dennis said later that he, too, had first noticed Karin a year before, when she was only in the eighth grade. "There was just something about her, I guess." But he never approached her. She was, after all, just a kid, the only distinguishing marks that someone older might note being the violin case always clutched in her hand and the large glasses that seemed to cover half her face. Besides, there were all the other girls, the Michelles and the Brendas and the Denises and half a dozen more, all more mature, who had moved through and filled that part of his life, one after the other, since he had reached the age when becoming involved with girls turns into a preoccupation.

At first it seemed only a momentary, inconsequential thing, an idle passing on a spring night. Dennis later said, "I fell for her immediately. I found myself somehow willing to give more than I had ever given in my life." But he did nothing to show it during those first days.

Nor did Karin. In the days after that first meeting, she later wrote in her diary, she used to see Dennis often out by his car in the parking lot. She watched his car speed out of the lot and then, sometimes, race back in a few minutes later. She began to look for him at school, in the halls, with people they both knew, coming and going to classes, in a lot of different places. She nodded, they exchanged a few words, but "it was no major thing."

Until, that is, one afternoon shortly before the start of summer vacation, when she was waiting for the school bus to take her home. In her diary Karin wrote that Dennis was standing nearby, alongside his car, talking with a friend. He happened to glance up, saw her and asked if she'd like a ride. She said yes. They started off, Karin in the front seat with Dennis, the friend in the back. It began to rain in torrents. For some reason she didn't understand, Karin started to laugh and couldn't stop laughing the whole way home. Dennis dropped his friend off, then put the MG's cover over her head to protect her; over his own head he wrapped a blue towel that blew out behind him, making him look, she thought, like an Arab. "Everything appeared so funny," she wrote. "Now, as I look back, that was the first day in a line of many where or in which I would spend most of my time with Dennis laughing." It was, she said, the high point of the year, her first in high school, and "I entitled it, 'the ultimate life experience.'"

It was the start. Within days he was writing her notes and she was writing notes back to him. They established a routine, complete with their private mailbox for delivering and receiving those notes, some just a few lines, some running to page after page. A friend, Dennis noted, "told me Karin liked me, and that gave me the confidence to 'pursue my heart's desire.'"

The last week of school, though as a graduating senior he had no classes in the morning, he drove her to school in the morning, picked her up and drove her home in the afternoon.

In the way of any romance, though, stood Joyce Aparo. She would have to be won, would have to see something in Dennis that made him suitable for Karin if the relationship were to progress beyond casual greetings. Almost unwittingly he won her over. "In my ongoing attempt to have parents (not mine) like me," he wrote in his own diary (which, unlike Karin, who rarely missed a day in recording the ongoing events of her life, he kept only sporadically), "I gave her mother a ride to Waterbury, and thank god I did. I guess she likes me now and I think she's a neat person."

The significance of that gesture was not lost on Karin. That particular day Joyce had trouble with her car and took it to a Volkswagen dealer near the high school. Driving by with Karin on the way to her morning classes, Dennis noticed Joyce standing in the dealer's parking lot. He asked if Karin thought Joyce might need a lift. Initially Karin said no, then changed her mind. So, once he had dropped Karin off, he returned, picked up Joyce and drove her to her job in Waterbury. That afternoon he reported to Karin what he had done. She was amazed and stunned, wanted to know everything they had talked about and everything they had done on that trip.

That ride and the conversation during it thawed Joyce. She was taken with Dennis and began to talk about him to Karin. Until then, Karin said, she had not really examined her own feelings. Now "I knew there was something there, though. It was different and it was special."

"I'd like to say," Dennis wrote in his own diary, "how glad I am that Karin came into my life just as graduation did. Sitting in the bleachers waiting to get my diploma, I constantly thought of her. Quite honestly, she was *all* I could think of. Anyway, I'm happy she was there for me to think of."

And Karin wrote in her diary that on the last day of school Dennis gave her one long-stemmed rose together with a note expressing his growing fondness for her. Now he began to see more and more of her.

So it grew, for the most part unplanned, just sudden whims, sudden chance that threw them together when they were free, no formal dates set days or weeks in advance. They might see each other in the condo parking lot, somewhere in the neighborhood, anywhere, come together and then go off somewhere, anywhere.

There were those three years between them, of course, teen years that to those who have grown old enough to forget seem a nearly unbridgeable chasm. Between Dennis and Karin, it was a gap as easily crossed as if it had not existed. It was more than certain shared interests or a physical attraction that drew them together. Each had a need, a desperate one, an emptiness that the other filled, so each became indispensable to the other.

15

"I think I'd like to tell you about me. As much as is remembered," Dennis Coleman wrote to Karin Aparo in August 1986, a long autobiography that is a mixture of fact and fancy, braggadocio and understatement, insight and naiveté. "Born Feb. 23, 1968, 8:32 A.M. Mom sort of woke up and there I were. At six months I helped move from East Hartford—a trailer park my first home and a tenement the second one. Imagine being conceived in a mobile home? TACKY."

It wasn't quite that bad. Dennis's grandparents were an old, established and financially comfortable Glastonbury family. Both of Dennis's parents, Dennis senior and Carol Louise, grew up in Glastonbury. They met in high school when the elder Dennis was a senior and Carol a freshman.

They fell in love. And as in most high school romances they fell out of love. After a time Carol still at Glastonbury High School, Dennis in college, Carol announced that they ought to end it, that she didn't want to see him anymore. He became distraught, made an abortive suicide attempt. When he recovered, Carol took him back. They married when she finished high school, Dennis senior dropping out of college, to the displeasure of his parents. "I only found out about [them] during all that happened [to me]," Dennis junior said much later. "It was a very similar situation to Karin and me. The parallels are creepy."

The newly married Colemans settled temporarily in a trailer park in East Hartford. Dennis went to work for the Travelers Insurance Company in Hartford, and Carol got a job at the Aetna. They were doing well, and soon after Dennis was born, they bought a house in Hebron, stayed there for little more than a year before they bought a larger house in Glastonbury. There a second son, Matthew, was born.

The marriage was breaking apart, had probably been destined to fail from the start. Two sons did nothing to cement it. "I was about five. I can only remember sitting in the living room and my dad trying to talk to us and trying to explain that he and my mom weren't getting along and he was moving out. I guess what happened was that they both just grew up. You know, they were kids when they got married and then they grew up and became different people."

He wrote in that autobiography to Karin:

We moved into an apartment on Griswold Street with Mom. Dad moved to Meriden. First day of school . . . I gain the edge I'm looking for. I'm the first to spot the sign with the banana on it. My official classroom symbol. There was a teacher holding the sign, so up I ran. I got to hold the sign. To me it was an honor, to her a relief, for she no longer had to hold that damned sign. Looked more like a picket sign than

anything else, come to think of it. The perfect start to
a glorious schooling career.

Quickly I gained friends. By 3rd grade, I had the
biggest muscles, could run third fastest and caused the
2nd most amount of trouble in my class. *Yes!* I was
also the best soccer offensive player that Naubuc ever
had, or will see.

He was also, he says, part of the in crowd, the elite
group of third graders. "All my friends were the best jocks,
the best with the books, all that. I fit in." Then it ended.

Tragedy strikes! We moved to Rocky Hill. Why,
I don't know. It was all over. My reign was finished.
Fourth grade—not bad. I was quickly advanced to 5th
grade English. I also fell in love for the first time. If
you think you are, then you are. Nicole—ah, Nicole.
Strangely enough, 100% Italian. Again I became sincerely popular with my classmates. I am the third best
at everything in my class behind Rick Gozzo and Mike
Lopez. Good enough. Then Gozzo steals Nicole and
they're "married" at home plate during recess. My
life was over. Crushed for the first time. Just to prove
what a nice guy I was, I became the best man. You
see—it started even then.

Their marriage wasn't to be, however. Within
days, I had them fighting. Ha-ha. Sixth grade—I jump
an unprecedented 14'-6" in the running long jump.
(Most high school people can't jump that now—even
track people[.]) SUPER JOCK. Needless to say, I was
on my way. After my fantastic jump I got in line to try
again—never satisfied—and while there, Nicole turned
to me and for the first time a female told me she loved
me. I'll never forget it. Some kid overheard her and
promptly yelled it out for anyone in the gym to hear if
they cared to listen. No matter. I ask her out—she says
yes. Life is great.

July 12 we move and off I go to Canton. The relationship lasts because my dad lives so close by and that's where I am on weekends.

Dennis senior had been married for a second time, to another woman named Carol Louise. Then the first Carol Louise, a single mother working and trying to raise two young sons, met a man. "She moved out to Canton with this guy," Dennis says, "and she was going to get married, and we moved out to his house. It was a total disaster." He wrote about it to Karin:

Canton. Again I am the best soccer player the school had ever seen, but popularity there suffered for me. Drugs everywhere and I had never been exposed to this environment before. A 7–12 grade school. The new kid on the block. Tensions were high. Then the fateful day behind the supermarket. The atmosphere in the town was such that a stabbing was no big thing. No big thing. Why did he have to ruin my life? No longer do I have the edge. I become withdrawn and alone. Empty. Why did he have to kill me? Basically that's what he did. A lot of the "old me" will *never* be back now. He took everything away except my body— gasping for breath as I lie helpless, unable even to yell or cry, as the sun went down and *everything* turned grey. Grey. Then black. Why? I can't forget it. I can't take off my shirt without reliving that instant. Ever. When you touch me there, *that's* what hurts. Forever. *Why?*

It was a nice dramatic story. Only it never happened. "The scar," Dennis says now, "is just where I had a mole removed. I never got stabbed. I got into a fight, but nothing like that. Karin wanted to know about the scar, so I invented a story."

As Dennis said, the move to Canton was a disaster. The prospective marriage never took place, the relationship ended badly after a short time and Carol and her sons moved back to Glastonbury, to the condo at 8 Butternut Drive. Dennis was nearly thirteen then, halfway through seventh grade.

Only a few remembered me and no one cared. By the end of the year, my only friend was Kevin Miller. Eighth grade was better. I formed various crushes on certain girls. I met the Hish [a fellow student who became a close friend] and everything was getting better, but I was still very much a loner. My grades, I found, were shot and gone for good. I wasn't first, or second, or third, or anything best at anything. I didn't even try.

Freshman year. *The* worst year of my entire life. Nicole and I finally broke up and I literally failed every class I took. I thought about suicide many times and began sincerely wishing I had died behind the stores. My emotions were so strong I almost died from them alone. Everyday I would come home, go to the basement and stare at the ceiling. I kept myself from crying and vowed never to cry again and never open up again. I just couldn't climb back up. It was over. I was beaten, but as will happen with prideful, young teenagers I refused to act it. Two of me formed and *every second* of my life I used to analyze myself. That is scary. My mind never stopped and I drowned in a sea of contradictions. Nothing fit.

The next year, in early March, Wheatley introduced me on a blind date to Denise Chicoine. Blonde, blonde hair though mutant. We had a good summer, but in the end I guess my inability to open up to her killed us. In September (the 19th) we broke up. "When you're lying awake . . . go ahead and cry. I love you." In December, I went to her birthday party at her house and ended up "with" her best friend on the couch. I later learned that she wanted to get back together . . . until that. What can I say? It just came *that* close again. I, again, fell apart. Music became my hobby and I wrote 11 songs and about 200 pages of notes to her during January.

Among the songs, the lyrics, he wrote for the departed Denise was this:

> *Shifting sands of time*
> *Erasing all the pain*
> *Blowing winds of change*
> *Bring on tears of rain*
> *Tides will rise and fall*
> *Waves will crash the shore*
> *Understanding will now see*
> *What the waves ignore*
> *The depth of the mountains*
> *The height of the sea*
> *The darkness of what's around us*
> *Creating light to see . . .*
> *The light in my eyes blinds me like dark*

In one letter to Denise he wrote:

Hi. Please don't tear this up. I just wanted to say hi. I also wanted to say that I'm sorry for what happened way back when. I did once, but I kind of took it back by the way I acted. I'm angry when things don't work out for me. It gets hard for me to relate to myself. This is actually the fourth letter I've written you. The first was back around Christmas and in it I apologized. The next became a warning and the third was just downright obnoxious. I didn't have the heart to send any of them though. Those who know about them think I sent them. I never really told them I didn't. I had to protect both my pride and my image.

I said above that I didn't have the heart to send those letters but in my mind I'm conditioned to say to myself that I can do anything. The other guy is always wrong. I can always find some way to come out looking better, or save my pride. If a teacher says, "I don't like the way you did this, please try it again," I say, "Fuck you. I did it the way *I* thought it should be done. I count, not you." The teacher gets pissed and I cop an attitude and fail the class. It always seemed like a game—but now it's gotten out of control and I find myself living it. I don't really regret it, but it does force me to change. You see that. That's why you broke up with me.

It got out of hand because I found new friends. The elite of our class. You saw me the other night with Chris, but that's the first time I've even talked to him in about a month. He got involved with Debbie and I split. They make me sick. With these new people you really have to be like them. To be like them I had to change, but it got out of hand and now I'm living in their world not mine. I underwent a change the same as I did last summer. For some reason I do that every six months or so. In between I'm an all right person, but during the change I'm an asshole because I feel insecure. I don't feel whole and I do feel vulnerable so I try to keep everyone out. Everyone. That combined with rumors added up.

Well anyway, that's why we broke up. I tried to think of a million excuses. That's what I do best. Well almost. Some things remain intact. In this letter I want to admit to all of my excuses. I was wrong obviously. There's a reason for everything, but sometimes just reasons aren't enough. Other things count too. To me you counted. I hate to admit it, but I still think of you everyday. It hurts to think of what I did. It still hurts to think of all the people I hurt. For you the hurt was the last thing you felt, but I hope I brought enough happiness to make up for it. I'm sorry.

A little later, in another letter to Denise, he wrote:

I'm not sure if you know anything about me, or what I'm doing now through various sources. Even if you do, I'll tell you anyway. I'm doing just fine thank you. The band is going well, my job got even better, although I'm still at Frank's [the store where he worked], and socially I'm peak. No problem.

Truthfully I know nothing about you now. I haven't been keeping tabs I'm afraid. Life and death struggles, heroic acts, and general citizenship have left me rather preoccupied lately. Such things as concerts, work, football games, ski club and everything. The little things in life.

I have a question. Why was I such a jerk last summer, like during August especially? I remember you wrote something about "I can look back now and smile when I think of" etc. . . . something like that, but all I can do is look back and say, "Oh god, what a jerk." Something like that. I'm sorry for being such a jerk. I already told you that though. Oh god, what a jerk.

You should come to one of our football games. I'm cheerleader (work permitting). Kind of cheerleader. It's keen. If it wasn't for work I'd be *starting* on the team. Problem is, *I have* to work. And rehearse. Oh well. My life as a jock. Working sucks, doesn't it.

Here's something you might appreciate. Through no fault of my own I am sustaining at least a "B" average in every class. Of course I have no math or English, but respectable all the same. I haven't even tried yet. I haven't done *any* homework yet in fact. It makes me wonder what I used to find so difficult. Maybe things will get back to normal soon.

As for my personal life which I'm sure you might, probably don't care about. I'm seeing a girl from work. She's twenty-two. I'm not so sure "seeing" is the

Joyce Aparo, the victim, a social worker and health planner described by some as brilliant and warm and by others as cold and abusive.

The late Hartford Archbishop John F. Whealon. Joyce told Karin he was her father, which Whealon strongly denied.

Karin Aparo listens as one of her love letters to Dennis is read aloud in court. STEPHEN DUNN/*The Hartford Courant*

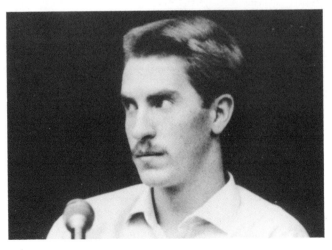

Dennis Coleman on the witness stand.
STEPHEN DUNN/*The Hartford Courant*

Left to right: Hubert J. Santos, one of Karin's attorneys, Karin, and Michael Aparo, her father, leave Superior Court.

JOHN DUNN/*Journal Inquirer*

Christopher Wheatley, the medical student who helped Dennis dispose of the body. TONY DUGAL/*The Hartford Courant*

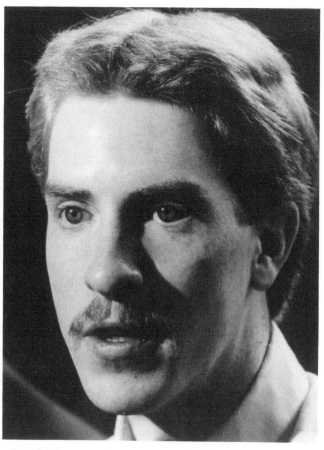

Dennis Coleman at the time of the trial.

Hope Seeley (*left*), another attorney for Karin, and Karin leave the courtroom after the prosecutor announced he would retry Karin on conspiracy to commit murder.

RICHARD MEI/*The Hartford Courant*

Dennis Coleman and the young woman he would later marry enter Superior Court for his sentencing. Coleman received a thirty-four-year prison term.

TONY BACEWICZ/*The Hartford Courant*

right word exactly, it's more of a "give/take" relationship. She's quite acceptable. For now. There's another girl I think I may decide to like more who's nineteen. I know—through sources—she likes me. I'm quite sure you don't have any info of that sort coming to you through Scott or anyone. No one *really* knows about it.

Wheatley is still a blow off. Debbie dumped him and now hates his guts. He doesn't know that yet though. Oh god, what a jerk. Did you see my name in the Courant, twice. I'm famous. Something about working a few (3 I think) sixteen hour days until 2 A.M. to get Frank's West Hartford store back in operation after the storm. Monday, Tuesday and Wednesday. Guess who's up for another raise. I got paid double time for most of it. The article wasn't about me of course, but mine and the manager's names were the only ones mentioned. You probably think I live for that store. *Wrong.* I just needed a $250 paycheck at the time. I'm an opportunist. You know *that* also, regrettably. Oh god, what a jerk.

As for the "revenge." I guessed you, at least, found it amusing. I'm sorry we can't get together, but I understand that we shouldn't. You get nostalgic? Our prom was on April 27th—ring a bell?

As for the "peer pressure." I'm sorry everyone else hates me so much. What I did was stupid, not unforgivable I think, but stupid. I certainly don't expect forgiveness. Please tell everyone, especially Theresa, that I'm sorry for all of it. *All* of it. Sometimes things can make a person insensitive. And as for your worst flaw—it's only understanding. For that I thank you. It was much more than I feel I deserved. Your letter touched me and even brought a tear to my eye for the first time since June. I also thank you for that. I guess (hope) we *are* better off with just some memories. I'll never forget what I've done, and never understand why. I'll always regret it. If you ever need someone to talk to, a guy's point of view, write or call *please*. For friendship's sake, how can people be friends if they don't communicate? Need feeds emptiness—the emptiness of being alone. Take care of *yourself*. There are still people that will always love only what they shouldn't. It's a hobby of mine. I do still love you. I *never stopped.*

Then he stopped, and Denise was the past. He explained to Karin Aparo:

One year later, I met Brenda. *The* most gorgeous perfect person I had ever known. I was a junior and she was a senior. Oh god . . . I fell in love with that girl. I was absolutely, and utterly hers. She went with me to my Junior Prom and quite honestly every guy there was in total envy. I had gotten the edge back. At last. I just may owe her my life. *Everything* in my life changed. All my friends I dropped. She, though, didn't want to have *that* much to do with it all. To put it shortly—we'll never talk again. My fault again. Now I had no friends. Except Kevin Miller. Not to be a fag, or anything, but I love that kid more than a lot of things. The thought of not seeing him again makes me just cry. Not much can do that. It's all over now, though. They're all gone forever. Well anyway, Kevin and I threw my party last August and about 300–400 people showed up. Even the most popular good looking girls in the class who are usually never to be seen. I was pleased and it *really* set up my senior year. This last took an upturn and now my life is good again. At last. Oh god, don't leave me. I've lost everything I've ever had, including myself. Please don't go. Ever.

16

Amid all the passion and hyperbole, in all the dramatics and overblown elaborate phraseology of that long autobiography written for Karin, in those letters and lyrics written for Denise, in other letters to others, something was wrong.

All his life Dennis Coleman had been searching desperately, not for something he had once had and lost but for something that had never been his, an essential ingredient in the creation of a personality. Perhaps it was because of the friction and incompatibility in his home in his earliest years, perhaps it was because of something in his psyche, but psychiatrists later said that he had never bonded, not with his mother or his father. He had been a difficult baby, had been difficult all the time he was growing up, refusing what comfort his mother offered, refusing even to let her take care of him, turning aside all her attempts at solace, all her shows of affection and caring. After a time both his mother, with whom he lived, who tried as best she could to tend him and his brother, and his father, with whom he spent weekends, turned into pals rather than parents, trying to spend time and do things with him as equals. Though he refused affection and bonding from them, he craved them from someone, as all children, as all people, do. As his letters clearly demonstrate, when he grew into adolescence, the usual crushes became not puppy love soon shed but intense and clinging attachments that sent him into despair and depression when they ended.

He was what the renowned Viennese psychoanalyst and theorist Helen Deutsch described in a classic groundbreaking study in 1934: an ''as if'' personality.* Deutsch wrote:

> The individual's whole relationship to life has something about it which is lacking in genuineness and yet outwardly runs along ''as if'' it were complete. . . .
> The first impression these people make is of complete normality. They are intellectually intact, gifted, and bring great understanding to intellectual and emotional problems; but . . . without the slightest trace of originality. On closer observation, the same thing is seen in their affective relationships to the environment. These relationships are usually intense and bear all the earmarks of friendship, love, sympathy, and understanding. . . . but [i]t is soon clear that all these relationships are devoid of any trace of warmth, that all expressions of emotion are formal, that all inner expe-

---

* Remarks delivered to the American Psychoanalytic Society in 1938 and published in 1942 in English as ''Some Forms of Emotional Disturbance and Their Relationship to Schizophrenia'' in *Psychoanalytic Quarterly*.

rience is completely excluded. It is like the performance of an actor who is technically well trained but
who lacks the necessary spark to make his imperson-
ations true to life. . . .

Consequences of such a relation to life are completely passive attitude to the environment with a
highly plastic readiness to pick up signals from the
outer world and to mold oneself and one's behavior
accordingly. . . .

The same emptiness and the same lack of individ-
uality which are so evident in the emotional life appear
also in the moral structure. Completely without char-
acter, wholly unprincipled in the literal meaning of the
term, the morals of the "as if" individuals, their ideals,
their convictions are simply reflections of another person, good or bad. . . . A second characteristic . . . is
their suggestibility. . . . Thus it can come about that the
individual can be seduced into asocial or criminal acts.

They matched. They fitted, Dennis Coleman and Karin
Aparo. Each had what the other craved, what the other
needed. It was not just the hidden yearnings and demands.
There were all the surface things, too.

They both were smart, with IQs that put them into the
special realm of the intellectually very superior, yet in
school both were underachievers, doing adequately sometimes, poorly at others, nowhere near as well as they should
have. Dennis, says one of his closest friends, "never did
homework, never studied. He was the average student as far
as grades went, but he never tried. He made out just because
of his intelligence. Like, we had a *Newsweek* course, where
the text was the magazine. Dennis never subscribed to the
magazine, and I don't think he ever read it, but he aced the
tests because he knew what was going on in the world. It
was like, if he was interested in something, he was about
the best, and if he didn't give a damn, he just kind of
squeaked by."

Dennis himself says, "When we moved back to Glastonbury, I was an outsider. My old friends remembered me, and they'd talk to me, but I wasn't part of that crowd anymore, and they were the guys who were at the top. I was just rebellious. I didn't like school or anything, so I never read anything. It was funny, the people I was trying to be accepted by, I resented them quite a bit at the same time. And then the college thing. I hadn't ruled out going to college. I always really wanted to go on to school. But by junior year this guy was going to Harvard and this guy to MIT or Yale, here and there, and I didn't think I could compete with them. I got turned off and disgusted with the whole societal thing."

Karin, too, did well only in those things she cared about, even though she was aware that her mother demanded perfection and that if she didn't perform to those standards, it meant trouble. But sometimes performing to expectations was just too hard; sometimes it was a way of rebelling, one of the few ways she had. "So I just finished failing a geometry exam. No problem!" she wrote in a friend's yearbook at the end of a school term.

Karin and Dennis shared a love of animals. She had two cats, Godfrey and Winston; there had been cats in her house as long as she could remember; affection for them was a thing she and her mother shared. Dennis's pet was more exotic, a ferret he named Meegan, and she had become essential in his life, something to which he could talk and confide secrets as he could to nobody else.

They shared—perhaps as important as anything, for it dominated their lives—a passion for music. His, though, was not for the classics. He had little use or appreciation for them, as she had little for anything but, although he tried to win her to what he liked. He was a trombonist in the school orchestra; he also played bass and was part of a rock group with some friends that played a few gigs here and there. "I never had a lesson," he says. "I taught myself. I could pick up the trombone, most instruments, and be able to play." He had a dream. He would be a rock star, a composer and performer. As their attachment deepened and became more intimate, as they began to look to the future, he wrote Karin:

> I have a dream of being famous like a rock star. I really want that for me, but I'm not sure you do. To begin with, it would mean extensive travel for me and a pretty hectic life. Most of the hard part will be while you're still in college. Hard meaning travel, low budget, cruddy living, etc. You know, struggling band stuff. But if all works out o.k., then the band will be at midlife and at peak forte by the time we get married in 7–9 years. I will be about 26 or 27 then and about 9 months out of every two years would be spent "on the road." That's 9 months straight through—then 18 for rest and recording. I dream of living that way, but there's no way I could ask you to live out *my* dream. You must live out dreams of your own. You have an incredible future for yourself. Don't follow my half-assed, fluke-of-a-life future when you've got so much more. By the time I'm 30, or 35, my career should be waning, or at an end, and I'll be rich enough to make us happy forever. Millions, Karin. What scares the hell out of me is, what if this doesn't work out?

Still, he wrote poems to her, lyrics, perhaps, for the rock songs he would compose:

> *You are my fantasy*
> *You are my friend*
> *Together we will be*
> *Beyond the end*
> *You are my love*
> *You are my life*
> *You are my density*
> *You will be my wife (ha ha)*
> *We'll always be special*

We'll always be right
But oh how I wish
You were with me tonight
I love you gorgeous. . . .

Classical music was her world, and in her dream she would be the star of the concert halls as Dennis would be of the rock arenas. But these were impossible dreams, fantasies, and both their lives were dominated by fantasies.

"Karin," her first teacher said a long time later, "was not as good as I first thought she would be. There was something blocking her talent and development as she got older. She did not live up to expectations. She became an average student, and she should have been a very good one."

As for Dennis, "His intelligence took over," a friend who played in a group with him says. "He could literally hear a song once he'd never heard before and follow along the rest of the song. I don't think I could do that, and I've been a musician all my life, both my parents are musicians. Playing with Dennis was really easy. He could just pick up out of nowhere. I'd play off the top of my head and he'd pick up. I play bass on and off, but I could never do what he did. But his intelligence took over, so it was no secret that he wasn't the greatest bass player ever."

That was, indeed, what he feared, for he realized it was true. "Where do I get a job and with what qualifications?" he wrote to Karin. "There's always the very strong possibility that I may take the safer, though probably not quite so lucrative, path that I'm on now. Give up my dreams for assured happiness with you. I *still* love you, my Karin. Still and always will." Giving up that dream, sooner or later, was something he knew he would have to do. "It was frustrating," he says. "I knew what I wanted to do, how I wanted to play, but there was a wall surrounding me and there was no way I could get through that wall. Almost everything I ever wanted to do, I wanted to reach out for, there was that wall surrounding me. So I knew I'd never make it in music."

They were sure, in these early summer days of 1986, that what they felt for each other was different from anything they had experienced in the past. This, they became convinced, was love, real love, true love. "I've always been more of an analytical person, covering my emotions," Dennis says. "Karin opened me. I never felt that before. She made me a complete person for the first time in my life."

Dennis had a job by then, a full-time one. He had worked at a supermarket since the time he was old enough, earning enough money to support his car, that MG, and have some to spend on what he wanted. But that wasn't the kind of job he wanted once he graduated from high school. College might lie somewhere in the future, but not now. He would pass it up for the moment and get a job that would make use of his skills with the computer and would earn him some money. He might have gone to work for his father's computer consulting firm, for which he had done work over the summers in the past. He decided to pass up that chance. At some time in the future he could always go to work there, just as he was sure he could also decide to go on to college if he ever wanted. Now he got a job with an insurance company, Aetna Life and Casualty, and he was earning $375 a week. It was enough money to buy anything Karin might want or anything he might want to give her.

Late one Saturday afternoon in mid-June they drove into Hartford and had what Dennis called a picnic. It turned into a momentous day in their relationship. "Not in a very long time have I enjoyed another person's company as much," Dennis wrote. "We *do* get along wonderfully. Our picnic turned out to be a sign stealing fest and secretly I was amazed and amused by her brazen talent, and iron nerves for this. What a good day."

Remembering the same escapade, Karin wrote that they wandered all over Hartford, having a wonderful time, particularly stealing signs off the fences and walls of the

Civic Center, the parking lot by the State Capitol and else-where.

With the stolen signs in the trunk of Dennis's MG, they were unwilling just to drive back home, say good-bye, and go their own ways for the rest of the evening. They went to a movie.

According to Karin, all they did was hold hands.

Dennis had fuller memories, as he confided to his diary:

> By interpreting what she said after the movie, we weren't gonna go home right away and she wasn't hungry. At my best guess, we ended up down at the Meadows. It made me happy to find her so over-whelmed by the area which I managed, for so long, to take for granted. Again I was amazed and amused and even grateful of her appreciation. It was a beautiful night. Now, in all honesty, what progressed in the car went *far* beyond my most aggressive feelings. Without getting intently graphic, I might say that what hap-pened did so *very* fast. Never were my intentions *that*. Not on a "first date."

In Karin's diary she wrote that once they left the movie theater they drove down to a field at the edge of the Con-necticut River. There Dennis kissed her for the first time. "Very interesting," she wrote. It was after two in the morn-ing by the time they reached the condos on Butternut Drive. Joyce was waiting up. She was furious. She lashed out at Karin with all her vitriol. But to Karin's surprise and de-light, Joyce did not declare Dennis off limits; indeed, she said that Karin could even see him again the next day.

After midnight the next day Dennis wrote about his reactions:

> Last night, when we got home, I was told a small battalion of police were combing the town. I didn't get

much sleep for the first four hours I lay in bed. Sunday, today, I was to call and see if we were going out for dinner that night. I'll not describe how scared I was making that call. I even talked, at first, with an odd voice in case her mother answered in wrath. I was prepared to say it was only Sean. But Karin answered and by some miracle, it seemed to me, her mother was forgiving and understanding about the whole thing. Dinner was off for *that* night, but I sensed some tension in Karin's voice. To me something else sounded wrong. The way she said, "Well, I guess I'll talk to you sometime . . . call me tomorrow," has unsettled me to no end. The fact that my brother later told me that Mrs. Aparo had wanted me arrested did not help. Oh god.

For the first time in over a year, or more, I feel emotion stirred deep, deep within me. For some reason I feel I just can't, no matter what, lose this girl. I've fallen for her completely, and it is the most unthinkable fear which causes my worst thoughts. All I want is to talk openly and honestly. To Karin I would be nothing other than open, honest, and sincere. We need a chance, because what's inside me now is a feeling much like love. *Please* understand. What am I going to say to her later this morning? *Please*.

One of the things he did say when he saw her was that they must make definite plans for dinner together. It would be, both decided, their first real date. They had been talking about it for a couple of weeks, since just before the end of school. He had even given her a list of possible restaurants and asked her to choose one. They settled on one of Glastonbury's best, Blacksmith's Tavern. "We planned," Karin said, "an evening that reeked of class." There would be that dinner, and then, Dennis promised, he would drive her to a hill from which they would have a spectacular night view of Hartford.

It didn't happen on the night they originally planned. But it did finally on June 25, 1986. They had dinner and then drove around the town, Dennis stopping and kissing her every few minutes. They parked on a hill with a breathtaking view, and Dennis told her he was falling in love with her. They talked about that and about trusting and respecting each other, and then they drove to an area where new houses were being built, where they parked in one of the driveways. They sat in his car and talked about the future, talked about going away together for what they called a honeymoon. She agreed, but on one condition. Before she could spell that out, he asked her to marry him. She said yes. And then they planned their wedding and reception, and a honeymoon trip to Vienna, and even the house in which they would live on their return.

They were home by ten. Karin went to bed. A few minutes later she heard a tapping at her window screen. It was Dennis. She turned out the lights and went over to the window. He had, he said, come to say good-night.

When he was gone, she took a piece of paper and wrote him a letter, then put it in their private mailbox in her window for him to pick up in the morning. She wrote that she wanted to tell him that she had just come home from a truly wonderful night with a wonderful person in a wonderful car, and that they had talked about wonderful things, and that even without the place and the car and the night, it would still have been wonderful, but the person she had been with had made it perfect. He was, she wrote, very special, and her only fear was that she might lose him. "I want to keep you around . . . yes, forever. Forever and a day."

But a separation lay just ahead, and even though only temporary, it loomed to them as forever. Karin had been baby-sitting for some neighbors, Kennedy Hudner and his wife, for the past year. In mid-July the Hudners were going to Cape Cod for vacation. They had asked Karin to go along with them, and she had agreed. It would get her out of the house and away from her mother for a couple of weeks, and that was, to her, a prospect much to be desired. Her relationship with her mother was at best volatile; Joyce's demands often seemed to her extreme, and nothing Karin did was ever enough, ever satisfactory. She needed room and rarely had it. The Hudners were offering her some of that necessary space.

But when the Hudners returned to Glastonbury, Karin would not be returning with them. Her mother had arranged for the two of them to go to Nantucket for a short vacation of their own, and that would mean they would be in close proximity all the time they were on the island. There would not even be the kind of limited freedom she enjoyed when Joyce was off at her job. There would be only Joyce. And Dennis would be far away, back in Glastonbury.

Then Joyce offered an option that made the trip inviting. Dennis had driven Joyce to her job at Athena in Waterbury on several occasions, they had talked during those rides and she had grown increasingly fond of him. Now she suggested to him, and he eagerly accepted, a chance for him and Karin to be together. Why, she asked, didn't he go with them to Nantucket? When he said yes, she booked a room for him at the same hotel at which they were staying.

Karin was delighted at the prospect, and not merely because it meant that she and Dennis would be together. He would also be a buffer between her and Joyce, for relations between mother and daughter had been deteriorating over recent weeks, another of those cycles through which she had lived as long as she could remember, things steadily getting worse between them until something happened to cause an improvement. Perhaps Dennis could be that something.

On July 6 she wrote in her diary that she was in trouble again with Joyce, though she didn't spell out the cause of the trouble, and had been grounded, forbidden to see anyone. She was, as a result, very lonely, missing Dennis and hoping that he hadn't forgotten her. "Could cry but no tears. Could scream but no voice. Could die but no heart. Must go on in silence, closed silence."

In another entry the next day she wrote that she was still, and again, in trouble with Joyce, that Joyce was threatening to take away her violin, was even threatening to hit her with the violin, as she had before. Karin didn't know why; she didn't know what she had done. "Being a teenager is *not my* fault!" Maybe if Joyce did actually use the violin as a club, it would clear the fog that seemed to envelop Karin.

That daze may well have been the result of the mounting intensity in her romance with Dennis as much as anything else. They were seeing each other constantly. Dennis had no time for anything but work and Karin. His friends saw him hardly at all, and when they did, he was not the old Dennis; he was distracted, interested only in Karin. Karin, too, had little time for much but the chores her mother set for her, her violin lessons and practice, the tasks Joyce set for her as a nursing home volunteer, the work for Archbishop Whealon—and Dennis. If they missed a day, it was as though they had been apart forever. When together, they seemed increasingly unable to control their emotions, and perhaps nothing is so uncontrollable as the sex drives of teenagers.

One day Dennis wrote:

To Karin: A Note
     Have you come up with a "sure fire" method of taking care of, well, my "problem?"
     I HOPE SO DEAR. I also love you.

The notes went back and forth, Karin responding in kind. Then, on July 7, while sitting at his computer at work, he took a piece of Aetna stationery and wrote:

Hi Karin. This program is bugging me out. Totally. I can't concentrate. Well, about 45 minutes after I left your house, I finally did regain my concentration. However, I am now suffering from something worse than that. There is a lewd term used among males, but it is generally not discussed among mixed company. Point is—it *is* painful and comes from being "stimulated" beyond or to the limits of concentration, but not quite totally. Pain doesn't quite do it justice. Agony— maybe. We'll *have* to find a solution soon. So, are you going to total my concentration now, or what? GO FOR IT!!! Oh my.

Two days later, on July 9, they took a ride early in the day to celebrate a new car Dennis had just bought. The MG was gone. In its place was a Triumph Spitfire, another sports car. And, he told her, he was about to get a special license plate for it. That plate would read DEN-KAR. They rode, and then they returned to the Aparo condo. That afternoon, Karin wrote in her diary, she and Dennis became engaged. The ring he gave her to seal the promise was a twist tie made of yellow and blue string. And then they made love— for the first time.

Dennis celebrated by writing to her, putting the note in their secret mailbox:

Yesterday morning was absolutely wonderful. You don't know how much mental anguish I've put myself through over the last few weeks concerning the subject. That is all over now, because you are wonderful. In my own way, I thank you from the bottom of my heart. Actually, I think that's the reason I feel lousy. I've been working myself up to a peak, or forte lately in preparation for our "special time." I peaked out, did well, and now I'm on a slide down. It's only because I have to concentrate on everything I do so much.

You're right—we deserve an "A" and you could've fooled me about not knowing any better. Oh my.

Over the next week they made love together several more times, both because it seemed natural and because they wanted to hold on to each other in anticipation of the absence to come when Karin went to the Cape. They took precautions, but suddenly it looked as though they hadn't worked. Karin's period was late. She was sure she was pregnant. They bought a pregnancy test kit to find out. She wasn't. Dennis wrote:

I love you, I love you. If I seem in "high spirits," don't think it's because I don't care. I care as much as you. Another thing, it's not *your* fault. All right? Now about this blood thing. Well, seeing as how there's six inches of you and eight of me, one is to expect blood. Believe me, I've heard this before. It comes with the territory, so to speak. It may last one or two days and *that* is why it stings. If it were *anything* else it wouldn't sting at all. I know these things. I love you, I love you. It's good you cried, but don't you worry. I know, I know—how can you not worry? Believe in us. It'll be o.k. I've really got a good feeling about this. There is no doubt. I WILL *NEVER* LEAVE YOU! Especially not now.

Now that Dennis was hers, she began to talk about things that she had only hinted at before. Again and again, in the days before she was to leave for the Cape, Dennis says, "she told me how she felt oppressed and possessed by her mother. She went into a lot of details about her life, about the things her mother had done to her, kind of telling me her life story like you do with someone. She told me about the time when she tried to commit suicide and a lot of other things. At first it wasn't like she was saying, 'Please kill my mother.' It was more, 'I wish my mother were dead, or I wish somehow I could change that relationship.' ''

How? he asked, pushing aside then any idea of death as a way to change the situation. Did she have any ideas?

If only she could move out, she said.

If she wanted to do that, if it were possible, then he would give her a place to stay. He would ask his mother or father, and he was sure either would take her in. Both of them had grown fond of her; she had baked bread for them, something she did well, something she had learned from her mother. She had done other small favors to win them.

She said, if only he could be her guardian, then he could be responsible for her and that would solve so many problems.

When they had time, they agreed, they would investigate to see if that were possible.

On July 19 Karin left for the Cape with the Hudners. Dennis promised to drive up for a day. He did just that, appearing at the Hudners' on a Tuesday. When he arrived, she wrote in her diary, she gave him a gold chain she had bought for ninety-seven dollars, a bargain because it was half price. He stayed over and that night crept into her room. They made love, taking precautions this time so that there would be no fear of pregnancy (the precautions, she wrote, did what they were supposed to, and she got her period two days later), and then he went to sleep in her closet. It was, she noted, the day that Prince Andrew married Sarah Ferguson. ''Yes,'' she concluded, ''Denny's mine.''

Indeed, he was. He had thought during the early stages of their romance that he was the leader, the dominant force, the white knight come riding on his charger to woo and win and rescue his lady fair, trapped, he believed from all she was telling him, in some dark tower. He had her wrapped around his finger, he told friends and later told a psychiatrist. All that changed now. Karin became dominant, Dennis, people later said, her slave. His letters to her were more

and more filled with pleadings: "Don't ever leave me . . .
I don't know what I would do without you . . . I need
you. . . . You are my life." Anything she wanted he would
get for her, he told her; anything she wanted him to do he
would do without question. "I promise to make you happy
and I'll try my absolute, most hardest to give you whatever
you want. And don't think I wouldn't give my life for you
right now if I had to. Even if you asked. But don't 'cause I
need to be with you."

What he didn't realize then was that she was about to
put those promises to the test.

17

On a Friday, two weeks after Karin left for Cape Cod, Joyce Aparo was preparing to make the trip there herself with Dennis Coleman to pick up her daughter and go on with them to Nantucket for the weekend. She went into her daughter's room and opened the drawer of the night table. It was a thing she did often. Karin never threw anything away, and neither did Dennis. Both kept every letter they had ever received and sometimes copies of letters they had written. And so in that drawer, Joyce Aparo found Karin's diaries and a stack of letters. She read them.

The phone rang in the Hudners' house on the Cape. The call was for Karin. The caller was her mother. "She was very angry and she was screaming at me. She told me that she had gone into my room and found notes from Dennis and now she knew we were sleeping together. She was calling me names and she said she was driving up to the Cape right then. And she said that when she got there she was going to take some drastic action." Karin was terrified. She said she began to cry, and the tears, of fear as much as anything else, flowed for the next forty-five minutes while the Hudners tried to comfort her. They didn't know what was happening; all they knew was that their baby-sitter was extremely tormented.

Six hours later Joyce Aparo arrived. With her was Dennis Coleman. It was his second trip to the Cape that week. Through the hours of that drive Joyce said nothing directly to him about her discovery in Karin's bedside drawer. "She made some sly little remarks that I would never have caught if I hadn't known," he says. But he knew. Karin had called him as soon as Joyce hung up. She had told him about Joyce's find and Joyce's reaction. As they traveled through the late afternoon and into the evening, he waited for Joyce to attack him. She didn't.

At the Hudners' Karin was sure she knew what to expect when her mother arrived. She was not looking forward to the confrontation. Her first surprise was to see Dennis. She had been sure Joyce would call off her invitation to him. Her second was her mother's demeanor. Joyce was in a good mood. She acted glad to see Karin, acted the loving mother, and said not a word about the letters she had found or the call she had made earlier in the day. "But then," Karin later said, "my mother had wild and wide mood swings, and she was very unpredictable."

They left the Hudners' almost immediately, drove to Hyannis and stayed the night in a motel. The next morning Joyce, Karin and Dennis made a detour, driving to Provincetown. Joyce left them alone and went shopping by herself. Dennis and Karin did some shopping on their own.

"We went to Provincetown," Karin wrote in her diary, "and Denny and I found a very nice diamond ring.

$1300.00. He wants to buy it for me. [He did, paying for it in three installments, the final one in November, at which time the store, Thunder Road, sent it to him at Glastonbury and he then gave it to her.] It looks gorgeous on me. I tried it on. We both love it. We are engaged to be engaged. How interesting. Mom would kill me if she ever knew."

Finished with their shopping, they drove back to Hyannis and then took the ferry across to Nantucket. They were to spend the weekend together on the small resort island.

That evening at the inn Joyce took Karin aside and handed her the letters and notes she had found in Karin's bedside drawer. Until then Joyce had held her rage. Now she vented it, though coldly. Cool it, she ordered Karin. It was all right if she continued to see Dennis, but no more sex. That was over. If she learned that they were still going to bed together, she'd take steps to put an end to the situation, drastic steps if she had to.

But in front of Dennis, Joyce still did not mention her discovery, made no mention, either, of her order to Karin. She was pleasant and friendly and told them to go out and enjoy themselves. They did not. They went to Dennis's room. Karin gave him back the letters, told him what Joyce had said. For more than an hour they debated the future, what they might do. They talked about Karin's running away, about getting married, about her moving in with the Colemans, about Dennis's becoming her guardian. It was something, they decided, they would look into as soon as they got back to Glastonbury. Then they made love; it was, according to Karin's diary and to the markings she later made on the wall calendar in her room, where she noted such things, the fifth time they had gone to bed together.

Through the rest of the stay Joyce did not again mention the letters or her threats. They were much together, went shopping often. Joyce was suddenly in a warm and generous mood. She bought Karin a nineteenth-century Victorian black jacket for eighty-one dollars, a full-length black

velvet skirt for her trips to New York and a diamond ring
with seven diamonds, one more than the ring Dennis had
bought for her. One might say she was competing with
Dennis for Karin, but of course she did not know about the
other ring then, found out about it only later. Still, that
element of competition was there, as it was always when
someone who might offer a challenge to Joyce for Karin's
affection and loyalty appeared.

It was an idyll, a momentary respite. On the surface
everything seemed calm, serene, no trouble. But under-
neath, the trouble was there. Perhaps the precipitating cause
was Karin's fear of what Joyce would ultimately do about
her discovery of those letters and diaries left so carelessly in
that bedside drawer. She would, being Joyce, do something. Karin was determined to find a way to stop her.

18

He believed everything she said, believed it though he did not see it. He saw a mother who might be over-bearing, even in his presence, but who seemed to care and be concerned about her daughter, a woman who was usually nice to him. But Karin was bitter and becoming ever more bitter; Karin was determined and becoming ever more so; Karin's expressed hatred of her mother was palpable and growing. He was in love with Karin. It was, he says, "like I'd never known any other person." He was willing, he thought, to do whatever she asked. He had told her that, had told her that he would die for her if necessary. Still, he was afraid of just how much she might ask, of where the asking might lead.

She began to put her thoughts into words, words he

didn't want to hear, words he wanted to shove from his mind and pretend had never been spoken. "The first time she brought it up," he says, "it wasn't like 'Please kill my mother.' It was like, 'I wish she was dead.' Then gradually it cropped up. Over the course of a few weeks it went from these little dreams she had to she had to kill her mother."

Dennis suggested an alternate way out. What if Karin ran away? "It's not worth killing somebody over," he told her. "I'll take you away."

"I've thought about that," she told him. "It would never work. She'd find me. She'd track me down. She'd kill me. I'm serious. I'm afraid she'd really kill me."

The fear was eating away inside him. In one of those notes placed in her window he wrote: "I went to see *Top Gun* again tonight. While there I got sick—again. It's only because I ate food. Went to see the doctor about it. I'm afraid. Bad news. I'm not gonna die, but I'm going to get another ulcer soon because of 'tension and a crumby diet.' So there it is. All that is only if I haven't already got one. My instructions are to relax and eat *good* food. I feel absolutely horrible."

Perhaps, he thought, it was still possible to head things off, to make her see another side, to turn her from that increasing determination. He wrote her:

Do you know what your mother did the other day when you played for us? She turned to me and said, "I just can't believe it. She is doing super. That was incredible, and she did it in *one* week. That was great." Then when you walked back into the room she turned to you and said, "That wasn't too bad." She then proceeded to remind you of this, that, and a hundred other things. Good story. She *is* terribly impressed by you even though she doesn't let on to you. Always remember that *that* is how she really feels no matter what she *says*. You *did* do great. Actually you're lucky. She supports you and pushes you to no end. Sometimes it's necessary and other times it's a pain. Understand, though, that she is trying her best for you. If my parents ever even cared that I played trombone and had done what your mom is doing to/for you, I could have been a great player. Enough so to want a scholarship through Yale and possibly a career with it. I'm not bad now and that's without *one* lesson *ever*. I hope you can look at what she's doing as being *for* you and not *to* you. She does love you, Karin. It's okay.

It wasn't okay, not for Karin, not as July was turning into August 1986 and they were back in Glastonbury, the vacation ended.

On July 31, right after they got home, it was off to the public library, to research Connecticut's guardianship laws. It was still Dennis's idea that if the search turned up something hopeful, Karin could be dissuaded from more extreme action and agree to run away, to move in with the Colemans and have Dennis as her guardian. She later claimed that Dennis went to the library by himself and only reported back to her afterward what he discovered. Dennis has always maintained they went together. "I was the one who spotted the book," he says. "I don't think she was even in the same room when I found it. But I found it and took it to her and showed her."

The language in the statute book was a little ambiguous. What it came down to was that at sixteen, if the situation called for it, a minor could request that a specific person be appointed guardian and the court might well approve that choice. At fifteen, however, while the minor could ask to be placed in the custody of a particular guardian, it would be up to the court whether or not to approve, and that approval was wrapped in a multitude of legal restrictions.

At first glance it looked as though there might be a chance, even though Karin was still fifteen. In her diary on August 1 Karin wrote, "Den and I have our plot." He had checked the statutes, and he could become her guardian if things worked out right. She also noted that the house was peaceful and there had been no trouble that evening, except that she had gotten sick after eating steak, ice cream, blueberry pie and grapes. She had to hide that because she thought she couldn't be sick when Joyce was home.

But the more she thought about the idea of guardianship and the more the legal restrictions became clear, the possibility that the plan could work faded. She understood all too well that escape, even if authorized by the courts, wasn't possible. "I was totally unrealistic," she says, "and there was no way I could do it." Joyce would certainly come after her and one way or another haul her home, and it was not pleasant to contemplate what would happen then. The next evening she appended a note to the bottom of the previous diary entry, saying that they would not carry out the plan.

They would, then, move on to the next step. Over the next days, expressed by Karin ever more frequently and openly when she and Dennis were together, was her conviction that Joyce would have to die if Karin were ever to be free. Dennis grew increasingly distraught. He says he tried to give her options; she rejected them.

He needed help. He was faced with a dilemma. There was nothing he wouldn't do for Karin, but this was just too much, this was incomprehensible. He went to his father, told his father that Karin was having terrible problems at home, that she was saying it was essential that she get out, that she was even talking about killing her mother and having Dennis help her. It was such an incredible story that his father wasn't sure he was serious. Kids always have trouble at home. Kids are always talking about running away. But murder? That was carrying it too far. If Karin was in so much trouble at home that her mind was even toying with such an idea, Dennis senior said, then she could come live with them; he would even, if necessary, adopt her. But he didn't really believe it could be that bad.

Dennis brought his father's offer to Karin. She turned it down. It couldn't work, she said. As long as Joyce was alive, she could never escape.

But if Joyce were dead, then Karin would be free. And if Joyce were dead, there would be plenty of money to live on. A year before, her mother had told her that if anything were to happen, there would be enough for her and that she wouldn't have to worry about having to live with her father. It all was spelled out in Joyce's will. Karin went to the closet where Joyce kept that will and other important papers, took them out and glanced through them.

Now she wrote to Dennis that they would do what had to be done soon, the sooner the better. School was to start in a month, and her problem should be taken care of long before that. They should get together and look over what she called "the crucial papers. Legal ones I mean." She had them, and when they examined them, they would be able to see just what they would have in the future.

Karin later said that what she was writing about in that note was her never-ending plan, her fantasy, that she could run away with Dennis. All her notes dealt with that and nothing else, certainly not the murder of her mother. As for the crucial legal papers, she said she could not remember what they were.

Dennis, however, maintains that the note had nothing to do with running away. That plan had vanished. A new one had replaced it. The papers, which he says he himself never saw, were Joyce's will, insurance policies, deeds and other documents. Joyce's estate, Karin told him, was sizable, and she offered to split the proceeds with Dennis if he helped her. Best of all, there was the fantasy that the condo would be hers and they could live there together.

On August 3 the plot became more than talk, more than oblique references in notes. "We had just been shopping, the three of us—Joyce, Karin and me," Dennis remembers. "We had just come home, and we were sitting in the living room. Joyce asked Karin to make her a sandwich,

and Karin went off, first to the bathroom and then to the
kitchen. She had a bottle in her hand. I got up and followed
her. She said, 'You wouldn't do it. Now I'm going to do it
myself.' I didn't help her then, but I didn't do anything to
stop her. She got a plate and put the sandwich on it and
carried it back to the living room, and she gave it to Joyce.
I thought, *oh, God.*''

Karin had taken a bottle of Joyce's prescription medicine, Seconal pills for her migraine headaches, from the
medicine cabinet, carried the bottle into the kitchen, taken
the pills from the bottle, crushed them and mixed the pow-
der into the sandwich for her mother. She said later that she
had crushed only two, perhaps three or four, just enough to
calm her mother down. Dennis says he isn't sure how many
pills she crushed for the sandwich, but the bottle was empty
when she showed it to him, and there was enough in the
sandwich to kill Joyce. What's more, Jill Smith, the woman
who had taken care of Karin when she was small and with
whom Karin lived for a time during the winter after Joyce's
death, says that one night that winter, on a ride home from
Hartford to her house, she talked to Karin about the pills,
talked about the quantity that Karin had put in the sandwich,
perhaps as much as the whole bottle. ''You could have
killed your mother,'' Jill Smith said to Karin. ''I know. I
know,'' Karin replied. And Karin's friend Kira Lintner later
said that Karin wrote her a note about the attempt, saying,
''I almost had my mom dead.''

But Joyce did not die from the pills. She took one bite
of the sandwich and made a face. ''The damn relish has
gone bad,'' she said. ''Throw it out, and the two of you go
to the store and buy some fresh relish.''

Karin and Dennis did as ordered. In the car an an-
guished Dennis talked about what he had witnessed. Karin
told him that since he wouldn't do it, she'd had to make the
attempt herself. She should never have put it to him anyway.

Dennis spent a sleepless night. ''I was distraught. I

was a wreck," he says. Until that moment in the living room he had thought that it was just talk, that Karin couldn't possibly be serious about killing her mother. He had tried to head her off whenever she came too close to the idea. It hadn't worked. Now he knew she meant it. The next morning he got up, got into his car and sped out of the parking lot without glancing in the direction of her window, without making any gesture toward it, as he normally did on his way to work. He just had to get out of there, get away, fast.

Sometime during the day his brother showed up at the office. Karin had come across the lot late in the morning and handed Matt a letter for Dennis. Since Matt was driving into Hartford, he decided to drop off the letter and not let Dennis wait until he got home to read it.

In the stillness of her room that morning, after he had sped away without a backward glance toward her, she wrote him that long letter about abandonment. "Where are you?" she began. "Have you stopped talking to me?" If, indeed, he had, she wrote, she understood. She had asked him to do something that never should have been asked of anyone, certainly not of someone she loved as she loved him. Now she wanted him to know she didn't really want him to do it. She didn't want him to have to live with the memory of committing such an act, murder. He had suffered enough as it was, and she didn't want to add to the suffering. Joyce, after all, was her mother, and she would deal with Joyce herself. But what really hurt her was that he had driven away that morning without even saying a word to her. She related then the story of the seventh birthday that never was and of her father's abandonment in that time of crucial need. She ended, "You both left when I needed you most . . . and you didn't even say goodbye."

If she wrote that letter to make him feel guilty, to turn him back into more than just an ally, into someone to help her do what she believed had to be done, she succeeded. Reading it, Dennis felt himself torn apart. "I felt I was dealing with a horror," he says. "She was playing on me, making me see it from her point of view. That's the way it came across when I got that letter. It was an emotional appeal.'' He could not abandon her as everyone had in the past. He would be there for her from then on, would do whatever she asked without question.

He read the letter several times. He dialed her number, and they talked. He was sobbing into the phone. She seemed cold and distant. When he hung up, he felt he had to answer her letter. During breaks through the day he wrote a reply he titled "Love and Death":

I read every note you gave me and remembered us in a simpler time. Our first kiss, our first meeting, and most special to me, the first time I ventured forth beyond limit of restraint and held your hand. The feelings that shot through me at that second. Today those same feelings have flourished to the point that I cry at the thought of you—every night. My heart feels like it's going to burst from the fullness in and around it. My innocent attraction has taken me like a tide and I lie happy and helpless in its wake. A love I have never felt, or even dreamed of. A girl I scarcely know yet I dream of. Karin Aparo—before you I felt love and life slipping to loneliness. My life was becoming void and my heart unable to love. Already had I lost the capability of trust. Consider it one of your greatest achievements to have me trust once again.

I love you. I want you. I need you. What more can I say? Any sacrifice I will make. My life is yours. Forever from now, my only goal is to make you happy in any way I must. Don't be afraid to ask. If you don't, how will I know you still need me. Soon—for you—I will give my soul to something black. Please, all I ask in return is that you keep my heart in the light. My soul I can do without. You I cannot. Today you almost took both our lives. Don't scare me like that again. When I saw that bottle empty, you can't imagine how incredibly terrified I became. I can honestly say, I've *never* been that scared. Please . . . promise me. I love you Karin. I'm here for you. Always. You know I would kill for you. You could ask nothing more, yet I could give nothing less.

I had a talk with my mom about things for you. Any time you need to you can stay here for as long as you like—she said so. There could even be the possibility (she kind of offered) to have you come live with us, permanently. If *anything* starts to look bad over at your house, don't wait. Come right over, whether I'm home or not. My mom said so. We can work things out dear.

When he arrived home, he put that letter in their secret mailbox. When Karin reached home later that afternoon, Dennis's letter was waiting for her. But she was not the only one who read that introspective struggle with love and death, that offer to die for her.

Joyce was furious. She summoned Karin into the living room and for an hour berated her. "She told me if I had anything more to do with Dennis, she would cancel me," Karin says. "She said she was not going to let me ruin my life over Dennis. Then she asked me to call Dennis and get him over."

While she waited for Dennis to appear, Karin picked up some odd pieces of stationery she was using as a diary until she bought a new book, and she scribbled some rambling reflections. Joyce had found the note in the window, so Karin was in permanent trouble. She wondered if the trouble came out of teenage rebellion. Her eyesight was changing, and she had to see an ophthalmologist. She had been so upset at Dennis that morning when he raced out of the parking lot without a word to her, so hurt and angry that she had written him the note about her seventh birthday and given it to Matt to pass on. Dennis had called, had been in tears, but she had refused to cry. She and Joyce were going to visit Archbishop Whealon, who was ill in the hospital. She weighed 116 pounds, which was too much, yet she craved ice cream. "Am in love with Denny," she concluded, "very much so. Miss Alasdair!"

When Dennis arrived, he says, there appeared to him to be nothing out of the ordinary. Joyce acted toward him as she always had. It was just their usual evening together. But, then, Joyce rarely, if ever, spoke severely to Dennis. "She never expressed anything to me but that she liked me and had a good opinion of me," he says. "All I ever knew about her thinking anything different was what Karin told me she said." Of course, Joyce rarely criticized or became angry at outsiders unless she thought they posed a threat, a danger to her of one kind or another. Because Dennis was hardly more than a boy, she considered him no threat; he was someone she could handle. She saved her rages for those close to her, like Karin, or for those such as neighbors who publicly criticized and thereby humiliated her.

Karin says, however, that Joyce sat both of them down on the couch in the living room and then told Dennis that Karin had better things to do with her life than sleep with him. She ordered them to stop. Karin says that they agreed, that they would just see each other socially but there would be no more sex. Joyce seemed satisfied with that, she says. They, of course, had no intention of keeping that promise.

Whatever happened that evening in the Aparo living room, whether Joyce spoke only to Karin or to both of them, gave her orders only to Karin or to both of them, the determination that Joyce had to go, and go without delay, became even more entrenched, although Karin later said that all they were ever talking about, that all they were ever planning, that the only determination was about her running away. Murder, she claimed, was not on her mind.

Perhaps. Perhaps not. For within days Karin and Dennis had devised a new plan. This time it would not be Karin acting on her own. This time they would work in concert. It was now the second week of August 1986.

It would go this way: Of an evening Karin would lure Joyce into the kitchen of the condo. Initially it was decided that Dennis would be lurking in a nearby closet, ready to come to her aid. Before it was over, Joyce would be dead, Karin doing the killing and Dennis supporting her in a claim of self-defense. Then that scheme was dismissed, and a new plan emerged, though with essentially the same elements. In this one Dennis would be watching from his window across the way. At the appropriate moment, when Joyce was distracted, Karin would take a kitchen knife and kill her. She would then flick the lights in the kitchen on and off to summon Dennis, and he would come running. The police would be called. Dennis would tell them that he had heard loud noises and come rushing across the parking lot. As he arrived, Joyce was viciously attacking Karin. In self-defense Karin had grabbed a knife and acted to protect herself.

When they finally agreed on this method, Karin wrote another note to Dennis, telling him, "I will do whatever is necessary. It is a decided thing and I will do it even if you won't help me. It is just another thing to do on my 'priority list' & right now it has a very high billing." As for the lights, she would take care of them, unless, that is, he wanted to help.

Out of nowhere, a non sequitur, she added that she had his socks, that school began on September 3 and she had her school schedule, was going to be taking chemistry even though she hadn't finished algebra.

Then, on a line by itself, she wrote, "My God, do you realize what we're thinking?"

Now Karin announced that she couldn't carry out the plan herself. Joyce was her mother, she said, and much as she hated her and wanted to escape from her, she couldn't kill her. Dennis said, "Okay. I understand. I could do it."

So the plan was revised once more. Joyce and Karin were going out for a day. When they got home, Karin would get Joyce into the kitchen. Karin would flick the lights on and off. Dennis would be watching from his window. When he saw the signal, he would come across the parking lot, enter the condo, take a knife and stab Joyce to death. The police would be summoned. Karin would tell them that Joyce had been attacking her. She had screamed. Hearing the screams, Dennis had raced across the lot to her aid. Joyce was strangling her. He had tried to help Karin, but Joyce was raving and could not be stopped. The only way he could stop her and save Karin was to grab the nearest implement at hand and go at Joyce. Unfortunately that implement happened to be a kitchen knife, and he had killed Joyce. He hadn't wanted to, hadn't meant to, but it was the only way to stop Joyce and save Karin.

Dennis agreed. Anything to placate Karin, anything to help her. "But I was a wreck. I didn't know what to do," he says. "I wanted to talk to someone, so I called Denise and I made a date to see her that night."

Then he waited and watched. It grew later. Dusk settled and then darkness. He heard Joyce's car pull into the parking lot. She and Karin had spent the evening at dinner with Archbishop Whealon, who was home from the hospital. These had been long and, for Karin, excruciating hours, filled with apprehension. She was sure she knew what would happen when they reached home. Dennis had said, "If I promise you something, I'll do it, no matter what."

Dennis says: "I was watching from the window right across the lot, and then I saw the lights go on and off. I thought, *Oh, god.* I went over to the phone and called Denise and said, 'I've got to talk to you.' I left right away, and we went to a bar, and I told her everything that was going on. She couldn't deal with it. You can't deal with something like that. I was freaked out."

He also talked to his friend Christopher Wheatley and told him what Karin wanted done. Unlike Denise, Wheatley didn't seem to be bothered by the idea. He listened, did not try to talk Dennis into walking away from the whole thing, merely listened and made no comment.

The lights in the Aparo condo had been flicked on and off by accident. Entering the condo's kitchen, Joyce had switched them on and immediately switched them off again. "I got scared," Karin says. "I thought Dennis would come over and do it then. So I went over and locked the glass doors and drew the curtains so he couldn't come in. And then later he told me he didn't even try."

Late that night, sitting at the desk in her room, Karin wrote to Dennis. What had she learned from the events of the day? she asked. She had learned that if she ever ran away from home and moved in somewhere else, Joyce would take revenge and would make sure, at the very least, that she didn't get into a good college. She would, for instance, go down to Yale and talk to the deans, talk to Alasdair Neal, and relate in detail the stories of Karin's delinquencies so that they would never want to speak to her again. Even now they probably wanted to have nothing to do with her because the word was spreading that she had a bad reputation; even as far away as California they must know that she had done things no girl her age should have done.

She had had a miserable evening, sitting with Archbishop Whealon and eating ice cream and wanting to talk to him, but she had been unable to do so.

What was left for her now? she asked. "Just more shattered dreams, eh? Remind me never to get my hopes up again about anything." She'd listened to too many promises only to see them broken. Promises were like water, a flood one day, a drought the next. People shouldn't make promises unless they intend to keep them, she told him. Maybe Dennis could not have done anything but what he did—which was nothing. "I told you that you wouldn't be able to. But you denied me. . . . I didn't ask you this time. You offered."

One thing was certain, she wrote: Any possibility that she could ever get away was gone now. Joyce wouldn't let her break free. If she tried, Joyce would have her committed to juvenile hall as a delinquent. Yes, she wanted to leave because she was terrified of her mother, but she knew there was no way she could.

"Don't promise freedom," she wrote, "when you don't have the keys to the cage. It's not fair!"

Then she added that he should not pay attention to what she was writing; he should just forget it and go to work in the morning, work hard and not think about her. He should go away and let her cry for a few days and get things in order, get her life in order.

"God," she concluded, "the pain is unbearable. It hurts so Goddamn much."

Dennis responded. He wrote that even though he had promised, he just couldn't go through with the plot to kill her mother. He reiterated the offer his father had made that if things were that bad, the Colemans were ready to offer sanctuary, adding that he had been so distraught when he had discussed it with his father, that he had broken down and cried. Perhaps, he suggested, the answer was not to carry out the plot but rather for Karin to seek psychiatric help to get her through these times.

She was furious. She wrote back that her initial reaction to his letter was utter rage. If he had been realistic, he should have known that there was no way they could really have murdered Joyce, that there was no way she could have just stood by and let him do it. What it came down to was that they were teenagers, and all teenagers, she realized, hated their parents at some point; it was just a normal part of growing up. Their problem was that they had carried it beyond the point of mere rebellion and had planned to act out that anger in a violent way. She asked him to thank his father for the offer of sanctuary, but she couldn't accept it because she wasn't going to hurt her mother by doing that. In the future she would just be the rebellious teenager behind Joyce's back. Besides, there was always tomorrow, and she could look forward to that. If the situation at home did become unbearable, perhaps she would take up the offer of a place to stay, but only for a night.

Yes, she said, she had wanted him for her guardian, because she wanted to spend her life with him. But the only way her life would turn out right was for her mother to raise her. To conjure up the idea of living with Dennis in a house and having lots of money was just the fantasy of a teenage girl smitten with love. He ought to understand the thing about dreams, that, after all, they were only dreams. She certainly didn't need a shrink to tell her that. She just needed a place where she could go when she got angry.

She wasn't mad at him, she assured him, for what he hadn't done, for not having come across the lot when the lights were flicked and carrying out their plan. It was right of him not to do it. She was mad at him, though, because he hadn't come across and talked to her through her window. She had wanted to tell him how glad she was that he hadn't done what they had planned. She was hurt that he had misunderstood her.

She had listened to "Desert Moon" on the tape he made for her, had then carried her Walkman across and put it in his window and let the tape play continuously, had stood there and listened to him sleep for some time. She was hurt, and she wanted him to know it. She was furious and then hurt and then understanding and then sympathetic. She felt fifteen then, and as she was writing this note, she felt forty. She was afraid he was tiring of her and losing interest.

Most important, she ended, they should put this whole thing behind them and start over, be happy and in love the way they had been. Joyce, she assured Dennis, still loved him, and "I still love you Dennis Coleman."

So the plot to murder Joyce Aparo and gain Karin Aparo her freedom in August 1986 came to an end.

19

Early in September 1986 Dennis received a letter from his friend Chris Wheatley. Wheatley had gone off to Syracuse University as a premed student, telling friends he dreamed of the day when he could help people as a doctor in a hospital emergency room. The letter from college was a rambling one, filled with news, the embarking on a new adventure. The main reason for the letter, he wrote, was that he was broke. He'd already borrowed more than he should have from his father and couldn't ask him for any more, especially since, he said, he'd lost the money gambling. Could Dennis send him a couple of hundred? Dennis did, and later sent him more when Wheatley asked again. "I found out later," Dennis says, "that he hadn't lost money betting; he'd gotten a girl in trouble, and he needed it to pay for an abortion."

In the course of that letter Wheatley wrote, "So, Dude, how's your woman? Is her mother still alive?"

Joyce Aparo was, indeed, still alive and, as autumn approached, in no immediate danger. She either had been unaware of or had blinded herself to the plot that nearly took her life during those first weeks of August. She probably would not have taken it seriously in any case. The plotters, after all, were mere children; she was an adult, she was trained in social work and psychology and she had always totally dominated and controlled one of the conspirators. Besides, her life was full; she had little time for anything beyond her immediate conscious concerns. The demands of her job at Athena Health Care were exhausting. Her jewelry designing business was booming; she was becoming a nuisance around the Glastonbury post office with her demands. One employee in the post office remembers how everyone groaned when Joyce Aparo walked in the door. It always meant trouble.

And there was still trouble at home. There was always trouble at home. Joyce's nagging at Karin continued unabated. Nothing Karin did was the way Joyce wanted it done.

"Whatever your mom says, or does," Dennis wrote near the end of August, the plot now put aside, "can't be helped. Just remember that it will end soon. She can say what she likes, but it won't affect our lives together. Not in the long run. When she gets angry, just know in your mind that it'll all blow over quickly and that I'm here waiting for you . . . forever. Because it means so much. Think of the long run. Please trust in us, and *hope* for us."

A little later he wrote, "I wish you could cope with your mom without getting upset."

Later still: "Right now I really feel bad about your state of affairs. Karin, do whatever you do only for you. Appease your mother for just a while longer. But know in your mind that what she says, or what she does, doesn't, shouldn't and won't ruin your life. You keep your dreams and ambitions alive—if you lose everything else: your violin, me (never), or anything else, never lose your dreams. Devote your life to them.''

Again: "Your mother is too unstable, self-centered and ignorant to be an obstacle to us. She may call me what she likes, and I don't care, because any opinion she has about me, or much of anything else is warped. Why she feels as if the whole world is out to get her is beyond me. Why should *it* or *anyone* care about her? I couldn't imagine being so closed and self-centered. She considers me to be 'that kind of company.' I consider her to be *no* kind of company."

Another time he wrote: "These 'bad times' with your mother go in cycles. There was Nantucket and now there's now. I understand. They will pass and you'll live. At this rate, I figure there are about one of these every 1½ months. Or about 8 a year—tops. Don't worry, you'll make it and I'm *always* and *forever* here for you."

Letter after letter from Dennis, advising, cautioning, entreating, understanding, agreeing, followed complaint after complaint from Karin. It became something of a ritual. Karin would relate to Dennis another of Joyce's foibles, follies, impossible demands. Dennis would try to calm her with one of his letters.

Karin was back in school, a high school sophomore now, her days filled with all the usual chores, the violin demanding more time, and now schoolwork, too, and baby-sitting for the Hudners a couple of evenings a week. It was hard to find the time for Dennis. She made the time.

"During school are we gonna have midnight visits or what?" Dennis wrote. "It'll be hard during autumn with leaves on the ground, and during winter with the snow. Feet make tracks in snow, you know."

The midnight visits, trekking across the parking lot, were not to be. In September Dennis's mother met a man and thought she was in love. The man was from Michigan. In order to be with him, she sold the condo on Butternut

Drive, packed up her belongings and moved west. Her younger son, Matt, went with her, though he returned before too long. Dennis packed up his clothes, the intricate model house he had been building for years, carving shingles the size of eraser heads and painting each individually, fitting every piece meticulously, never finishing, and all the rest of his personal effects and moved in with his father and stepmother in the house that had been his grandparents' in South Glastonbury.

That first night in what was now his permanent home, he wrote a sad letter to Karin:

I miss you already. We all had a very nice dinner and I told my mom I loved her. I don't think Matt will stay out there. To tell you the truth, I don't think my mom will either. She's already decided that if she doesn't like it, she's gonna come back. What hurt the most was looking out my window for the last time, out at your window, and I backed out of my spot for the last time. It made me miss you. We'll still be together just as much as always. Please stay with me now and forever. In many ways, you're all I've got to hold on to. I'm supposed to be pulling away from my family. That's what happens at my age. And it still really hurts to have lost all my friends. I feel I'm moving through one chapter in my life and starting another. Besides you, I'm all alone in my life.

To the end of that letter, he appended one of his love poems:

> I had a dream
> And it would seem
> I only dreamed of you
> Forever I could always dream
> And only dream of you
> Try as I might to get in the dream

The dream would only have you
I don't know what this obsession with
You has got to do with my dreams
But if I were you I'd know what
I'd do . . . I'd go to you with my life
And to you I would give
My promises, my hopes, and my dreams
To make life what it seems.
We'll travel together, on the road of life
While stopping along the way
So I won't take for granted my own wife
And we'll love now, day by day.
I love you.

It was a drive of several miles to see Karin from then on, to pick up the notes she left for him in their mailbox, to leave notes for her. It was not easy. Still, they found ways. There were notes waiting for Dennis in that mail slot often: "Wanna fuck?" she scribbled in the course of one, to which he appended, "Hi Kar—Now that you put it that way, YEA!!!!!—Love, Den." Or another, in which she told him to think of the two of them when he was in bed that night, adding a postscript, "Thanx for the fuck."

The quality of their sex was changing, though. "I know what you're saying," Dennis wrote that fall. "You're saying, 'But I'm too embarrassed to ask about kinky sex. . . . I'm afraid of what he'd do.' I'll tell you what I'd do. I'd give more than all the kinky sex you could take in a week. I'm here for *anything* . . . for*ever*."

They tied each other to the bed with nylon hose. Dennis bought handcuffs, drilled holes in the posts of his bed, and they locked each other to the posts with those cuffs. Karin asked for and Dennis bought a metal dildo. Karin wrote an illustrated letter, detailing their sexual activities. "It wasn't one of us taking the lead," he says. "It was mutual."

*   *   *

They had their arguments, of course. Dennis was filled with an almost unreasoning jealousy if Karin talked to somebody else, looked at somebody else. He was even jealous when she paid attention to his brother:

> Call me insecure maybe, or call me anything you like, but it *is* the way I feel. I love you so much. Something like this shouldn't and won't come between us, but please just try to put yourself in *my* place. Reverse the roles, so that every time your sister came over I turned around and ran to her to talk to, or do things for her. To be more excited around her than you. It just really hurts, and really tears me up. You're not trying to do it on purpose, I know, but please understand. . . . You say that you like him because there's so much of me. That means I'm not enough, or possibly you prefer the package it comes in with him. . . . You're upset because you're afraid that I don't trust enough in us to be secure about this. I understand that, and I do believe in us . . . forever. I do, I do, I do. Do you even want to know what I'm afraid of? I'm afraid that you have the room in your heart to like someone else right now, or ever. I'm afraid that you have the capability to put me in the background be it only for a few minutes. . . . I'm not mad, I'm scared, literally, to tears. I only ask as much as I give to you. . . . I'm very sorry and very much in love with you. Karin, I need you so much. I'm out of words. Stay with me forever.

Karin could be jealous, too, but in her jealousy she was stone, not tears. One day early in the fall, she says, she was in Dennis's room, cleaning it for him, when she found a note he was writing to Chris Wheatley. In what was an attempt to show Wheatley that he was still his own man or in a fit of braggadocio, he wrote that he was going to spend a weekend with one of his former girls and, if possible, have sex with her. Dennis was in tears when Karin faced him with that note, begged forgiveness, swore that it wasn't true, that he would never betray her in any way. The discovery of the note gave her another hold over him.

The most serious argument and the closest they came to an irreconcilable difference, though, arose in November, over one of Dennis's closest friends and a member with him of the rock group. His name is Mike, and he was close not merely to Dennis but to Karin as well. "I used to sit with her for hours outside school," he says, "and she would just talk and talk and talk and talk about her relationship with Den. I used to talk to her practically every day, buddy-buddy, take walks outside, talk about this, talk about that. It was like she couldn't talk to me enough, like I was her best friend."

There was one thing about Mike beyond school and the rock group. "Back then," he says, "I used to smoke a lot of pot, and when I was really on, I was selling it. It was a really stupid thing to do. And one day out of nowhere the police showed up at my door and arrested me for dealing. Which was pretty much to be expected. But I never knew how they found out. So I thought I must have been pretty stupid about the whole thing. Then, after it all happened, Dennis told me that Karin told him she had gone to a pay phone and made an anonymous phone call about me and told the police that I had so much of this at such and such a place and told them everything, and fifteen minutes later they drove up to my house and I was arrested."

Karin was sure, she told Dennis, she had done the right thing. Mike was selling drugs. That was a crime. Who knew to whom he was selling the pot? The temptation was there for anyone who wanted to experiment, and Mike's stash made it easy to give in to that temptation. She had even thought about it herself, and that scared her. So she had an obligation, to herself and everyone else, to turn him in, even if anonymously.

Dennis was furious. Mike was his friend, one of his

closest friends. Mike played with him in the rock group. And Karin had turned him in. He wrote her:

. . . Where I come from a friend is the most important thing in the world and not something to abuse. Ask just about anyone our age or older and they'll say you are wrong. And if you're not wrong, why are you afraid of it getting around? If you had to do something you could've told a school administrator to look into it more carefully and if they found pot let them call the police. I understand your side of it and I know you tried to help—in your way, but you acted very rashly. Why not try to help Mike in his way, not your way. We won't talk about it no more. I'll love you forever.

Like most of their other disputes, this faded, too, for angry as he might become at something she did, he could never hold that anger, he forgave her anything, the anger giving way to increasing espousals of love and devotion and a torrent of more and more expensive gifts.

There was little doubt now who was the dominant force in their relationship. If Dennis had thought himself in the preeminent position when they met and began in the spring, if he had thought they had come into balance by mid-July, even he no longer had any doubts over who powered the engine. "I was hooked," he says. "I lost all my friends. There was work, and there was Karin, and that was it; there wasn't any time for anything else." He wrote to her constantly, even though he was seeing her most days. He was fantasizing about the future, sketching plans for a large, lavish house on a hill that he would build for her and where they would live in paradise forever. Under unrelenting pressure from Karin and even from Joyce, he was reconsidering his decision to forgo college. Karin was at him all the time about it. He capitulated and wrote away for applications. Considering his far from outstanding scholastic record in high school, he knew there was no chance for the Ivy League, no chance probably at any of the better colleges. The thing to do, Karin said and he agreed, was go to a college nearby, make a good record there and then aim higher. The choice was Central Connecticut University, in New Britain, not far away; it would have the advantage, too, of keeping him close to Karin. He began to fill out those applications.

"It was like religious worshiping," says a close friend of Dennis. "He alienated almost all his friends. You'd never see him out anymore. The only time you'd see him out was with Karin."

It was a heady thing for Karin. All her life she had been the slave to Joyce's master, a reluctant, unwilling, resentful inmate to her warden, forced to do her mother's bidding, forced to abnegate herself, to have no will of her own. Now, for the first time, she was the master with a slave of her own, not a reluctant slave but a willing one. All she had to do was ask and he gave. There was nothing he would not do for her or give to her. And she was not slow to ask. Did she want flowers? Dennis bought them. Did she want jewelry? Dennis got it for her. Did she want expensive dinners out? Dennis took her. It was not Joyce who drove her down to Rowayton, a round trip of more than 130 miles, and then to Manhattan, another round trip of nearly 230 miles, for her violin lessons. Most times it was Dennis. "I'd drive her to Markov's in Rowayton on Friday night after work and after she finished school, and she'd have a lesson for an hour or an hour and a half, and I'd hang around, and then I'd drive her home," he says. "And then at six-thirty on Saturday morning I'd pick her up and drive her down to New York for her lesson at the school there."

He turned his room in his father's house in South Glastonbury into what he called "my Karin Shrine." "You walked into his room," remembers a friend, "and there were photos of Karin all over the walls and memorabilia she had given him everywhere. There were dead flowers; there was packaging from gifts he had given her, lots of photos, everything you could think of. Three of the four walls were papered from floor to ceiling, from the cracks in the corners, with pictures, all sizes, all different kinds, class photos, photos of her in a car, in this and that, snapshots, eight-by-tens. They were everywhere."

20

All through the winter and into the spring Dennis was there for Karin whenever she needed him, whenever she wanted him. He wanted only her protestations of total love and commitment to him to the exclusion of anyone else.

That winter there were episodes of jealousy. In the Aparo living room in January Dennis listened as Joyce carried on about Michael Zaccaro: He was only twenty-nine and such a success, president of Athena and that was just the start; he owned his own home, ate his meals off Lenox china and sterling silver, drove a beautiful car, dressed in the latest fashions. And, she told Dennis and Karin, Zaccaro had expressed to her deep feelings toward Karin, had said he was going to wait for her to grow up and then marry her. Dennis sat and inwardly was racked with anguish, until Karin assured him in private that Zaccaro really didn't feel that way about her; besides, she loved Dennis.

He was jealous of any mention of Alasdair Neal, grew frantic with jealousy when Neal reappeared briefly at the beginning of January. In her diary Karin wrote that wearing a yellow sweater over a white shirt with red stripes, gray tweed slacks, gray socks and black shoes, Neal had arrived that day to conduct the orchestra in which she played. "He looked wonderful! My heart *still* can't believe it." But there was a downside. She had to leave the rehearsal early because of a violin lesson, and she was on the verge of tears when she left. Still, Alasdair Neal "is so perfect in every way! Absolutely wonderful! I am so much more in love with him than I could ever be with the rest of the world! Ooohhh heavens."

What she wrote in that diary she reported to Dennis, including her renewed love for Alasdair Neal. Dennis felt lost, abandoned, in deep depression. He pleaded with her:

I love you. You know a lot has happened between us lately, and so far we've come through it o.k. Not great, but o.k. Karin, I know that in some ways you *do* love me, but in others you don't. And it's usually easier for anyone (me in particular) to look at the bad half of things. I ask you to please understand that there's a lot in me. A lot of dreams, hopes and desires. They drive me and what I do. You also have your own, and part of that is how or with who you'll be happy with in the long run. There are a hundred things we could do to make each other happy—in the short run. But they all include some sort of compromise. We can't just keep giving up this and that forever. It won't work. I will compromise my dreams to be with, and stay with you. But understand, please, that I have sacrificed much of my self-esteem, and pride as well. I did not sacrifice my dignity—that you have, in effect, taken from me.

As long as you still love Alasdair as much, if not *much more* than me, how can I have anything? How? Why must I live as an afterthought, or a second choice? How can I do those things and retain any dignity or self-worth, when, what you're asking me to do is give up those things to "better myself?" I'm sorry. All my life people have been asking me to compromise and to change. They have promised to help me and to stay behind me. And all those people (me included) they have let me down and cast me out, leaving me with the remnants of what I was. Leaving me, and making me put the pieces back together and each time, each person took more and more. Bit by bit until I became so bitter that I all but dropped out of school and decided to *ruin* my life as best I could and live in the bitterness. Survive despite the extravagance of my loss and the consequence of my choice. Become part of the terrible hate in me which fed upon itself. Not just give up and die. That was not the answer, that was too easy. No, I had to stay alive to punish myself for having given of myself too much. For having compromised my very moral fiber. I had to give in and give up. I had compromised too much.

Then came a girl named Karin Aparo. Of course I fell for her immediately. And again I found myself, somehow, willing to give more than I had ever given in my life. I told her I loved her—because I did. I gave her what I could—because I did. I resigned my life to the sharing of hers—because I did. I still do, and always will. But no matter how I feel, or what I do, it's happened again. Even as I have begun to give and compromise and try as hard as I could, her lover eyes have been looking beyond me. She loves another and doesn't want to be near me. Her eyes look beyond me. Yet I give—for her—because I do.

Now I think about it and wonder. I can't bear to think of what would happen to me when/if she leaves me with more pieces than ever. Shattered. Would it multiply my hate or drain everything out of me? Even that I do not know. Yet, amidst my present rage, there is love. The one remaining pinnacle of devotion to which I cling. Hanging for my life above a sea of images. Of hate, and envy, of power, and corruption, of disease and rage. Of emotions so strong they could consume my mind. And I recognize these images. They are the frail and poorly mended pieces and fragments of my life. The ones that had been broken so many times before. The sea which with each storm grows deeper. The sea into which she might cast me into, my own self breaking the surface and not returning up again for the air. The air I call love, life and happiness. Immersed, and surrounded by the broken pieces of my life . . . once again. And never again. Karin, oh Karin, I need you. Can't you hear me? Why don't you see? I'm sorry I am what I am. You ask so much. So much. Yet I shall always give for you. Forever, and ever and ever.

I know you love Alasdair and that you've had a "crush" on Rob [a boy from school] for some time. I know you're only 15. You can see other guys than me if you want to. Maybe it would be better. I ask only one thing. Please don't kiss him, or anyone. I've been struggling with that image now for days. *Please* dear. The one thing I ask, and not give. I love you gorgeous. Please understand me. I need you.

Alasdair Neal was soon gone after that concert, and Rob was put to the side, and Karin once more assured Dennis of her love and devotion. And so they resumed, Dennis more deeply dependent on her than ever.

She offered him a prize, a way in which she would make up for those hurts of January. Through the previous years Joyce had become increasingly friendly with Albert Markov, Karin's violin teacher. She had hinted to people at

Athena that a romance was in progress, a romance not deterred by Markov's wife. From all evidence the romance was just another of Joyce's tales, though she and Markov had indeed become friends, drawn together by a mutual affection for stones and climbs. And as their friendship developed, she began to talk to him about joint ventures, about their becoming partners and opening a music school. At the beginning of February Joyce and Markov went off to Colorado for a week, to climb, to search for stones and to explore the possibility of forming a music school.

Karin was left home alone. She did not remain alone long. Hardly was Joyce out the door before Dennis was in. "We played husband and wife for that week," Karin said. "We got up in the morning and I made breakfast, and when Dennis got home from work, we had dinner and watched movies on television."

They also took a trip into Hartford and went shopping for a wedding dress. Her sixteenth birthday was approaching, and both of them thought it a fitting gift. They went to several stores, finally found one in a shop on Franklin Avenue, a formal gown. Karin tried it on. She wanted it. Dennis made a down payment. The dress would be ready in a few weeks. "We were planning to get married," Dennis says, "but not in a couple of months or anything like that, not for years. She had school to finish, and I was going back to school and I had to finish, and then we had careers to think about. So it wouldn't happen for quite a while. Shopping for that wedding dress and putting money down on it was just part of our fantasy life."

Sixteen, sweet sixteen, a pivotal year. It could not be ignored, nor could it be celebrated like any other birthday. They would have to do something special. Karin wanted to have dinner at Cavey's, one of the best and most expensive restaurants in their part of Connecticut. Dennis made the reservations. Karin wanted flowers. Dennis bought them. He bought her a costly piece of jewelry. He hired a limousine to drive them to the restaurant. Then Karin told him she wanted her best friend Shannon Dubois to be part of the celebration. Dennis did not demur. He changed the reservation from two people to three, and they all went out to dinner, a meal that cost him close to two hundred dollars.

"All Karin had to do," says Shannon, "was ask Dennis for something and he'd get it for her. He was spending all his money on her." In about six months he spent more than ten thousand dollars on jewelry, clothes, dinners and more on her.

Hardly was the birthday party over before Karin told Dennis that the whole idea of buying a wedding dress was ridiculous and she had canceled the order. He knew it had been a foolish fancy, but nevertheless, he was upset. "One day you ask me to buy you a wedding dress," he wrote her, "the next day you ask me to let you grow up. Karin, all I ask is that you think. You decide, Karin, are you 16 or 23? You cannot be both. You ask too much. What you did, so you say, was play a game. My love, my life, my pride and everything we share are not a game and not something for you to play with. No games like that. What good is it?"

They made up after that, as they always seemed to make up. As much as Dennis needed her, she needed him. Her relationship with Joyce had deteriorated once more, and Dennis was a prop to support her.

Someone once called adolescent love one of life's great tragedies or, if not a tragedy, at least one of its sorrows. It lasts only a moment and envelops those who are stricken with a white flame, passion so intense they are sure no one has ever experienced anything approaching it, agony so excruciating it is unbearable. Teenage lovers are certain their love is eternal and will never die. Yet it burns too fast, and in its dying, it afflicts those who suffer with such anguish they are sure they will never recover. No one can escape it, no one can be immunized against it and there is no antidote. Yet for most people, adolescent love is a necessary thing, a stage of growing up, of turning from dependent child into independent adult, a passing through so that someday mature and lasting relationships can form. Perhaps Karin was beginning to accept that. Dennis was not. For him this love was the only love.

But they were drifting, and things were changing. In April he got his first real sense that something had passed beyond his control. Joyce had gone away again to Colorado with Albert Markov to continue their search for a music school. Karin was left home alone once more.

"One night we went out to a movie," he remembers. "On the way we stopped at a Pizza Hut in East Hartford to get something to eat. The place was very crowded, and we had to share a table with some other people. We were sitting there, and suddenly she said, 'Well, you're not going to sleep in my bed tonight. You're not going to share my bed while my mom's away.' Everybody at that table, and I think everybody around us, heard her say that, and they started staring at us. I got very embarrassed. It's the way I am. I didn't like things discussed out in public for everyone to hear. I said, 'Karin, shut up.' She got very angry with me. Our whole relationship changed after that. Nothing was ever the same again."

On a Friday evening a few weeks later Karin told Dennis he shouldn't bother to drive her down to Rowayton for her lesson that night and go to all the trouble of driving her home and then down to New York early on Saturday. She had her own car by then, a used Volkswagen Rabbit; she had gone shopping for it with her mother and Archbishop Whealon when she got her license in March, soon after her birthday. She would just drive herself, she told Dennis, stay over at the Markovs' and then drive into Manhattan in the morning with Albert, return with him to Rowayton, pick up her car and drive back in the afternoon. He protested, complaining that she was spending too much time at the Markovs'. She was adamant. Her lessons were going well. Besides and perhaps most important, she said, Albert Markov had become a father figure for her, a real father figure such as she had never had before. Dennis accepted that, but he didn't like it.

"One time I called the house, and Joyce told me she was down there," Dennis says. "I called again on Saturday, and Joyce told me she was still down there and was staying over another day. I remember the next morning waking up at five-thirty and driving down to the Markovs' house and hanging around the house, just driving around. About seven-thirty or eight o'clock I went over to a pay phone and called the house. Alex Markov answered, and then she came on the phone, and she was really pissed at me for showing up. I got out of there. I made it back to Glastonbury in about forty-five minutes. It usually took more than an hour. I had my foot on the gas and the needle as high as it would go. I just didn't care."

21

There was something in Rowayton to attract her, to keep her there longer than usual. It wasn't Albert Markov and the violin lessons. It was Alex Markov.

He was the personification of Joyce's fantasies for Karin even more than Alasdair Neal had ever been. Despite what Joyce said, her attempts to lure Michael Zaccaro for Karin had failed, and she knew it. Alasdair Neal was no longer attainable. Alex Markov was handsome, young and exotic, even more exotic than Neal. The Russian-born violinist fitted Joyce's dreams closely. If he was not in the first rank of concert virtuosos, if he did not have a catalog of recordings of major concertos, chamber pieces and solos, nevertheless he had won his prizes and he had his tours. He was successful and seemed on the verge of greater renown, and he was in demand for performances on the concert stage and at festivals around the world. Joyce saw him as the perfect match for Karin.

She did everything she could to throw them together as often as possible. She made sure that Karin spent more time in Rowayton with the Markovs, without Dennis along, arranged that Karin spend nights and weekends there. She talked about Karin constantly to Alex, piled praise upon praise about her talent and her beauty, let Alex know that Karin was developing deep romantic feelings about him. She talked about Alex to Karin unendingly, lauding his talent and his looks, and let Karin know that Alex was more than mildly interested in her. "I wouldn't mind if Alex got you into bed," she told sixteen-year-old Karin. "Just make sure I don't become a grandmother."

Joyce had been having some medical problems. She went to her doctor. She had to have a hysterectomy. The operation was scheduled for May 20, and she was to be in the hospital for about four days. She arranged for Karin to spend those days in Rowayton with the Markovs.

A few days before she was to enter the hospital and Karin departed for Rowayton, Joyce summoned Karin and Dennis into the Aparo living room and sat them down. She was, she said, very worried and nervous about the outcome of the surgery. "If I don't come out of it," she said, "I want you to know that I've arranged for Karin to be taken care of." She turned to Karin. "You know where all the papers are, in the hall closet. If anything happens, you should get them and get in touch with Michael Zaccaro. He'll take care of you and everything else."

The next day Karin and Dennis met for lunch, at Karin's request—or demand. As they were eating, Karin looked at Dennis and without preliminaries announced, "I want to break up. I'm in love with Alex Markov."

Dennis couldn't eat. His stomach turned over. His world was falling apart. He begged her to reconsider, pleaded with her not to take such a drastic and final step.

She thought it over, then said, "All right. Then I want us to go incommunicado for a month."

"What do you mean?"

"I mean, cut it off for a month. I won't see you, and you won't see me. We won't see each other for the next month, and then we'll see how things work out. They'll work out. Don't worry. I promise that we'll be together again once this is over."

When Dennis left that lunch to drive back to his father's house in South Glastonbury, he was at the lowest point he could ever remember. Everything was going sour. Karin was out of his life for the next month, unless he could do something to change it. Without her he felt his life had lost meaning. And he had just lost his job at Aetna; his department had been hit by budget problems, and thirty employees had been scheduled to be laid off. With practically no seniority, he had been one of the thirty. He had gone to work for his father's computer consulting firm, but that wasn't panning out well. "I was just overhead," he says. "It was a small business where my dad contracted his people out to do work for other companies. I did pretty well at it, but there wasn't that much business, and so there wasn't really a place for me." Still, he had intended that only as a stopgap. He would be going to college, to Central Connecticut, at the start of the new term, first classes scheduled, he remembers, for August 7. But that $375-a-week salary, almost all of which was gone as soon as it reached his pocket, spent on Karin, and on his car, wasn't there any longer. He needed some temporary job at least to tide him over the next months, to keep him in funds. Eventually he found one, as a short-order cook at the concession stand at the Tallwoods Country Club. It wasn't much, certainly didn't make any use of his abilities, but at least it paid a little, about $200 a week.

In his room the night he accepted Karin's offer to go "incommunicado" for a month, he began to write her a log that he did not give her for some time. It covered most of that month.

This is just a little diary of my doings from that fateful day, May 20. *Goodbye.* . . .

It happened suddenly to me. We had to say goodbye. Something I had always hoped and prayed we'd never have to say in such a context. When the idea of not seeing each other first popped up, I accepted it rather bravely (or so it seemed to me). Deep down inside I knew it might help us. I've never been torn and hurt so deeply though. And as I sit writing with burning eyes, and a lump in my throat, I remember saying to myself, "I can do this if I must." But when it finally came time to say "goodbye"—I realized just how difficult it is all going to be. I have never been so scared in my life. I have been shaking pretty badly since this afternoon.

I wish my mind didn't work the way it does. Immediately I started to make myself more scared, thinking that this is the beginning of the end of everything. Then I started thinking about what I could do in one month. Not do for me, but do for you. Fix the Triumph so I could give it to you on the 26th. Or buy the synthesizer from Todd [a friend] to write some songs for you. Save up all my money to get you some wonderous gift upon our return. But then I realized that that's not the point of this whole thing. You want me to do something for me, while you do something for you.

I'm living on your promise that you'll come back. And stay back. Living on it. Should I be scared? I don't see how I can't be. So many things dear. Number 1 on this list: I love you . . . always, more each day. This is going to be a long month. Oh god. . . .

My first full day without you. How lonely I felt. I did find, however, that keeping very busy helped me. Shannon and I talked a bit, but I'm not sure it helped me. Maybe if I was thinking the way I should, she would have been a great help. But right now I'm just so scared and depressed nothing helps. I'm tired so it's off to sleep. Have a good night, stay safe and well. I love you. . . .

I spent today down on Groton working on the boat. I got a pretty bad sunburn and I think my left pinky is either broken, or chipped. My finger has turned blue. I found out my mom is moving back here next Friday. She wants me to drive out to Michigan and back. I miss you. I wonder about it Kare. About the years we could have. All I need is your love and your faith. Oh please, please need me. I'm so scared. Love me. I love you. . . .

I slept until noon today and worked on my model after that. Ripp [a friend] called me and we went for a ride in his new car, and then went up to Cotton Hollow. We're planning to go skiing tomorrow. Denise called me this evening. I hadn't talked with her since December. I'm afraid of going to bed. Once the light goes out, I lie here and think of you. It makes me feel terrible. I'm *so* afraid of spending time alone. I keep telling myself that it'll all be o.k. soon. *We'll* be o.k. I hope so. I *know* we can make it. Forever . . . and ever . . . and ever. . . .

I drove by your house about 8:00, but no one was home. I went skiing with Ripp today. Up at Killington. It was fun. I figured it would take my mind off "things." All that happened was that as we drove north, I counted the miles increasing between us. You never left my thoughts once today. I did a number on my hands today in the ice and rocks. I managed to hack a good bit of skin off my fingers. Not to mention my aching back. Anyway, I hope your weekend went better than mine. (Actually I don't.) I love you silly. See you soon. (I hope.) . . .

I stopped by your locker this evening. I wish you could've at least said hi this afternoon when you dropped Shannon off at work. I know you were in a rush, but it hurt. I drove by your house this evening and you looked out and saw me. That made me feel *much* better. Tomorrow is my big trip to Michigan. I'll miss you even more. I love you silly Kar. Goodnight. . . .

I got back from my trip to Michigan a couple of hours ago. Glad to be back as well. Dear this is getting bad I'm afraid. I'm not sure how much more of this I can take. Oh it hurts *so* badly. The drive from Michigan took 17 hours, and I sat and cried for about 10 of that. It hurts. Please come back to me. Please. At first I thought I would be able to do this, but instead of getting better, it's getting worse. Much worse. Oh how I need you. I just want to hold you in my arms forever . . . and ever . . . and ever. Goodnight beloved. Stay safe, and wait for me. I can't bear this without you. . . .

I talked to Shannon tonight. Sailing was fun yesterday, We did o.k. I got absolutely burnt to a cinder. One of my worst burns yet. My entire face is a blister—literally. My legs are so bad I can't bend them, or even lie on my side. Sleeping on your back is tough. I'm gonna try now. *Love you muchly.*

Karin relented. She would see him, but with a condition.

Early in June, just after the anniversary of the first time Dennis had driven her home from school, she wrote to him. She began by asking how his life had been going. She and Shannon were going to Rowayton for the weekend. Alasdair Neal had reappeared after a stay in Japan, and he was going to join them on Saturday and meet Alex Markov. "How about we make a deal?" she wrote. "No more sex. O.K.? At least until 7–9."

She was sorry the month they had been apart had been so hard on him, but that was the way things went, that was life and he shouldn't put all his emotions on her because she certainly wasn't the most important thing in the world and shouldn't be the center of his universe. When she thought about it, it seemed that the year since they met had flown; perhaps if he took up with another girl, time would pass even faster for him. He was right that the three years between them was a big gap, but that was a simple fact, and nothing could be done about it. He should just take it easy.

He agreed to whatever she suggested, whatever she wanted. He was sure he had no other choice. To celebrate her return to him, even on these terms, on whatever terms she set, he decided to give her something special. School was coming to an end for the summer. He drove up to the high school in a rented Bentley; the backseat was filled with flowers; in the middle of those flowers was an expensive gold bracelet. Karin accepted the gifts as her due. But, she told Dennis, she was a little disappointed. Why had he rented a Bentley and not a Rolls-Royce?

Karin, someone said later, was playing him like a fish on a line, and he was offering no resistance. She was manipulating him and his emotions as far as she could. In her friend Kira Lintner's yearbook Karin wrote:

So I just finished failing a geometry exam. No problem! Hope that you enjoy the summer & get to spend some time with Chris. Just the two of you together, you know? You guys are great with each other so I hope it works out & I *expect* to be in the wedding party! As you may expect to be in mine. Although you have yet to meet the groom. No, it's not Dennis. Surprised? No, not really. His name is Alex. Yes, the very same Alex who is down in Rowayton. He is really very special & we get along great together. He is Russian, as you know, with an accent that could stop a train, a body that stops my heart & just the sweetest disposition in the *world*! I haven't gotten him yet, but I will soon you can be sure. You don't know how close it was this weekend though. I have news for you. Alex talks in his sleep! *That's* how close it was. O.K.—so yes, our first son will be named Kevin Alexander. What do you think? Den & I are still inseparable friends though. He buys me things, lets me drive the Triumph & takes me for rides in Rolls Royces & Bentleys. It's a cool life. But we'll never be like you and Chris. What you guys have is special & I admire it. Stay cool O.K. If you're around during the summer, we'll talk. Enjoy senior, your *last* year in this place. Well, I'm happy to be 1/2 way through & still surviving. Take care kid, Karin Aparo.

Kira Lintner, who was then involved with Dennis's friend Chris Wheatley, says that about this time Karin passed her a note in school. Would Kira agree to sleep with Dennis? Why? So she'd have an even tighter hold over Dennis, be able to control him even more firmly than ever; if Kira slept with him, Karin would be able to go to Dennis and say, "I know what you did with Kira." Dennis would feel so guilty he would have no resistance to anything she asked.

Kira refused. Karin asked her if there was someone else in the class who might be willing. "After class," Kira said, "we went to the cafeteria, and Karin asked several other girls if they'd sleep with Dennis. At least two of them were friends of Dennis, not Karin, and she went over to them and asked if they'd sleep with him. They said, absolutely not, they were Dennis's friends and not hers."

She didn't need that to control Dennis. She didn't need anything. On the surface, she didn't even need Dennis any longer. She had Alex Markov. On June 20 she slept with him for the first time. Yet she would not give up Dennis or her hold on him. "My feelings toward Dennis were very mixed," she said. She still loved him, but she needed to get away from his clinging, needed some freedom. Besides, though she didn't say it then, she might well need him in the time to come.

22

A crisis was approaching, the worst crisis of her life. She was going to abandon her mother's most cherished dream, the fantasy that they had shared for more than a decade, since she was five. She knew now that it had always been nothing more than a delusion, a goal she could never reach. Hearing the other violinists at the Manhattan School, working at her lessons with Albert Markov, listening to Alex play, she understood at last that the small talent she had was not enough, that she would never play on the concert stage, that a career as a professional musician was closed to her. She would have to find something else. Worse, she would have to tell Joyce, sometime and in some way, and prepare herself to deal somehow with the inevitable reaction and consequence.

At first she held the decision to herself. Then she told Maria Bonaiuto, the school nurse who had become her adult confidante. "She was," Bonaiuto says, "beginning to develop an idea for the future. She had felt so desperate so often I was truly worried that Karin felt she had no future and might commit suicide. Now she was really talking about college and becoming a psychologist. She said she only had to get through two years and then she would be in college and then she could get counseling and there would be no more problems once she was in college and away. She was beginning to sound much more adult and real. She seemed to have something she could hold on to."

She revealed that crucial change of plans to Dennis as well. Deep inside, she explained, she had never really wanted to be a concert violinist, and she had known, really, that she didn't have the talent or the drive to succeed. That actually had been her mother's plan, her mother's dream. She had used the fantasy and the violin to get what she wanted, which was now to be a psychologist.

Everyone else might accept Karin's decision, might consider it admirable and mature, a sign that she was growing up and finally becoming independent, especially when she told Shannon and others that no matter how bad things got, she knew she only had to get through another two years and then would be free. Still, there were those two years, and at sixteen even a month can seem a very long time. And there was the question, How would Joyce take it? If the past is prelude, there was little doubt that Joyce would not take it well.

Karin says that she did tell Joyce, did discuss it with her not once but several times and that her mother's response was to suggest that they both get psychological counseling. That is what Karin says. No one knows for certain.

And Karin maintains that from late May on, she and Joyce were actually getting along better than they ever had before. If so, the reason was Alex Markov. Joyce adored him, and Karin's growing attachment to him was a source of enormous pleasure; even if Karin discussed abandoning the violin with her, it was always possible that the Markovs, Albert, the teacher and Joyce's friend and Karin's father figure, and especially Alex, the son and now Karin's lover, could be a palpable influence in turning her back to that first dream, that first love.

But even as Karin's affair with Alex blossomed and flourished, a crisis loomed there, too. Despite whatever protestations he might be making, the affair was only an interlude, a temporary thing. In August Alex was going to leave for an extended concert tour that would take him out of the country. It could not have been pleasant to look forward to the time with Joyce when both Alex and the violin were gone.

On June 26 Joyce was in Greenwich on business. She had driven Karin to the Markovs', dropped her off and gone on her way. The plan was for her to retrieve Karin in the afternoon and drive her home. It was the anniversary of Karin's first date with Dennis, and they were going out to celebrate. But on the way from Greenwich Joyce's car was rear-ended. Karin was called at the Markovs' and informed that Joyce was at Middlesex Memorial Hospital, that though she had not been seriously hurt, she would have to remain in the hospital at least overnight. Alex offered to drive Karin to the hospital. She accepted. Joyce greeted them, said she was in some pain and then told Alex to drive Karin back to the condo in Glastonbury, stay the night and drive her back to the hospital the next day. Alex agreed.

Knowing nothing about Joyce's accident or the arrangements she had dictated, Dennis drove up from South Glastonbury to the Aparo condo early in the evening. "I went up to the back and knocked," he says. "Karin opened the door, and I could hear the shower running in the bathroom. I asked her who was there, and she said Alex was taking a shower and I couldn't come in. She said her mom had been in an accident and was in the hospital and Alex had driven her home and was staying over so he could drive her back in the morning. I asked her where he was going to sleep, and she said on the couch or in her mother's room. She said, 'Don't worry, he isn't going to sleep with me.' I was on my little cloud, so I accepted it, but I didn't like it, and I was upset by it.''

Dennis couldn't get it out of his mind. He worried it constantly, and the more he worried it, the more he became concerned that Karin was having an affair with Alex Markov. At the end of June he put the question to her.

Not an affair exactly, she said. She had gone to bed with Alex once, she told Dennis. "It was just a physical thing," she said. "I had to get it out of my system. Now I've done it, and I don't want to do it with him anymore.''

Dennis began to cry, sobbing bitterly, uncontrollably. But she was still seeing Alex, he protested.

Yes, she said, but it was purely platonic, and that was the way it was going to remain. She still loved Dennis.

He convinced himself that she was telling him the truth. Inside, he couldn't really believe it, was filled with doubts and fears, but he tried as best he could to push them away. Still, the effect on him was apparent. He was nervous, edgy, had trouble concentrating, his stomach was acting up again, he wasn't eating, he was losing weight, had lost perhaps ten pounds since the time they had gone "incommunicado" in May, was to lose another ten over the next month, and he could not afford to lose weight.

On July 1 Karin began a new diary. Over the next twenty-eight days she wrote regularly, filling the pages in a 7½- by 4½-inch book with a red plaid cover, on which appeared:

> *This book belongs to*
> *Karin Aparo*
> *Date*
> *7–1–87*

Each day when she finished writing, she put that diary into the drawer beside her bed, the drawer where she had kept the letters from Dennis Coleman that Joyce had found nearly a year before. The entries in this diary were a rambling compendium of the surface events of her days. At the center were Alex Markov and Dennis Coleman: Alex, strong, self-sufficient, talented, dominating, independent; Dennis, weak, dominated, clinging desperately, doing anything to hold on and easily manipulated. But for anyone who might have read Karin's writings over the year previous, since her meeting with Dennis, there was something odd about this volume. There was little of the introspection that had filled the earlier pages, few of the recriminations, no attempts to relate and juxtapose the present with the past and so draw parallels and emerge with insights. Missing, too, was Joyce Aparo. The references to her were few, and those were in the blandest of terms.

Among other things in that first entry Karin noted that she was sixteen, a terrible violinist, in love with nobody, having an affair with Alex Markov, seeing Dennis casually and very fat and weight-conscious. She was planning to go away with Alex for a week to Woodstock, New York, to baby-sit for the children of his cousin. July 9 would be the anniversary of the first time she had slept with Dennis; she had slept with him eighty times since. He had just bought her some diamond earrings and a pearl necklace. Though she hadn't spoken to Alex Markov in two days, they were in the midst of a wonderful affair and had slept together five times since that initial experience on June 20. She was very happy about this affair because she had gotten something she wanted badly and because she was the first girl he had ever had sex with. She thought he was very strong, and she died every time she saw his chest and arms and especially his back. Her marks had come from school, mainly A's and B's, except in chemistry, for which she got a C.

A day later she noted that she was listening to Alex play Paganini, at which he was brilliant, and though he had been trying to help her with her practice, she felt hopeless compared with him. She felt particularly hopeless because she had been working on a Bach gavotte that he had played as an encore at a concert he had given at New York's 92d Street Y. Listening to his tapes, she felt frustrated, but, then, it didn't really matter anymore because now she intended to become a psychiatrist anyway. She had bought Alex some posters of Led Zeppelin, had even found one to hang in her own room, and she was going to help Alex write up a patent he was hoping to get for an electric violin.

On July 4, she wrote, she and Dennis were supposed to watch the fireworks in Hartford but, instead, had driven down to Rowayton in the Spitfire with the top down and watched the fireworks at the beach there. Later they drove by the Markovs' house and saw an American flag hanging from the porch. Dennis had barbecued hamburgers and hot dogs for them, and they went shopping and he bought her a pair of pink pants and white shoes, and then they watched some television and played with Dennis's ferret, Meegan. She had a long talk with Alex, and they both were excited about the pending week in Woodstock.

For Dennis that Fourth of July was not such a pleasant day. He remembers the drive to the beach at Rowayton. "All the way down," he says, "she was being very clinical and asking a lot of questions. 'How does it feel? What would you do if I did this, like sleep with Alex again?' She was trying to get me to explain what was going through my head. I just kept telling her I didn't really understand it myself. I used the term 'territorial'; that was how I felt about her. But I didn't really understand it. I was getting very hurt by what she was doing, and she just kept pushing buttons, acting like the little psychologist she wanted to be."

One of the things that they talked about, that Karin pressed him about, was her impending week in Woodstock. She had agreed, she said, as she had told him a few days before, to go to Woodstock with Alex Markov. They would be leaving on July 7 and would be gone until July 14. The reason was simply that Alex had been asked to baby-sit for his cousin's children, and Alex knew absolutely nothing about children, so she was going along to do more than help, to do the actual work. She was not, she insisted, going to be sleeping with Alex during that week. She was just going to baby-sit.

Despite her explanations, Dennis was not happy. He was, both he and Karin agree, extremely upset. "He said he was getting tired of my going away so much and spending so much time with Alex," she says. Still, she insisted that she still loved him and this whole thing was just temporary and they would soon be back together again.

He felt he had no choice but to accept. While she was away, he said, he would call her often. And one of the reasons he would call her was not simply that he missed her and wanted to be in constant touch, to hear her voice. "She told me," he says, "that when we came back on the Fourth, her mother was suspicious that we hadn't really gone down to Rowayton but had gone to my house. She said her mother was yelling at her, that she'd been yelling at her for a while, that things were really starting up again with her mother. She said she had to get away from her mother."

On July 7 Karin and Alex Markov went to Woodstock. That night in her diary she wrote that listening to him play Paganini caprices made her realize that she was passionately in love with the man who played that music, not necessarily Alex Markov, but the Alex Markov who was playing the violin. Doing that, he was different, more sophisticated, more giving, incredibly tender.

The next day, she wrote, she went shopping, bought Joyce a kaleidoscope and saw a diamond ring she wanted. She talked to Dennis on the phone and told him about it, and he agreed to buy it for her.

On July 9 she noted that it was the anniversary of the

day she had slept with Dennis for the first time. The total for the year was still eighty, and that was all right with her because there was no need for any more or any less. While she was writing, Alex was in the shower, but when he emerged, he was going to throw her out of his room so he could sit on the floor, stare at a candle and meditate. She and Alex had made love twice that day, "concerts" she called the experience.

On July 10 she and Alex made love again. Dennis called to tell her that he was going sailing and that he had sent a money order off to the store in Woodstock for the diamond ring. Hearing the call, Alex Markov flew into a rage, told her that he was extremely jealous and that she was being unfair and ruining their vacation, which, she noted, were just about the same words Dennis had used to her. Alex told her that this might be their last week together because once school started, she wouldn't be able to spend so much time in Rowayton, and besides, he would be gone; he had a concert in Binghamton, New York, at the beginning of August, and then he was going on tour, first to Wisconsin and then to Vienna.

On July 10 Karin and Alex made love twice more. Dennis called her, and, she wrote, she was very happy to hear from him.

During that week Dennis tried to keep himself occupied. He had his job at Tallwoods to fill part of the day. He called Karin often. During one of those calls she mentioned that she had seen a diamond ring at the Jewelry Store in Woodstock she loved and wanted very much to have. It was only $327. Dennis sent off a money order that day.

And Joyce Aparo helped fill the empty hours. As Karin's affair with Alex Markov intensified, Joyce began to pay increasing attention to Dennis; it became almost a courtship. She called him several times and asked if he would go with her to the supermarket and help bring the groceries home. She called him and asked him to go to the movies

with her. She invited him to have dinner with her, once at
Blacksmith's Tavern. "It wasn't like with the mothers of
other girls," he said a long time later. "She'd invite me
over and I'd get there and she'd be in the shower, and then
she'd come out wrapped in a towel, and she'd just walk out
into the living room. She was like that. Then after a while
she'd get dressed."

Asked if he thought she might be trying to seduce him
or, perhaps, entice him into making a move toward her,
something that would give her a weapon he could never
deflect with which she could end his relationship with Karin,
he looked shocked and surprised. "She never made ad-
vances or anything like that," he says. "But right on the
edge of things. But she was the mother of the girl I was in
love with, so I never even thought anything like that. Besides, I thought she was a nice person. There were things
about her that I didn't like, but she was also a nice person,
at least to me."

During their evenings together and during their dinner
at Blacksmith's Tavern she talked much about Karin, about
her hopes and dreams for her daughter, telling Dennis that
she wanted only the best for Karin and that nothing should
come in the way of her realizing that ambition to become a
great concert violinist. He did not mention that he knew
Karin no longer had such ambitions, that she was aiming in
a different direction now. And, he says, "I never got the
impression that she was warning me off. According to
Karin, she was trying to break us up, but she never said
anything to me face-to-face about it. Maybe once or twice
she told me we should cool it, but that was all."

What was really on his mind in those days was the
future, a good future that was soon to arrive, he was certain.
"All I could think of was that she was going to be going
back to school pretty soon, and I was going to be at school
again, and we were going to get back together really again
and have time, and I couldn't wait until the day school
started."

*   *   *

On July 15 Karin was back in Glastonbury, at the desk in her own room once more. She was extremely glad to be back, she wrote in her diary. She and Alex had made love once more before he drove her home; it was either the thirteenth or fourteenth time, she wasn't positive, and it had been a wonderful experience. They had talked about her staying over in Rowayton, but the elder Markovs' being home she felt ruled out the possibilities. The ring Dennis had bought for her had arrived, and she was ecstatic about that.

Her next entry in the diary was four days later, July 19. She had been to Rowayton with Shannon on Sunday, had seen Alex that day. She had also been with him the previous one, and over the weekend they had made love six times, bringing the total, she wrote, to twenty. Michael Zaccaro had been to the condo for dinner that evening, and she had cooked a herbed fennel lamb and corn sage cakes, which were wonderful. "So much to think of & to do!" she wrote at the end of that page.

Karin went to Rowayton that Sunday not only with Shannon but with Joyce as well, in Joyce's car. Shannon remembers it clearly. "We had gone to the beach for the day and to meet Alex," she says. "On the ride back we got into the car when we were in the Markovs' driveway and Mrs. Aparo noticed that there was no gas, or the gas gauge was on empty. She had told Karin to fill up the tank, and she got angry, and she yelled and screamed at Karin for not getting the gas when she had been told to. But she got the car started, and we found a gas station and filled up. On the way back, Karin reached back and grabbed my hand and held it very tightly because she was afraid of her mother and what her mother might do when we got home."

Joyce did nothing, perhaps because Michael Zaccaro came to dinner. And that night Shannon slept over, taking Karin's room while Karin slept with Joyce. "During the night," Shannon says, "I heard laughing and talking between them, and I thought it was strange because Mrs. Aparo had been so angry earlier and now she seemed happy."

The next evening Karin and Shannon went to the movies together. They talked about Joyce's response to the empty gas tank the previous day, about her unreasonable rage. "Gee, Karin," Shannon said, "she treated you so awful I just wanted to push her out of the car and drive away."

Karin said, "Well, I think I can deal with it. There's no more physical abuse. I think I can make it for two more years, and then it's off to college and I'll be okay. Things are getting better."

At least that's what Karin told her best friend. But she was saying something else to Dennis Coleman. According to him, soon after her return from Woodstock, relations between mother and daughter turned even worse, as bad as they had ever been, and they were going downhill. "I asked her right after she got back, 'Are you all right?' She just sort of freaked out. She turned around and said it was bad. And she started to push." For the first time in nearly a year she began to talk about killing Joyce. The situation in the Aparo house was intolerable, she said. Joyce was forcing her to stay in Rowayton more and more often, she told him, and she didn't want to but had no choice. And the violin was becoming an increasing source of tension, Joyce putting ever more pressure on her about it, forcing her to practice longer and longer hours, criticizing with ever more severity. "She told me the situation was desperate," he says. Her only hope of escape, the only hope she and Dennis had to be together again as they had been, she told him, was for Joyce to die. "I told her this was not a good idea. But she kept at it. She didn't stop."

It became, in those weeks toward the end of July, a ritual incantation, recited with fervor whenever Karin and Dennis were together: Joyce was coming between them;

Joyce was trying to break them up; Joyce was forcing her to go to Rowayton and be with the Markovs when all she really wanted was to be with Dennis; Joyce was trying to force her to sleep with Alex. Escape, freedom, the only chance for them to be together again was for Joyce to die.

Every once in a while the song changed, a change that ripped through Dennis and sent him reeling into a nightmare world. They went for a long ride one afternoon. "I asked her if she was in love with Alex, and she didn't say anything, and I asked her again, and she said yes, and the bottom sort of dropped out of me. I dropped her off at her house and drove away, and then I drove back, and I sat outside her bedroom window and cried for about five hours, and she didn't know I was there, or she pretended she didn't know. She didn't come to the window."

Writing in her diary on July 26, Karin noted that she and Dennis had driven up to Boston the morning of the previous Saturday, had lunch, bought a lot of clothes, taken one of those old-fashioned tintype photographs and just had fun. After Dennis had dropped her off at home, she drove down to Rowayton. She stayed the night and slept with Alex for the twenty-first time. When she told Joyce that she was staying over, Joyce wanted to know whether the Markovs were going to be there. Karin told her they were. Joyce said that was fine, then, because if it were just Alex and Karin alone in the house, Karin would look like a slut. There had been a good party for Alex, but Karin had to leave early because she had Joyce's car and Joyce wanted it. Joyce had seen her wearing the ring Dennis had ordered from Woodstock, had said she didn't like it, and she didn't like the one from Thunder Hole he had bought for her a year earlier, and she told Karin to take them off.

The last entry in the diary was written on July 28. The first item she thought worthy of mention was that she had slept with Alex again, for the twenty-fourth time, which, she noted, added up to once for each year of his life. This particular session, though, had been special; he had held on to her when they were through as though he really cared for her. Still, she had promised him that she wouldn't get attached to him. Then she turned to Dennis, writing that he was desperate and on the verge of suicide; that was too bad, but she wasn't really sorry for him. He might have a lot of problems, but she couldn't understand why he had let her bother him so much. Perhaps Alex had given her a false sense of security. Her car had died and was beyond repair. But she didn't really mind because she could just ride her bike whenever she wanted to go somewhere or even walk; besides, they were about to buy a new Volkswagen Fox. She was looking forward to the trip to Binghamton over the weekend for Alex's concert, particularly because she would get to wear a special white dress when she went to receptions with him. They had made love three more times that day.

The pressure on Dennis was mounting; it was unbearable, and he felt unable to resist. He was not sleeping or eating. He was still losing weight. He was too pale, his eyes red-rimmed and haunted. He didn't know what to do, and he felt he knew all too well what she expected him to do.

On July 28 they took another ride. As they were returning to her house, Karin says she asked, ''What would you do if I told you I'd slept with Alex twenty times and not just once?''

''I'd drive off the road and kill us both,'' he said.

''No,'' she said, ''it was only that one time.'' Later she said, ''I wanted to tell him the truth, but I couldn't because I was afraid he was really going to drive off the road and kill us.''

23

July 28–August 5, 1987: Karin Aparo's Story

She loved Dennis, and she loved Alex. Alex was going away, and so she was going to lose him. But she would still have Dennis, and she wanted him. She wanted and expected everything to be as it had been before. "We would have the rest of the summer together, and that was what I wanted," she said.

And, she says, she loved her mother, and "we were getting along good. She approved of my relationship with Alex. We weren't having any trouble."

After Dennis's suicidal threat in the car, she worried more and more about him. On Thursday night, July 30, she was packing for the trip to Binghamton. It was a trip she was looking forward to. It was to be her last time that summer with Alex Markov, and she intended to make the most of it.

Dennis appeared outside her window. He was dis-

259

traught. She moved about the room, taking her things from drawers and putting them into suitcases, talking to him all the while. She and Joyce would be leaving in the morning, she said, driving to Greenwich for an anniversary party at a nursing home that evening. From Greenwich they would travel to Binghamton for Alex's concert, and they intended to be back home in Glastonbury on Tuesday morning.

"I don't want to go," she told him, "but I have to. Mom's making me go, and I don't want to."

"Then don't go," he said.

"I have to. Mom says I have to. But you don't have to worry. This is the last time I'll have to be with Alex. Then that's over, and we'll have the rest of the summer for us."

Outside the window Dennis was crying uncontrollably, begging her not to go, pleading with her to stay home and be with him.

"I lied to him," Karin says. "I did want to go. I was looking forward to the concert and the reception afterwards and being with Alex. But Dennis was so jealous, and I didn't want him to think I wanted to be with Alex. I was afraid of what he might do."

She sent Dennis away, assuring him passionately that she loved him and would be with him always once she returned.

On Friday, July 31, she and Joyce drove to Greenwich and that evening went to the nursing home party. She called Dennis from one of the offices during that party, without Joyce's knowledge. The reason she called him, she says, was that she was worried about her two cats, Godfrey and Winston. "Mom had said I wasn't to worry about the cats because they could take care of themselves. But the weather was very hot, and I was afraid they would run out of water. So I called Dennis and asked him to please go into the house and feed Godfrey and Winston; otherwise they might not make it through the weekend. He had his own key. He had made a copy before of mine. He said okay, he would take care of them."

The only other thing they talked about, she says, was when she was coming home. "I told him we'd be home on Tuesday, which was August 4."

On Saturday, August 1, she, Joyce and Albert and Alex Markov drove to Binghamton. They stayed in a hotel for three days. "Alex had a rehearsal and then a concert and then a reception party afterwards. I had a very good time. Alex was the soloist, and the reception was held in a big hall, and everybody got all dressed up. It was wonderful."

Early in the morning of Tuesday, August 4, they left Binghamton for Rowayton, Karin and Alex in one car, Joyce and Albert Markov in another. They reached the Markov house about four in the morning and went to bed. "My feelings toward my mother were very good then," she says. "We had a good weekend together."

About nine-thirty that morning Joyce woke her, told her she was leaving for Saybrook, where she had a business appointment, and then would be driving home. Karin, she said, should stay on in Rowayton for another day. Joyce would drive down in the Volkswagen Jetta that Athena was leasing for her and pick her up Wednesday (Karin's car had gone to the scrap heap).

About three o'clock that afternoon Karin called Dennis to tell him they were back, but not in Glastonbury. They had reached the Markovs' very early in the morning, she told him, and she was going to stay on until Wednesday. There was no need for him to go back to the Aparos' condo to see to the cats, she said, because Joyce would be home and would take care of them herself.

"Why are you staying?" Dennis demanded. "You're supposed to be back here. You told me you were coming back today."

"There isn't anything I can do about it," she said. "Mom is making me stay over." That wasn't true, but she says, "I didn't want Dennis to be mad."

As they were talking, Dennis mentioned that he had left a note for her when he had been in the condo over the weekend. "I hope," he said, "she doesn't find it."

"Where did you leave it?" Karin asked.

"Between the sheets of your bed."

She told him not to worry. Joyce wouldn't find it because she never looked there.

Later that afternoon Joyce called Rowayton to tell Karin that she was home and that she was making out a list of things for Karin to do. The whole house was filthy, she said, and she wanted Karin to clean it when she got home on Wednesday. The best thing would be if Alex would drive her up to Glastonbury in the morning; otherwise Joyce would drive down late in the afternoon and get her.

Soon after that call from Joyce, Karin phoned Dennis again. She told him Joyce was home, was complaining that the house was dirty and demanding that Karin clean it. Joyce intended to pick her up on Wednesday afternoon. Dennis was very unhappy about the delay in her return. He complained that she should already have been home. He sounded upset.

At midevening Karin called Joyce, who told her that Shannon had called, they had spoken for about a half hour, and Shannon wanted to see Karin when she got back to Glastonbury. Joyce said that was all right with her, but before they got together, Karin had to do the laundry. "Then my mom said she was very tired and she was going to bed early."

About nine that evening Dennis called. "He said he didn't understand why I wasn't there. He said, 'If she's making you stay there, she's coming between us. I think I should kill her. When you come back, you'll never have to go to Rowayton again.'"

According to Karin, all these calls were made from and received in the Markovs' living room, and Alex was in and out all the time.

After the last call from Dennis she stayed up for a while, then, very tired, went to bed.

About eleven the next morning the phone rang. It was for her. The caller was Michael Zaccaro. He told her that Joyce's car had been found abandoned in Massachusetts.

24

There is a different version of what happened that week. On July 28, after their traumatic ride, Dennis returned to the Aparo condo and stood outside Karin's window. "She began pressuring me," he says. "She began telling me that she couldn't live with her mother any longer. She was crying and saying she couldn't take it any longer, and she was begging me to kill her mother. And I was standing outside, and I was crying, too, I was so upset about what had happened and what was happening and what she wanted me to do and that she was so upset."

He stood outside the window for fifteen or twenty minutes, Karin inside crying and pleading with him, Dennis crying and trying to discourage her, to find some way to turn this thing, the idea of murder, aside. Then, he says, Karin came up with a plan. The way to kill Joyce, she proposed, was to cut the brake lines on her car; that way she wouldn't be able to stop, would have an accident at some speed, for she was a fast driver, and would be killed. "She was pleading with me to do it, and I was telling her I was not sure it was a good idea and I was afraid I was going to get caught. She assured me I wouldn't."

The pleading and the pressure were too much, and at last he agreed. He turned from the window, got into his car and drove away, went to an auto supply store and bought wire cutters. He drove back to the Aparo condo, into the parking lot and sat in his car, staring at Joyce's Volkswagen. "I couldn't do it. Every now and then people would be coming by, but that wasn't it. I just couldn't do it. So I gave up and went back over to Karin's window and it was dark and I tapped a few times, but she didn't move or come to the window. I gave up and went home."

The next day, Wednesday, he says he spoke to her briefly, told her that he hadn't been able to carry out the plan, that he had gone to her window and tapped, intending to tell her, but she didn't appear. Her response was anger.

Thursday night, at nine o'clock, he was back outside the window. "She was packing, and I was watching her pack, and she was pleading with me. 'This is it,' she kept saying, 'it has to be tonight.' They were leaving for Binghamton in the morning, and she told me she didn't want to go and she couldn't go, but her mother was making her. I was in tears outside the window, telling her I couldn't do it, and she was in tears inside the house on the other side of the window, begging me to do it, and her mother kept coming in and out asking for help or something, and she kept going off to talk to her mother, and then she'd come back and it would start over."

As they talked, plans, details, contingencies began to emerge and be spelled out. A week earlier, when Karin had first begun to press him on the necessity for murdering Joyce, a method had come up about creating a poison gas by mixing ammonia and bleach. "I can't remember who brought it up first," he says, "but I didn't really know that much about the ammonia-bleach thing. I may even have brought it up first because I thought of it, but she helped me with the ratios and exactly what was going to happen. It was three to one, but I can't remember whether it was three parts ammonia and one of bleach or the other way around."

So they worked it out. Before they went to bed, Karin would leave the door unlocked, and after everyone was asleep, Dennis would enter the condo, soak a rag in the mixture of ammonia and bleach, go into Joyce's bedroom, put the rag over her face and kill her. There was an alternative plan. If the ammonia-bleach combination didn't asphyxiate Joyce, Dennis would strangle her. When Joyce was dead, Karin "would stay in the house and clean up, get rid of the fingerprints, vacuum, wash the sheets, dust, make sure there were no traces of me left in the house."

Dennis's job at that point would be to get rid of Joyce's body. He would have to take it away somewhere and dump it. There had to be a body found, Karin said, because of the insurance; she couldn't collect without proof of death. And while he was disposing of Joyce's body, she told him, she wanted him to take the rings off Joyce's fingers: They were valuable, and she wanted them for herself.

Finally the plotting ended. "I left not sure of myself. I was not sure whether I was going to go through with it or not, and she was not sure whether I was going to or not either. She was assuming that I was going to show up that night. I never did. I went home and went to bed. I couldn't do it."

So the murder did not come off, and the next morning Joyce and Karin left for Greenwich and then went on to Binghamton.

Karin called from Greenwich. "At first she was upset. She asked me why I didn't show up and do it. I told her I couldn't. She said, 'I just don't understand,' And then it was kind of weird. She asked me to go into the house and take care of the cats while they were gone, and that she'd be home on Tuesday morning."

He went into the condo, using his key, the next day to feed the cats and do other chores. While there, he walked into her bedroom. "I saw the picture of her and Alex on her dresser. I didn't like it at all, and I walked out of there."

He returned to the condo on Monday afternoon. He fed the cats again, went back into her bedroom. "That's when I picked up her diary. I held on to it, and then I put it back without opening it. It was her private property, and it wasn't right for me to look inside. I should have. If I had read that diary, I wouldn't have killed anybody, not Joyce, not Karin, not anybody. Because she was telling me, on the one hand, that her mother was making her do all those things, and on the other hand, if I had read the diary, I would have seen there was nothing in it about her mother making her do anything; she was doing all these things—going to Rowayton, sleeping with Alex—because she wanted to. And there was the stuff she wrote about me. If I had read the diary, there wouldn't have been any reason for me to kill Joyce or anybody."

Later the question of whether or not he read the diary was raised again and again, debated and argued endlessly. Those who insist that he must have read it say that what he found there so shattered him that it spurred him on to take revenge and so to kill Joyce Aparo. They also maintain that since there is nothing in the diary about Karin's feeling a desperate need to escape her mother's domination, nothing about plots and plans to kill her mother, it is patent that she did not feel that need and did not beg or plead with Dennis to murder Joyce Aparo.

But there are people who find Dennis's story believable. As he said, what was there in the diary that would have driven him to murder the mother? There was nothing about Joyce's forcing Karin to spend time in Rowayton, nothing about Joyce's fostering an affair between Karin and Alex Markov, little even about disputes between Karin and Joyce, nothing certainly about wanting her mother dead. If what was written there was reason for murder, it was not for the murder of Joyce Aparo but rather for the murder of

Karin Aparo or Alex Markov. And Dennis Coleman did not murder Alex Markov and would never have considered murdering Karin Aparo.

Yet another question hovers over the diary. Why was it left so openly in that bedside drawer, where anyone who entered the room might find and read it? Karin was certainly not blind to the fact that her mother often entered her room, was not hesitant about opening her drawers, searching through them and reading whatever she found. Realizing that at any time Joyce might come upon and read the diary, would Karin have written in it anything about her anger, about her bitterness, even about her disenchantment with the violin or about a desperate desire to be free and have Joyce out of the way? Among all the mundane events that fill those pages, the major subject is the affair with Alex Markov, an affair of which Joyce Aparo fully and enthusiastically approved.

Karin also understood Dennis well enough by then, had enough experience with him, to know that he indeed respected her privacy, that she could leave things in the open and he would not look at them without her approval. She had been witness to it often over the previous year.

So Dennis says he didn't read that diary. Instead, he sat down on Karin's bed and wrote her a note beginning, "I will 'do the deed.' " He had been thinking about it, had been thinking about little else since she left, and was now determined that he would do it. "The whole thing wasn't real," he says. "It was surreal, fantasyland. I was in a nightmare, and there's nothing you can do about it. It's happening, and you're not in control of it. Just watching it happen and nothing you can do to stop it. My back was against the wall, and there was nowhere to run. The only option I thought she gave me was to kill myself or do that. All this time later I don't know if she thought I would really do it, but she kept pushing me to see how far she could push me." In his mind, variations on the plot had jelled. She and Joyce would not be home before Tuesday, so nothing could be done before they arrived. Once both were home, he and

Karin would have time to talk more about his revised plan.

He wrote it down in detail, a schedule of just how everything should go and how much time it ought to take. It went like this: He would go into the condo about one-thirty on Wednesday morning, after Joyce was asleep, and then with Karin's help, kill Joyce, either with the ammonia-bleach combination or by strangling her. It should take about ten minutes to kill her. Then he and Karin would carry Joyce's body out to the Volkswagen. Karin would return to the condo and clean up, wait twenty-four to thirty-six hours, then call the police to report her mother missing.

Dennis would drive away in the Volkswagen, Joyce's body in the back. At a prearranged rendezvous point he would meet up with a friend whom he would enlist to help him. They would drive in two separate cars to a remote section of the Bronx or perhaps Harlem, he wasn't sure which, clean all the evidence out of the car and then abandon it. Considering the normal pattern with abandoned cars in such areas of New York, it would be days, perhaps even weeks, before the body was discovered and identified; the car would probably be stripped before anyone thought to look inside and see what was in the back, and even if someone did while looting the car, it was doubtful if that person would call the police. Thus, by the time the body was discovered, it would be impossible to pinpoint with any degree of accuracy the date or time of death, so there would be nothing to implicate him, Karin or anyone in particular.

According to Dennis's timetable, the trip to New York, the ditching and cleaning the car of any evidence and the trip back ought to take something less than five hours, bringing him back to Glastonbury by seven in the morning, in time to go to work as though nothing had happened.

There was, of course, the necessity of recruiting someone to drive that second car. On Sunday he approached his friend Chris Wheatley, home for the summer from his pre-med studies. "He owed me one," Dennis says, "because of what I'd done for him when he needed help with money."

He laid out for Wheatley the plan to kill Joyce as it was developing in his mind.

"What's in it for me?" Wheatley asked.

Dennis offered him a thousand dollars from Joyce's insurance, though he'd have to wait for it until the insurance companies paid up, and Wheatley could have whatever loose money might be lying around in Joyce's purse.

Wheatley didn't say yes, and he didn't say no. He told Dennis he would think about it and give an answer in a day or two.

On Tuesday, August 4, Dennis arrived home from work at the country club at midafternoon, expecting that Karin would be home and he would be hearing from her momentarily so they could discuss how they would implement the plan, which he now set for that night, and to fill her in on the final details as he had formulated them. When she called, at three thirty-six, it was not from home but from Rowayton. She was still there; she was going to be there another day. In the background he could hear Alex Markov moving around, talking. Dennis had a funny feeling, he said, that Alex was overhearing all their plans. He didn't like it, but he didn't know what to do about it.

Once again, during the conversation, which lasted about ten minutes, Karin told him that Joyce would have to go; there was no other way. But, she said, it would have to wait until Wednesday night. Joyce would not be getting to Glastonbury until very late that Tuesday, and Karin would still be in Rowayton and unable to help. He told her he had left a note for her between the sheets of her bed, telling her that he had come up with a nearly complete plan. If she wasn't going to be home, he was afraid Joyce might find it. She told him not to worry, Joyce would never look there.

At six-oh-six that evening Karin called again. Once more Dennis heard Alex Markov talking in the background. He wondered how Karin could be so open in her talk with Alex around. She had been thinking about what they were going to do, she told him, and she realized that she just couldn't be in the house when he killed her mother. She just couldn't be there. Since she was coming home the next morning, the murder would have to take place that night, Tuesday. He should do it and not worry about leaving anything behind; when she got home, she would clean the condo thoroughly so that when she did report Joyce missing a day later, if the police decided to search, there would be nothing for them to find. He should remember to take clothes to dress Joyce in. She shouldn't be found in her nightgown. That would tell everybody that she had been killed at home and then moved. If she was dressed, there would be no way of knowing where she was killed; it would be just as possible the cops would think that she had never reached home that night, that she had been waylaid someplace, killed and left. At the beginning of that conversation she was breathing heavily, and he heard Alex Markov in the background. He didn't think much of it at the time. Later he became convinced that they must have just finished making love when she called him.

It was essential now that he win Chris Wheatley's agreement to help. Otherwise there was simply no way he would be able to drive away with Joyce's body once he had killed her, leave it and her car far away and be back in time for work. He went looking for Wheatley and found him at Kira Lintner's house. He asked Wheatley to go for a ride. They got into Dennis's car and drove around Glastonbury. Dennis told him the murder was now definitely set for that night. He would need Wheatley. He wanted a commitment. Wheatley said he hadn't completely made up his mind. He would think about it and let Dennis know later that evening.

Dennis dropped Wheatley off at Kira Lintner's and drove back home. At seven-thirty he called Karin at the Markovs'. He told her he had talked to Chris Wheatley, but Chris hadn't made up his mind if he would help. It was vital, she said, that the plan be carried out as they had agreed; a body had to be found if she was going to collect the insurance. She said, "If you can't get Chris, then get your brother, get Matt to help.'' He would try to get Wheatley, he said, and call her back later and let her know.

''I was determined to find somebody,'' Dennis says, ''anybody but Matt. But if I couldn't, if Chris hadn't agreed, I would have asked Matt. I wish I had. Because he wouldn't have. But I was desperate. I thought this was the only way I could save myself. If everyone had said no, this never would have happened. But everyone didn't say no.''

He went out to find Wheatley once more, to press him to make a decision. He found him, they went for another ride and this time Wheatley agreed. They drove around, looking for a place to buy some beer, couldn't find an open store and drove to the Coleman house in South Glastonbury to grab some beer from the refrigerator. They took a few cans; Wheatley carried them out to the car while Dennis called Karin. It was nine-oh-three.

It was on for that night, he told her. Wheatley had agreed to help, to drive the second car. All he needed to know now was when Joyce would be home.

She was already home, Karin said. They had talked an hour earlier, and Joyce had told her she was tired and was going to bed early.

Dennis went out to the car. He and Wheatley drove back to Kira Lintner's. She and another friend, Frank Manganaro, were there. Over the next few hours they sat around, drank beer, watched a couple of horror movies, including *Friday the 13th.*

About eleven-thirty, the movies over, the beer gone, Kira and Manganaro went off to try to buy a Garfield mug. Dennis and Wheatley discussed what would happen over the next hours. They agreed that Wheatley would pick Dennis up at the Coleman house about one in the morning.

Dennis left then. On his way home he stopped at a Wa-Wa convenience store and bought a pair of L'eggs panty hose, a black wig, work gloves, a box of plastic garbage bags and a pack of Marlboro cigarettes. He did not smoke. He began to smoke that night.

Once he was home, he burned the schedule he had written out. He changed into black pants, black shirt, black socks and shoes. He grabbed a black ski mask, a black hat, a pair of goggles and the box of plastic bags and put them in a duffel bag along with a change of clothes for later, for after. He wore all black, he later said, so that he would blend into the night darkness as he crossed lawns and entered the Aparo condo. The ski mask, the gloves, the goggles, the plastic bags all were a precaution against leaving any evidence behind in the condo, in case Karin didn't get around to cleaning as well as she should, and in Joyce's car. "I knew something about forensics," he later explained. "It was a question of hair falling out, things like that, leaving traces of myself around. You can never be too careful." He had learned about forensics, he said, when he read a book about the Atlanta child murders. "They eventually caught the guy who turned out to be the guilty party through forensics." He put his duplicate key to the Aparo condo and the unwrapped panty hose in his pocket. He would now "do the deed." There was no turning back. "That's the way it had to be. I thought it had to be done. She had put a tremendous amount of pressure on me. There was nothing, literally nothing I wouldn't have done for her. If I did the deed, there would be the insurance money, there would be the condo and I would be getting Karin."

Then he waited. A little after one in the morning Wheatley drove up. In the car with him was Kira Lintner. "I was very upset when I saw her. Chris said he had told her what was going to happen. I don't know why, but she insisted on coming along."

He got into the backseat of the car. Wheatley drove to Terry Brook Drive, a block from the condo, and parked. Dennis opened the duffel and removed the things he would need. As he did, they went over the final plans. He would be in the house about twenty minutes, he figured. It would take him that time to murder Joyce and then put her body in the backseat of her Volkswagen Jetta. Wheatley agreed to be outside the house about then, and they would start the trip down to the Bronx.

About one-twenty Dennis opened the car door and started away, toward Butternut Drive and the Aparo condo, dressed all in black, the ski mask over his head, the gloves covering his hands. He had decided against the hat and goggles and left them behind. Five minutes later he was at the front door. He put the duplicate key in the lock. There was some trouble with it. It was making what to him seemed like a terrible racket as he tried to turn it, and he was afraid the noise would wake Joyce.

At last the door swung open, and he entered the dark condo. He went into the living room and laid the box of garbage bags on the coffee table. He took off the ski mask; it was too hot, and he was sweating beneath it, the sweat dripping into his eyes and blinding him. He took the panty hose from his pocket and started into the bedroom. Joyce was lying on her back. He paused. "I was afraid she was awake and waiting, because people don't usually sleep on their backs. I was afraid she had heard me."

Then he started forward. He could not stop. "It was like a time that didn't exist in my life," he said. "It was as if it wasn't really me in the room, as if I was standing outside my body. It was surreal." A psychiatrist later said, "If there had been a cop in the room at that moment and he had ordered Dennis to stop, he would not have stopped. The only thing that would have stopped him and prevented the murder was shooting him."

As he neared the bed, Joyce suddenly woke and sat up. She shrank back in terror. "Please don't hurt me," she gasped. "I have no money. Please don't hurt me." Dennis doesn't think she recognized him. It was too dark in that room.

He pounced on her, wrapped the panty hose around her neck, twisted tighter and tighter, bracing himself with his knee on the bed. She began making gasping noises. "I was going shh, shh, shh. I was trying to quiet her. I didn't want a lot of noise." He grabbed a pillow and put it over her face to deaden the sound. He kept losing his grip on the panty hose, regained it, twisting and strangling. His finger pained him; he was developing a blister on it from the pressure. "I thought about stopping, but it was past the point of no return. I wanted to stop, but I couldn't."

At last she was dead. He looked at the digital clock beside her bed. It was one fifty-six. She might have been dead for several minutes by then. He had no way of knowing. All he knew was that it was 1:56, that the deed was done, and it had taken twenty-five minutes, far longer than he had estimated.

He was in a hurry now. He had to get the body off the bed, out of the condo and into the car. Chris would be waiting outside. They had a long drive ahead. He tugged her body off the bed, across the floor to the entrance to the kitchen. He went for the box of plastic bags, opened it, took out a bag and tried to slide her body into it. Her body slid right through. The bag was not strong enough to hold it. He gave up, went into the living room, took two afghans she had made and covered her with them.

He moved to the sliding glass windows facing onto Griswold Street and looked out, expecting to see Wheatley's car. It was not there. What he did see threw him into a panic. A police car was cruising slowly along the street. A moment later another police car appeared and moved past. The first police car reappeared, returning and passing. "I was flipping out. Chris wasn't there, and there were just those police cars. I didn't know what to do." He had no way of knowing that police were all over the area, cruising back and forth along the streets, up and down the culs-de-sac. The cops were out in force to catch the cat burglar.

He grabbed Joyce's purse, pawed frantically through it until he found her car keys. He took them, went out the front door, relocked it behind him and raced into the parking lot and climbed behind the wheel of her car. For the next fifteen or twenty minutes he drove around the neighborhood, frantically searching for Wheatley. But Wheatley was nowhere to be found. Finally he drove back to the condo, parked the car on the street just outside and let himself back into the house.

In the living room, Joyce's body lying nearby, covered by the afghans, he reached for the telephone and called Kira Lintner's house. He figured Wheatley would be there. He wasn't. What happened? he asked. Why wasn't Chris outside the Aparo condo waiting for him, as he had promised?

There'd been some trouble, Kira said. While they were parked on Terry Brook Drive, a cop had pulled up beside them. He had written a ticket for Chris for littering; Chris had thrown something out the window. Then the cop had told them to get out of there. Chris had started the car, and the cop followed them as they drove around Glastonbury. Finally Chris gave up and dropped her off at her house and just went home to his.

"Get Chris and have him call me here, at the Aparos'," Dennis practically screamed. He sat by the phone and waited. While he sat there, he could see through the window more police cars cruising back and forth. "I was falling apart," he says.

Five or ten minutes later Wheatley called. Dennis answered on the first ring. All Dennis was sure of at this point was that the original plan was no longer possible. It was too late to drive to New York and be back in time for work. He didn't know what to do. Wheatley took charge, tried to calm him down, told him to get the body into the car and drive to a parking lot across from a 7-Eleven store on Main Street in East Hartford, just off the exit ramp from Route 2. Wheatley would meet him there, and they would decide what to do then.

Now Dennis had to get the body out of the house and into the car. He dragged the body across the floor to the sliding glass windows and left it there. He turned and grabbed some of the plastic garbage bags, raced out of the house to the car and spread them across the seats. He started back toward the house to get Joyce. He froze just as he reached the middle of the yard. Another police car was coming down the road, its headlights sweeping across the area. He sought frantically for cover. There wasn't any. He was out in the open, too far from any place to run to and hide. He dropped flat on the ground. The cruiser went slowly by. It did not stop. He jumped up and sped back into the house. As he approached Joyce's body, he could hear sounds coming from it, gurgling noises. They were the sounds a dead body makes as the air leaves the lungs for the last time. He was terrified. He didn't know what to do. He went into the kitchen, grabbed a yellow paper towel off the roll under the sink, the last sheet on that roll, and stuffed it into her mouth to silence her. He covered her again with one of the afghans and began dragging her body through the doors, closing them behind him, and then across the lawn to the car. He had a lot of trouble moving her. He couldn't believe how heavy she was. The sweat was pouring off him in rivers, nearly blinding him, soaking his clothes. His eyes were straining up and down the road. He was praying he would reach the car before another police cruiser appeared.

He made it. He heaved her body onto the backseat, covered it with the afghan and some plastic bags and shut the door. For a second he remembered that he had left some things behind in the condo: the garbage bag box, garbage bags, perhaps other things. He didn't go back. He didn't care. Karin would be home in the morning and would clean everything.

It took him another ten or fifteen minutes to reach the parking lot in East Hartford. He sat in the car and waited. About five minutes later Wheatley arrived. Kira Lintner was with him. Dennis didn't care any longer. Wheatley got out of his car and walked over to the Jetta. They both knew there was no way they could drive south now. "I wasn't concerned about the insurance or anything anymore," Dennis says. "The only thing I was concerned about was getting rid of the body, and I didn't care if it was discovered or not." Wheatley suggested that they get on Interstate 91 and head north along the edge of the Connecticut River. At some point they'd stop and dump the body in the river.

So they started out, moving north, looking for a spot, Wheatley leading, Dennis following. Alone in the car he was filled with dread, with an unnatural fear. On the back-seat, under the afghan and plastic bags, Joyce's body was emitting sounds. Every time they went over a bump, there was another noise. "I was afraid she wasn't dead, that she was going to leap over the seat and strangle me," he says. He was afraid to look around, afraid of what he might see. He turned on the radio to drown out the sounds. It didn't help.

They drove steadily north for about an hour and a half. "I'd been up and down ninety-one many, many times, but I wasn't paying attention, and I had no idea where we were." They lost the river, and still they went on. Finally Dennis just couldn't go any farther. He flashed his lights at Wheatley and pulled over to the side of the road. Wheatley pulled over, got out and walked back to Dennis.

"We have to get rid of the car, get rid of her now," Dennis said. "If I'm going to get to work in the morning, we have to do it now. We can't keep on going."

Wheatley told him to follow and they would find a place. At the next exit Wheatley led him off the highway. They drove for a few minutes, searching for the river so they could dump the body into it. They couldn't find the river. They stopped and talked again, decided to dump the body wherever they found some out-of-the-way place. They came to a bridge. Both cars pulled off the road. Wheatley and Kira Lintner got out of the lead car. Dennis got out of the Jetta and walked toward them. He told them to drive away for a little while and he would take care of the body. They should return in five or ten minutes. They agreed, returned to Wheatley's car and drove off.

Dennis went back to the Jetta. He dragged Joyce's

body from the backseat, down the embankment beside the bridge and then under the bridge. He scraped up some leaves and brush and covered her. He turned away and climbed back up the embankment to the car.

Wheatley's car returned. Dennis went to it. Wheatley said that as he and Kira had been driving around, they'd found the perfect place to ditch the car, down a slope on a dead-end dirt road. Dennis got back into the Jetta and followed Wheatley to the spot. He drove the car off the road, down the hill and into a small stream. Wheatley clambered down the hill and pulled the plates off the Jetta. Together they went through Joyce's car and cleaned everything out of it, put it all into a trash bag and carried it back to Wheatley's car. Dennis got into the backseat, and Wheatley started driving back to Glastonbury.

In the backseat Dennis opened the duffel and changed his clothes. He searched through Joyce's purse, which he had taken from the condo, found seventy-five dollars and several credit cards. He gave them to Wheatley, as the down payment on the promised thousand dollars that would come from Joyce's insurance.

For a long time Dennis sat in the backseat sobbing. "He was crying," Kira Lintner says, "and he was telling us what he had done, and he kept saying, 'Karin made me do it. I had to do it. I didn't want to do it. I had to do it.' He was totally distraught."

After a time he stopped crying. Drained, nothing left in him, he fell asleep.

They reached Glastonbury about six in the morning. Wheatley made an unexpected detour. He stopped at Frank Manganaro's house, and Kira Lintner got out, went inside and after a few minutes reappeared. Dennis didn't know why they stopped. Later Wheatley told him it was because Kira wanted to tell Frank all about it. Wheatley drove her home and then dropped Dennis off at his house in South Glastonbury.

Dennis ran inside, ran upstairs. He carried the duffel

and the plastic garbage bag. He shoved them into his closet. He went into the bathroom, brushed his teeth and washed his hands and face. He ran downstairs, got into his car and sped off to Hebron. He arrived at the Tallwoods Country Club at seven. He was right on time.

PART FOUR

WHAT THE DEED COST

25

All the conspiring, all the planning, all the scheming had come to nothing. Early the morning of August 5 Joyce Aparo's Volkswagen Jetta was found, not in the Bronx but down a hill beside the home of the police chief in Bernardston, Massachusetts. By afternoon her body had been discovered a little distance away. Karin never got home that morning to clean the condo. That night Glastonbury police stenographer Beverly Warga overheard the incriminating telephone conversation between Karin Aparo and Dennis Coleman and overheard another as they sat talking in the police station near her desk a few hours later. Within a few days Karin had turned over to the state police the "I will 'do the deed,' " note, and on August 12, the day of her mother's funeral, she had gone to them with what she said was

Dennis's confession to her, down to the smallest detail, given only an hour before in the bathroom at the home of her closest friend Shannon Dubois, that he had murdered Joyce Aparo. Dennis never got to start classes at Central Connecticut State University. The day he was to begin, Friday, August 7, he drove instead to the Glastonbury incinerator and dumped the clothes he had worn two days before and everything else he took from Joyce Aparo's car. Less than a week later he was arrested and charged with her murder.

He was in jail over the weekend, until his $150,000 bond could be posted. On Monday, August 17, he was released and sent home, to wait for what would come. As soon as he was back home, he went to the phone and called the Duboises' number and asked to speak to Karin. "I was very upset, and I wanted to talk to her. I asked if I could see her that night."

During that call she told him everybody was putting pressure on her not to see or talk to him again. Still, she wanted to see him and talk with him, and they arranged to meet at the Gallery restaurant. Karin arrived first, with Shannon and a few others. Dennis drove up a little later. She saw him as he entered, got up and went to meet him. They walked out together to his car, got in and drove away.

They drove into South Glastonbury, by his house. He was sure they were being followed. They kept driving around until they lost whoever was behind them, then turned onto a field near the Connecticut River and parked out in a deserted area behind a barn in the woods. They stayed there for about two hours.

She asked him what jail was like. It wasn't good, it wasn't bad, he said. They talked about what lay in store for him. "If I went to jail," he says, "would she be around when I got out. Writing and things like that. She told me that she had found out from one of the police officers that the victim's next of kin had a lot to do with the person's final sentence if they were convicted and that when it came down to it, when she went to court, she would make sure that I stayed out of jail, she would try to keep me out of jail as long as possible." They talked about all that had happened in the past ten days. She talked about turning the note over to the police, told him they had found it and taken it from her when she sat on the bed and they heard the sound of paper crinkling. She told him about going to the police with his confession and so turning him in.

"It didn't upset me very much," he says. "I knew she had done that, and I told her not to worry. Whatever happened, I wouldn't ever say anything about her part. I told her I didn't want to see her go to jail and I would take all the blame. I had already told her before that if the police started to ask her any questions or started to consider her as a suspect, she should give a statement and lay the blame totally on me."

She agrees that he did not seem disturbed by what she had done. "He really seemed like the same old Dennis," she says. "I had very mixed feelings about him. He was all I had left, and I didn't want to lose him. But he had killed my mother. I didn't know how to deal with those two things."

And then they made love. "We hadn't had sex in a while," she says, "and so we did." One of the reasons she had sex with him that night, she later said, was that she was afraid of him, afraid of what he might do to her if she didn't.

"She asked me to make her pregnant," he says.

She says she never asked him to do that.

After a while they drove back to the restaurant, parked in the post office parking lot nearby, and Dennis took her inside to her friends and then left.

With Dennis gone, Shannon wanted to know what had happened, why Karin had even gone with him, what they had talked about all that time. "She said he accused her of turning him in. She said she told him she had to because the police made her. She said she was afraid because he was angry with her; she was afraid he would do something to her because of that and because they were all alone away off by the river.''

They did not see each other again until Saturday. Then Dennis called her. He was going down to Mystic to spend the day on his father's boat. She agreed to go along. They spent the day and the evening together. They made love again. Then he drove her back to Glastonbury and dropped her off.

It was months before he saw her again. Alex Markov had long since departed on his concert tour. She would not see him again. She had put the violin away, along with all those fantasies that her mother had conjured and they had shared. She had been arrested by then. He had talked to the police by then, had finally told them about her. Both were out on bond with the stipulation that they not see each other, speak to each other or communicate in any way.

They had one brief telephone conversation. Shannon called and said that Karin wanted to speak to him. He got on the phone. ''It was maybe thirty seconds long,'' he says. ''I said hello, and she told me to write to her. I didn't.''

But she wrote to him. Soon after their last meeting, during a time when he was still determined to protect her, before he decided to talk to the police, he received a note. It was inside a formal card whose cover contained the printed message ''To thank you for your kindness and sympathy at a time when it was deeply appreciated.''

He opened the card. Inside, she had written him a short note, addressed to ''my Denny.'' She was sorry about all that had happened. She would try to keep him busy for the next quarter of a century. She was sure things would work out. She begged him not to believe all he heard about her because half of it just wasn't true. She still loved him and forgave him for loving her.

There was one more letter. It was a long one. She wrote it on August 20. He received it a few days later.

She began by calling him "dearest." She asked how her love was making out and hoped he was well. It was nearly ten-thirty in the evening as she was writing, and she was listening to a song on the radio whose lyrics went: "I'm all out of love, I'm so lost without you." Those lyrics, she said, were true. She was sitting there remembering the time when the romance between the two of them was just beginning, when he was eighteen, young and sweet, and she was just falling in love with him. She was remembering all the things they had done together, ordering clothes for her from Victoria's Secret, going to Cape Cod and Nantucket and Boston. They had had so much fun, and he shouldn't worry, because they would still have fun together. "I really believe," she wrote, "that we'll turn out O.K. Even if we both have to spend 25 years in jail." But she didn't think that would happen. She had always been sure she would have a good life. The psychics had predicted it, and she was certain that they were right.

"Let's spend this good year together, O.K.?" she told him in that letter. "Then, next year, we'll worry about court." Unless forced to, she would not testify against him. But if the worst happened, he could depend on her to do what she could to make his life bearable. She would visit him as often as possible and write to him; she would bake him cookies, cakes and breads, would send him books and a lot more. And when he got out, they would make a good life together and do all the things they had planned and dreamed of. They would go to London, and they would see Venice in the year 2013. Above all, she didn't want him to miss New Year's Eve in 1999; they would party like crazy that night, to celebrate the changing of the millennium. Their children would be part of that new age; they wouldn't know anything about what had happened, and she and Dennis would be special for those children, just as they were special for each other now. "I love you, Denny. So damn much it hurts," she wrote.

She was feeling very lonely. She might have his voice

on tape, but that wasn't enough. She might have a lot of people around her, helping her, but she didn't have the one person she wanted, him. He should always stay close to her and never leave her. If she had to testify against him, she would, but only because she didn't want his lawyer to tear her apart when she got on the witness stand, and above all, she didn't want to go to prison. She wanted to thank him for making her the tape and for taking care of the ferret, Meegan, whom she adored. She promised that before September 1 she would give him a gold chain, with all her love and apologies, to wear around his neck. What lay ahead for them now was his going to court and her going back to school, and during recesses they would somehow manage to have lunch together at a Chinese restaurant.

"God, I love you, Den. You're my sweetie. My endless love," she wrote. She was sorry that words couldn't say precisely what she meant, and she was sorry that she had lied to him about Alex Markov. But he should ignore what she had told him and think only about what he felt. "God will be with you, Dennis. If not we'll be together in hell. Forever."

She loved him and missed him, wanted and needed him and thanked him for things he had sent her. She signed it, "Humbly, Karin."

And then she added a postscript: "You can send the Victoria's Secret clothes back!"

26

Christopher Wheatley was not just a smart young man. He had a powerful father who got him a good lawyer. So, in a corner, the evidence of his involvement in the murder of Joyce Aparo overwhelming, facing a long term in prison as an accessory, he looked for a way out. He made a deal. And the state of Connecticut made a blunder.

On August 24 Wheatley and his sixteen-year-old girl friend Kira Lintner and their attorneys showed up at the office of State's Attorney John Bailey and Assistant State's Attorney James Thomas, who had been handed the prosecution of the Aparo cases. Wheatley and Kira Lintner would tell everything they knew, everything they had done, would tell the truth, would appear as witnesses, if necessary, in exchange for a deal. The deal was that neither he nor she would ever be charged as accessories to murder, that nothing they said could ever be used against them, that the only charges that could ever be laid against them were those of hindering prosecution and perjury and that if hindering prosecution charges were brought, the state would not object to his receiving a suspended sentence or probation or to her being tried as a juvenile offender, with the proceedings closed and the verdict sealed.

It was not an unusual bargain to gain the cooperation of essential and potentially convicting witnesses. There was just one thing that was left out. It happened to be crucial. In their haste to strike this deal, the prosecutors forgot to include the stipulation that any agreement would be null and void if either of them lied to the authorities and that if they did, they could then be charged and tried as accessories.

The papers signed, Wheatley and Lintner began their song. Only, as far as the authorities were concerned, that song had more than a few false notes in it, was more than a trifle off key.

For instance, Wheatley never mentioned that the first time Dennis Coleman asked for his help, he wanted to know what financial arrangements Dennis was prepared to make in exchange for that help, an omission Detective Cavanaugh, who conducted the interview, characterized in his report as "definite, calculated." Among other "calculated" omissions from Wheatley's statement were his failure to mention the substance of his conversations with Dennis Coleman the evening of the murder and his failure to mention what happened in his car just before Dennis left to "do the deed." Further, Cavanaugh was of the opinion that Wheatley deliberately lied when he said, "I did not know that Dennis was going to kill Mrs. Aparo that night."

He had his doubts, too, about Kira Lintner's claim that she knew nothing about what was going to happen, that all she knew was that "Chris asked me if I wanted to go for a ride. Chris said we were going to New York City. When I asked why, Chris said don't worry about it, he just had something to do, and Chris said, 'Just go with me.' '' As far as Cavanaugh was concerned, it was far more believable that Wheatley had told her all about it before and that she had heard a lot more about it while Dennis was in the car preparing to go off to the Aparo condo.

In fact, little in either statement went beyond, in general outline, what Cavanaugh and the other investigators already knew or surmised. About the only thing either one said that was new came from Kira Lintner. She said that Karin told her that when Dennis told her the precise time of Joyce's death, the time he read on the digital clock at her bedside, Karin was struck by a coincidence; she had been in the middle of sex with Alex Markov at the moment.

Lintner had something else to relate. She said that in the days after the murder in a discussion with Karin Aparo, which dealt in large measure with the murder, Karin said that she was going to ask, or maybe had already asked, Alex Markov to kill Dennis. (When the police asked Markov about that, he denied that any such thing had ever been proposed to him or that he would ever have considered it had it been.)

When Wheatley and Lintner were finished, Cavanaugh was enraged. The state had gotten nothing for its bargain, he felt, except deliberate and calculated omissions and some outright lies. As far as he was concerned, that was grounds to throw the plea bargain out, indict both of them for accessory to murder and proceed to prosecution. He would have liked nothing better. Wheatley, particularly, with his superior and flippant manner, had gotten to him from the first day they met up at Lake George. The more he learned about Wheatley and his role, the more convinced he became that the law ought to move against him. ''Of all the kids involved in this thing,'' Cavanaugh says, ''he was the worst. He had no excuse. He could have stopped the whole thing by just saying no. He didn't. He went along. And the only reason he did was for money.''

Just about everybody who knew anything about the

murder agreed. But they could only bridle with frustration. For the state had neglected to put into the plea bargain the little item saying that if Wheatley did not tell the truth and the whole truth, the bargain was void and he could be prosecuted as an accessory to murder. A bargain, even when one side has blundered in the making, is still a bargain.

Soon after signing those deal papers and making their statements, however incomplete, misleading and fudged, Wheatley and Lintner checked themselves into private psychiatric hospitals. During their stays their attorneys pressed State's Attorney Bailey to live up to the agreement, despite what misgivings he might have, and Cavanaugh and other law enforcement officials pressed just as hard to have Bailey throw it out. Reluctantly Bailey decided that he had no choice. At stake, he said, was the reputation of the state as a responsible and principled entity. "When you enter an agreement with us, it will be honored," he said. Otherwise, it would be a "breach of our promise of immunity."

Wheatley and Lintner were off the hook. In February 1988 all the murder-related charges against both were dropped. Kira Lintner was granted youthful offender status, and her case, on the charge of hindering prosecution and making false statements, was transferred to juvenile court. Behind closed doors a hearing was held, though the record was sealed. She could have been sent away for three years. She was not. She was freed on probation.

As for Wheatley, in the late summer of 1988 he was in court on that same relatively minor charge. He could have been sentenced to up to five years in prison. His lawyer told the court he was a responsible young man and the state would not be served by locking him up. What Wheatley should receive was what in Connecticut is called accelerated rehabilitation, meaning that in the year since the murder of Joyce Aparo, he had become a good citizen and was totally rehabilitated. Without objection from the state, which said it had no right to object, Wheatley was rehabilitated instantaneously and put on probation for two years, at the end of which his criminal record was to be erased.

There was a public outcry. The Hartford *Courant* spoke for many. In an editorial, entitled ''Getting Away with Murder?'' it wrote:

> Judge Quinn did not even order Mr. Wheatley to perform community service. He said the charge against the 20-year-old Glastonbury man was ''not of a serious nature.'' That may be true, but only because the judge never got to consider Mr. Wheatley's participation in planning and executing a murder. . . .
>
> A terrible crime was committed. Investigators believe Mr. Wheatley played a part in it. But there will be no determination of his guilt or innocence, nor will there be any record of his involvement if he completes his probationary period satisfactorily. That's not justice—for Mrs. Aparo or for Mr. Wheatley.

But nothing could change the court's decision. It stood. In September 1990 Christopher Wheatley, having done nothing wrong, having gone back to his studies after initially being expelled from his college, was a totally free man, his record wiped clean.

27

M. Hatcher Norris was faced with a very big problem. It was not just that he had taken on a client who had committed a particularly brutal murder. He had done that plenty of times over the previous decade, since going into private practice as a criminal lawyer. If the case went to trial, he almost always won; if the evidence was insurmountable, he was usually able to plea-bargain a sentence that was something less than onerous. But this client didn't seem to want to do anything to help himself or help Norris defend him, even though if the state wanted to get full measure, it could send him to prison for the next eighty years.

Dennis told him, yes, he had done the deed. Dennis related the details of the deed. Dennis told him about Chris

Wheatley and Kira Lintner. "I wasn't going to protect Chris," he said later. "He was already talking, and I was going to let him hang in the wind. I figured he could take care of himself." But beyond that he would not go.

Anything else Norris was finding out from Detective Cavanaugh and other investigators, whom he cultivated and who talked freely to him, though he would not let them talk to Dennis. From them he learned about all those letters from Karin to Dennis and from Dennis to Karin, he learned about Karin's diary for July 1987 and what it contained, he learned that suspicion had fallen on her.

He tried to talk to Dennis about this, but Dennis did not want to listen. And though the police were forbidden to talk to Dennis about the crime, about anything surrounding it, they made some hints. Dennis remembers an afternoon when he and Detective Revoir were sitting on the lawn in front of his house, waiting for the arrival of a search warrant, which Revoir had forgotten to bring with him. They were talking about baseball, about a few other things. "Then Revoir looked at me," Dennis says, "and he got a little serious, and he said, 'You know, kid, there's a big difference between love and obsession. Think about it.' "

"Initially," Norris says, "he didn't want to hear the truth about Karin. Yet to allow him to take the rap and protect her—I just couldn't do that. That's not doing much lawyering for your client, at least not in my book. We have obligations to give our clients the best defense and the best representation, and if you believe the client has deluded himself, you've got to bring him back to reality and say, 'This is the fact.' I got him out on bond, and as you can imagine, I told him, as any lawyer would, to stay away from her. But he calls her, and they make love that very night. So much for the control of a lawyer. It makes you feel rather insignificant. Obviously my words and my advice were not enough to overpower her influence and the way he felt about her."

So Norris had a meeting with Cavanaugh. If

Cavanaugh would come to his office and bring along that diary, Norris would have Dennis there and let him read it for the first time. Once he had read it, maybe he would see some light, and maybe he would finally tell not just what had happened but why things had happened, why he had done what he had. And Norris would have no objections to Dennis's making a statement.

On September 3 Dennis showed up at Norris's office, in a small house set a little way back from New London Turnpike in Glastonbury. Norris and Cavanaugh were waiting. The diary was handed to Dennis. Norris and Cavanaugh waited while he read it slowly. "This wasn't someone else sullying the reputation of Karin Aparo," Norris says. "This wasn't someone saying bad things about Karin. I don't think Dennis would have listened to anyone. It had to be in Karin's own hand. It had to be Karin who burst the bubble herself. As he read it, the tears just flowed down his face. Until that moment it had been inconceivable to him that Karin would ever do anything to harm him, that she would ever have set him up and that he might have been a victim of her."

When he finished reading, when he discovered at last that Karin had lied to him about the number of times she had slept with Alex Markov, that she had lied to him about her feelings for Alex Markov, that she had lied to him about her concern for him, that she had used him and taken advantage of him and then written about that in her diary, that all she had promised him was a fiction, that if the diary was what she really felt and believed, the murder itself had been without meaning, he was stricken, in shock. He looked at Norris, a plea in his eyes. The lawyer nodded encouragement. Dennis began to talk. He went back to the time he and Karin had met, talked about the summer of 1986, talked about the last weeks of July and beginning of August 1987 as he had lived them. When he stopped talking some days later, he had put Karin Aparo at the center of a conspiracy to murder, had made her its core and its reason. He gave

Cavanaugh, and John Bailey, what they wanted in detail, enough detail so that when added to what Shannon Dubois had already told them and what Chris Wheatley and Kira Lintner had given them, they could charge her with conspiracy to murder and accessory to murder.

What he also did was give his attorney something to bargain with. Not much, but something. Dennis was going to go to prison for a long time. No one doubted that; no one argued with that. The question was, How long? Would it be for the rest of his life, or would he someday, with some life still ahead of him, be free? Norris began to deal. If Dennis testified against Karin, and he would be the major witness, what was the state willing to give? The state, Bailey replied, would not ask for the maximum, would not ask that he be sent away for eighty years; that would mean, if Connecticut precedents were followed, he would have to serve at least forty before he was released. Rather, the state would recommend a prison term of forty-two years, meaning he could get out in about twenty.

Norris tentatively accepted. He kept some options open, though, by entering a not guilty plea at a preliminary hearing at the end of September. Had he entered a guilty plea, Dennis could have been sentenced immediately, or as soon as a probation report was compiled, and sent to the state penitentiary without delay. This way no one worried that free on the $150,00 bond, he was likely to run; he would have a little time before the steel doors slammed behind him and the long years of his youth vanished in the limbo of a cell and bars. "There was no rush," Norris said. "He was going away, no doubt about it. But I figured I'd try to keep him out as long as I could."

It was also to the advantage of the state at that moment, though it would never admit it, to have Dennis enter a not guilty plea, be still free, remain not convicted. As a witness against Karin, he might appear as a self-confessed killer, but he would not appear as a convicted one, which would cast ever more doubt on his credibility.

*   *   *

As he was doing his bargaining, as he was meeting often with Dennis, Reese Norris was a troubled man, and not only because of the impossibility of his client's situation.

There was something wrong, and it was not just that Dennis had committed a murder. It went beyond that. Norris sensed it the first time he sat down with Dennis over the dining-room table in the Coleman home and listened to his confession of murder. Dennis was calm; Dennis was forthcoming; Dennis was articulate. Yet something was missing; something just wasn't there. Norris didn't know what. But he was enough disturbed and confused by it to call Gerald Faris, a man with a Ph.D. in clinical psychiatry, an expert in the study of schizophrenic children, whose specialty was diagnosing, evaluating and treating personality disorders over the long term.

He asked Faris to see Dennis, but not necessarily to search out and discover some mental disease or defect that he might use as a defense. It was not his intention then to use an insanity defense when and if Dennis came to trial. For one thing, he had been in practice long enough to know that insanity defenses rarely work, that juries seem to have a built-in bias and skepticism when they are told that a defendant is not guilty because he didn't know what he was doing, that he didn't know right from wrong, that he couldn't help himself because of something in his psychological makeup. For another, there was the nature of the crime itself. It was horrifying, not a shooting or a stabbing in which the victim died in an instant, but a strangulation that took perhaps twenty minutes, minutes in which the victim struggled and suffered intolerably. Thus, even if a jury bought the diminished capacity idea, the details of the murder, when spelled out, would undoubtedly work against any leniency.

Norris sent Dennis to Faris because he wanted to know what, if anything, was wrong with Dennis and because he was convinced that if Dennis were to survive this horror and the nightmare years that lay ahead, he was going to need a lot of help. Faris was not a forensic specialist, a man used to dealing with people charged with crimes and looking for reasons that might be used in court, either for or against the defense, depending on who did the hiring. He had never even appeared in court as a witness before. He was simply a therapist who tried to deal with the problems afflicting his patients.

Faris saw Dennis for the first time a few weeks after his arrest, and he continued to see him at least once a week, usually more often, for the next two years and more. When Dennis arrived for his first session, Faris saw a pleasant, friendly, articulate, calm, matter-of-fact all-American boy. Yet, Faris said, he had the immediate feeling, which grew stronger session after session, that this was all surface and that the expressions of turmoil, intense feelings of rage, betrayal, guilt, self-hatred that began to emerge were only an inch beneath that surface, if not on the surface itself. Something was missing. It was all intellectualizing. And then, Faris said, he understood that inside, there was a blank. "Dennis was not blocking his feelings. Inside, he is empty and dead. His inner world is a dead and empty one." All that surface friendliness, everything that he revealed to the world "is an unconscious procedure he has learned from us. He hides. He almost has to appear typical."

They talked. "His whole mind," Faris said, "was on Karin. He talked about her constantly. No matter what the subject was, everything came around to Karin." Faris gave Dennis a battery of psychological tests. "Can you imagine taking an ink blot test and coming up with Karin no matter what? It's very difficult to do." But, then, Dennis told Faris, "Karin was more meaning than I was."

Karin might betray him, Karin might lie to him, but still, he came back to her. He needed her desperately, Faris said, "to fill in the blanks, to take away his sense of being dead. Are we talking about a mature concept of love? No, because mature love requires an integrated personality, and

Dennis was anything but.'' That was as apparent in his attachments to girls before Karin as it was with Karin, apparent in the fact that he never had crushes but always developed intense, clinging relationships from which he could not free himself without agony. ''It is very clear that Dennis lost himself in this relationship, and that was very easy for him to do. He was totally compliant and vulnerable because of the inner terror that gripped him.'' Thus a mere suggestion from Karin was enough to compel him to act in order not to lose her. ''She told him to enroll in college, and he did. If she had told him to go to Montana and raise sheep, he would have. If Karin had asked him to kill himself, there is no doubt in my mind that he would have done it.''

Faris was fascinated enough by what was unfolding in his treatment room to discuss the case and his diagnosis and to seek some advice from another expert. He called Dr. Rima Brauer, a psychoanalyst who often serves as a control and consultant to other analysts. It was not an unusual step, especially when one therapist is confronted by a difficult or an unusual situation. They talked often, Faris going over his notes in detail. Brauer confirmed his feelings.

Finally, both concluded that while Dennis knew what he was doing when he murdered Joyce Aparo, that while he was aware of the consequences, he had little choice. ''As summer wore on,'' Faris said, ''and it became clear to him that she would leave him if he didn't commit murder, it was do it or die. His will was subjugated to her. He lost any capacity to act of his own free will.'' He was, at the end, Faris said, ''the vehicle and not the driver'' or, as Brauer said, ''the gun and Karin pulled the trigger.''

It was not for more than a year, not until September 1988, that Reese Norris learned what the psychiatrists were thinking. It was then that Faris called to say that while he had agreed to take on this case only for the purpose of treating Dennis, he now thought it appropriate to tell the lawyer what he and Brauer had diagnosed. Dennis Coleman, they said, had a borderline personality disorder, he was an "as if" personality, as defined by Helene Deutsch.

Norris read up, thought a lot and then told the state's attorney and the court that he was amending Dennis's plea. He was now going to offer a psychological defense of his client, though he didn't tell John Bailey or James Thomas, who was handling the prosecution, that he still had no intention of going to trial. What he was hoping was that with such a defense the state might agree to a better deal. He was praying it would agree to a plea of manslaughter, which would mean a maximum of a twenty-year sentence, with Dennis out in ten. He hoped, but he knew that wasn't a very realistic hope. Still, maybe he could win the state to agree to something less than forty-two years.

28

I n Hartford Hubert Santos was trying to frame a defense for his client, Karin Aparo. It was not an easy job. The public perception of her had hardened; she was, in the phrase repeated widely, a girl with no heart, a vicious, unfeeling, sexually promiscuous teenager who for some unknown reason had manipulated a nice, popular, all-American boy into murdering her mother and then had turned on him.

Reese Norris had done a good job in swaying opinion toward sympathy for Dennis and antipathy toward Karin. Norris, with nothing to lose, since there was no argument over his client's guilt or that Dennis was going to prison for what he had done, and fond of publicity anyway, gave interviews, on and off the record, articulating Dennis's story and reasons.

Santos kept his silence, as was his way. A onetime public defender, once corporation counsel for the city of Hartford, in private practice since 1974, he was widely considered one of the best and most expensive criminal lawyers in Connecticut, his retainers in important cases ranging upward of a hundred thousand dollars. He is an unprepossessing, rather ungainly man in his mid-forties, about six feet tall, though his perpetual slouch, sometimes with shoulders hunched, sometimes with stomach thrust forward, makes him appear shorter. His trousers are usually a little too long and baggy; his jackets, rumpled and just a trifle ill-fitting. It appears to be a deliberate costume, designed to enhance an image of the common man little concerned with clothes or other material things. His graying, thinning hair is close-cropped in a manner more appropriate to another era. He wears his spectacles low on his nose and often takes them off when he reads, takes them off and waves them to make a point. On his round, pleasant face there is invariably a slightly whimsical or sometimes a skeptical expression, and that can be heard in his orator's voice. He tends to be overdramatic, can be rambling, sometimes seems indecisive and uncertain, occasionally looks toward judge, jury, spectators for what seems to be help, as though he had lost himself. It is all a piece of the manner in which he has garbed himself, as is his willingness to try the unorthodox, if he thinks there is a chance it might work. What stands out as much as anything is a passionate devotion to the defense of his clients, and in that defense he will risk the anger of a judge by overstepping the bounds of courtroom propriety, doing so as if by accident, as if the heat of the moment had caused the slip, though again one senses that he does so with a certain calculation and deliberateness. In the courtroom all his devices and techniques come together, and by the end of a trial he emerges as the most commanding and dominating figure on the scene. He has won victories when causes seemed hopeless. People said that for what Santos did, his fees, no matter how high, were low. If you could afford him, he was the man to get.

Karin Aparo got him. Meeting his fee was not much of a problem. Her mother's estate, more than three hundred thousand dollars, to which she was the sole heir, remained in limbo as long as she was under indictment for her mother's murder, and she would lose all rights to it if she were convicted since under the law one cannot profit by a crime. But there was a way around this. Karin waived all rights to her mother's estate. It then devolved on the next of kin, Joyce's mother, Karin's grandmother. An arrangement was made whereby once the grandmother, Rose Cantone, had come into the proceeds, she agreed to simply send the money to pay Karin's legal costs and other expenses. It might be shading the intent of the law, but it was strictly legal. Ironically, Joyce Aparo's money was going to pay for the defense of the daughter charged with her murder.

That defense was not without its problems. For one thing, there was that public perception of Karin, so masterfully orchestrated by Norris. Nothing could be done about that. Even if Karin decided to tell her side, it might have little effect; it was too late, and the damage was already done. Besides, telling it could well dissipate the impact it might have when and if she came to trial. And it seemed certain that one day she would stand trial. Santos made a calculated decision. It was time to stop all the leaks, all the rumors, all the distortions. He asked the court to institute a gag order, preventing anyone involved in the case—the prosecution and its witnesses, the defense and its—from saying anything in public, to the press or anyone. The court agreed. The gag order went into effect. It didn't stop the rumors and speculations, didn't stop the press from recapitulating what was already on the record, but it sealed the lips of those who had once been so free with anyone who approached.

In private Karin was insisting to Santos and to those close to her that she was innocent. She had never asked, or begged, Dennis Coleman to murder her mother. She had not even been in or near the condo when the murder was committed; she had been far away, in Rowayton.

As the evidence in its possession grew to what seemed ever more damaging proportions, the state made a decision. It was sure that if the case went to trial, it would win a conviction on all the counts of the indictment: accessory to murder and a two-pronged conspiracy to murder, one conspiracy beginning in the summer of 1986 and extending to August 5, 1987, and the second and overlapping one beginning on or about July 15, 1987, and extending to the day of the murder. But trials are expensive and time-consuming. The state dropped hints that it might be willing to offer a deal if Santos were ready to listen. Any good lawyer is always ready to hear what the other side has to offer, so Santos asked just what the state had in mind. If Karin pleaded guilty, he was told, she would be sentenced to fourteen years. That meant she would be out of prison in about seven; she would still be young, in her twenties, and would have most of her life ahead of her.

On its face it seemed an irresistible offer. Santos urged her to accept. Santos's law partner urged her to accept. Others urged her to accept. They argued with her, implored her, tried to convince her it was the best way. Karin adamantly refused. She was innocent, she proclaimed, so why should she have to go to prison? She would stand trial, and she would be acquitted.

So that was out; there would be no deal. Santos had to maneuver in other directions. He explored a dozen. Because the first prong of the alleged conspiracy had begun when she was fifteen, she should be tried as a youthful offender, not as an adult. It was an argument that on its face had considerable merit. But the court thought not enough, that the nature of the crime, murder, overrode the fact that one part of the conspiracy had begun when she was, under law, a juvenile. Besides, there was the second part of the indictment, accessory to murder. She had been sixteen, an adult for purposes of the law, when the murder took place. Therefore, she was not entitled to be treated as a youthful offender. Santos appealed and appealed, and lost and lost.

He asked that she be granted accelerated rehabilitation and put on probation, citing the example of Christopher Wheatley, and in a hearing he brought her aunt and uncle and teachers and others who knew her, and had known Joyce, to ask that his petition be granted. The court listened and then said no.

He asked for a change of venue, claiming, with some justification, that because of all the publicity, so much of it adverse to his client, it would be impossible to pick an unbiased jury and give her a fair trial in Hartford. His motion was denied.

He took other tacks, every one he could think of, every precedent he could find in the lawbooks. He lost them all.

So there would be a trial, and he would have to prepare. And he would have to formulate a defense when that day came. Like Norris, he turned to the psychiatrists for help. Only, unlike Norris, he did not seek shrinks who specialized in treatment and were strangers to the courts. Santos went to men who knew their way around the legal system and whose opinions he could use when the day came that he needed them. He went to forensic specialists.

Those two experts were the psychologist John Cigalis and the psychiatrist Walter Borden. They interviewed her, talked with her, listened to her and gave her a battery of psychological tests. And then they reported their findings.

Though Karin, in Cigalis's opinion, was "cold, unemotional, stand-offish, anxious, hypervigilant, mildly paranoid, overly controlled in feelings, very difficult to relate to on a personal level," though "she was extremely angry, to the point of homicidal wishes toward her mother" and though she suffered from a variety of borderline personality disorders, she was telling the truth when she said,

"I did not assist Dennis Coleman in the murder of my mother," and was in no way involved in the murder.

Borden agreed. All her actions, all those letters before and after the murder, even her sleeping with Dennis twice following the murder, all of which to the layman might seem consistent with involvement and guilt, were actually consistent with her psychological profile as a battered child. She slept with Dennis, wrote to him, called him after the murder, Borden said, and Cigalis seconded, not because she was part of the plot but because she felt a certain degree of responsibility: Joyce and Dennis would never have met had it not been for her, and if they had not met, there would have been no murder. But, Borden insisted, she had actually played no role in the murder.

Neither Cigalis nor Borden, though, made any mention, if they even knew, of the crises that were overwhelming mother and daughter in July 1987—the imminent departure of Joyce's favored Alex Markov and the more important departure of Karin's violin—and what effect those crises may have had on the events that ensued. But they both were uncompromising in their view that on the basis of everything they had learned about her, through interviews and psychological tests, Karin had told them the truth and she was not guilty.

Before the trial was to begin, with those reports in hand, Santos filed notice that he might, just might, rely on a psychiatric defense. He wasn't sure, but he wanted to be on record that he was holding that option open.

With that notice the state had the right to bring in its own psychiatric experts to examine Karin and offer their opinions, to counter Cigalis and Borden. It decided not to exercise that right.

Psychiatry, of course, is an inexact science. Nowhere is it more inexact than in dealing with criminal cases. There the psychiatrists are ubiquitous. Some are employed by the state and some for the defense, and invariably they come up

with conflicting opinions, reflecting the positions their em-
ployers hold. The state's experts say the defendant knew
precisely what he or she was doing and was completely sane
and responsible for the act. The defense's experts say, not
so. The defendant didn't do the deed and played no part in
its doing, or suffered from such severe mental defects or
emotional disturbance as to be unaware of what was being
done and of the consequences, or was unable to control
himself or herself from doing the deed and so was not
responsible for it.

Nowhere was this dichotomy more clearly evident than
in this case. Dr. Faris and Dr. Brauer said Dennis acted only
because of Karin's manipulation of and control over him.
Dr. Cigalis and Dr. Borden said, nonsense, Dennis did it on
his own, and Karin played no part. A state-appointed psychiatrist concluded after examining Dennis briefly that he
was perfectly sane and normal and knew precisely what he
was doing. He offered no opinion about Karin's role. But
then neither he nor any expert on the state's side talked to
her.

One was left to wish only that somehow Cigalis and
Borden had spent time with Dennis Coleman, that Faris and
Brauer had spent time with Karin Aparo and then that
Cigalis, Borden, Faris and Brauer had spent time together,
comparing notes, arguing, listening—an idle and futile
dream, on a par, perhaps, with Joyce Aparo's fantasies.

29

Trial dates came, and trials were postponed, and so trial dates passed, and the cases against Dennis Coleman and Karin Aparo dragged on inconclusively for more than two years. It was as though no one wanted to bring either of them to final judgment, as though no one wanted to write a finish to this tragedy.

Dennis remained free on bond. He did not go to college as he had once planned. He got a motorcycle, and he roared around Glastonbury, his red hair flying, a sight to be recognized and pitied. He kept his appointments with Dr. Faris. He was in and out of Reese Norris's office. He worked on his model house, carefully shaving shingles, adding to it slowly. He wandered often through the woods behind his father's home, creating campsites, carving trails, spending long hours in loneliness. He spent time with old friends, who had returned to him in this time of trouble. He played a few gigs with his rock group. He took a trip now and then just to get away for a few days. John Bailey remembers a summer evening when he and his wife were vacationing on Martha's Vineyard. They were in a bistro when he felt someone staring at him. He looked up. On a balcony, eyes focused on him, was Dennis Coleman. Dennis tried drugs, smoking marijuana, taking cocaine, LSD, more, was stoned every day, trying to blot out the memories of what had happened and what would happen. And he waited.

One day late in the fall of 1987 he took a large box and went to his room and slowly took from his walls all the photographs and all the memorabilia of his time with Karin Aparo. He put everything into that box, which he took and stored in the attic. His room suddenly looked a lot larger and a lot barer.

Karin Aparo, too, waited, tried to create a new life for herself. In September 1987 she went back to Glastonbury High School, to begin her junior year. She remained only a few days. The cruelty of those who knew her, who knew about her was unbearable. She left. She transferred to a high school in Hartford where nobody knew her, though many knew about her. She was anonymous. She rarely saw the people who had been friends with her mother and with her, Michael Zaccaro, Jeff Sands, and others. She lived for a time with the woman who had taken care of her when she was small, Jill Smith. It did not work out. Smith was something of a spiritualist, sometimes held séances in her home. She was persuaded that Karin had brought evil vibrations into her home. She asked Karin to leave. Karin found an apartment for herself in the south end of Hartford. She got a part-time job in a bank; she did well, and the people liked her there, though initially they were a little leery. She gave up the violin and talked more about a career as a psychologist, a psychiatrist, even as a nursing home administrator. She planned to go to college when she graduated from high school, first to Central Connecticut and then, when everything was finished and when she was free, as she was convinced she would be, to Yale or some other good university. She, too, waited.

After their last meeting, that trip to Mystic and Dennis's father's boat in the week he got out of jail, Dennis and Karin did not see each other again until January. Then it was in court. The state of Connecticut some years earlier had abandoned the grand jury system as the way to hand down indictments. Instead, it has instituted what it calls probable cause hearings, held in open court during which the state lays out the outlines of its case, calls enough witnesses and presents enough evidence to show there is probable cause to bring the defendant to trial. Karin's probable cause hearing was held on January 5, 1988, in a small courtroom on the third floor of the pedestrian-modern criminal court building in Hartford, a three-story structure. To the rear of the first floor, across a hall from each other, are the offices of the state's attorney and of the public defender. In the center of the building is an atrium that rises from ground to ceiling. On the second and third floors, ringing the atrium, are the courtrooms; those on the third floor are reserved for jury trials, sentencings, major arraignments and important hearings. The courtrooms are small, holding fewer than a hundred people. They have no windows, only stark brick walls and light-colored benches and carpets.

"I came up the steps into the hallway outside the courtroom," Dennis says, "and she was standing there. It was the first time I'd seen her. And I didn't care what she did, I still loved her. I thought in the months before that I hated her, but everything came into balance then, and I still loved her. I sat up there on the witness stand, and I testified against her, and when I looked at her, I knew I still loved her."

The court heard Dennis and Shannon and the police and a few others, and it decided there was probable cause to bring Karin Aparo to trial.

30

Then no more delays were possible. In the fall of 1989 it was announced that trials would be held before the end of the year, first Karin's and then Dennis's. The last thing Norris wanted, naturally, was a jury trial for Dennis, a trial at which, despite whatever psychiatric testimony he might bring in as mitigation, all the details of the strangling would be spelled out. But neither did he want Dennis to go to prison for forty-two years. He met with Bailey and prosecutor Thomas. They discussed and argued and finally came to an agreement. If Dennis would change his plea to guilty, the state would not hold him to the terms of the original compact: that he accept those forty-two years. A hearing on the sentence would be held in open court. Norris could present whatever evidence he wanted, could, in essence, present what would have been the defense in a trial. He could ask the judge to impose a lesser sentence, but no less than thirty years. The state would still ask for forty-two years. It would be up to the judge to make the final determination.

Just before Thanksgiving the hearing began. It lasted three days, with one break for the holiday and then another while Judge Raymond Norko considered what he had heard and what he should do. Norris was given latitude, and he used it. He spent a day with Detective Cavanaugh, who testified to all he had discovered about the crime and the relationship between Dennis and Karin. He spent another day eliciting testimony from Shannon, Kira Lintner, and his two psychiatrists, Faris and Brauer. Then it was up to Norko. He was to announce his decision on Tuesday, November 28.

On Monday Dennis tried to prepare. It was to be the last night he would spend in his father's house, in his own room, in his own bed. It was to be his last night of freedom. He left the house early in the afternoon and wandered through the woods, stopping at the campsites he had carved out, following the trails he had created. It was dark by the time he returned home. He went to bed early.

On Tuesday morning, just after ten, he was back in court. He was dressed neatly in a dark suit. He wore a dark raincoat over it. His red hair was neatly combed. His face was too thin, thinner than it had ever been, almost hawk-like. It had no expression, no show of emotions. His eyes appeared lifeless, hopeless. With him were his father, mother, stepmother and brother. They all looked lost and helpless, stricken, especially Dennis's mother, on the edge of collapse. With him, too, was a tall, attractive blond girl. Her name was Margaret. Matthew Coleman had met her in New Haven a few months before and brought her home because, she said, she wanted to meet his brother, Dennis. It was something that happens often in notorious murder cases: the sudden appearance of young girls attracted to the murderer, for one reason or another. From then on she rarely let Dennis out of her sight. Some of his friends thought she was manipulating him just as Karin had. She said she was in love with him and he was in love with her and they planned to marry.

Norris spoke eloquently for Dennis, castigated Karin for enslaving Dennis, for taking away his will and giving him no option but to "do the deed" or die. He noted that Dennis had cooperated with the state and would be a major witness in the "final act of this tragedy" when he testified against Karin. Dennis had to pay for his crime, yes, but how much should he be asked to pay, considering all that the court now knew? The minimum sentence in Connecticut for murder was twenty-five years in prison. Norris asked the court to send Dennis away for thirty years. If he served even two thirds of that time, not unusual in the state, "he will be my age when he gets out. He will have lost the best years of his life." But, Norris added, no matter what the sentence, Dennis's file should be flagged to alert the prison authorities that he required special ongoing psychiatric treatment. Further, he was very concerned about Dennis's safety. He ought not to be sent to the state's maximum security prison at Somers, an overcrowded place inhabited by hard-core career criminals, where violence was the rule rather than the exception. Some better, more fitting place should be found for Dennis, someplace where his life would not be in danger and his many talents could be put to use profitably.

Jim Thomas spoke for the state. The crime, he said, "was murder, pure and simple." Dennis had acted with intent, and he had known what he was doing. His explanations of why and all the opinions of the psychiatrists didn't mitigate what he had done. "It is easy to look at him and feel some mercy, but there was no mercy for Joyce Aparo. This is a horrendous, horrific case. It is a brutal, brutal case. The state asks for the maximum under the bargain it made with the defendant, a sentence of forty-two years. Any sentence less severe will not serve the people of the state of Connecticut.''

Then Judge Norko, a tall, burly, balding blond man who bore a remarkable resemblance to the football quarterback Terry Bradshaw, who had been a public defender before going on the bench, looked down at Dennis. He seemed as stricken as anyone. He noted that he had been the judge who arraigned Dennis on August 14, 1987. ''You and I,'' he said, ''made eye contact that day, and I cannot forget it.''

A few nights before, Judge Norko had been reading a mystery story in bed before going to sleep. He came across a passage that burned in his mind, a passage he paraphrased as ''No crime is so detestable as a murder. It contaminates and pollutes all the lives it touches, and no one can ever be the same again.''

This case, he said, was especially disturbing. Dennis was not a child of poverty, nor were any of the others involved. They all were children of the middle class. Yet he had listened to some of them testify, and ''watching them sent chills up my spine. They spoke of murder as if it were a candy bar to be reached on a shelf. Why none of your friends tried to reach out and stop this tragedy is beyond me. Why did they let you do it? Why there was no parent, no educator, no one in the church, no one in the community you could turn to I'll never know.''

He shook his head. One could see tears glistening in his eyes as he said, ''When I sentence you, part of me goes with you. I don't forget I'm sending you to Somers, probably one of the most dangerous places on earth. I've wrestled about this, slept on it, woke on it. Everyone would agree whatever I do to you, I'm throwing away your youth. Indeed, I accept Mr. Norris's recommendation that we find a better and more suitable place for you than Somers.''

He looked at Dennis, seated beside Norris, staring intently at the judge. ''Dennis,'' he said, ''resolve to yourself to survive and come out and become a citizen like the rest of us. Don't lose all hope. There are peers of yours who should go to jail. But I can't do anything about those agreements that they made with the state. Now, before I pass sentence, do you have anything you wish to say to the court?''

Dennis rose slowly. He stood rigid and looked at Norko. He spoke in a very low, soft voice. "If I could turn back time, I would. I'm not a cold-blooded person, and this was not cold-blooded. It was the opposite. It was passion. I felt very much like it was a choice between committing suicide or committing murder. I can't tell you how much I regret it.''

That was all. He stood there, Norris standing beside him. Norko looked down at papers before him. He looked back at Dennis. He shook his head. The back of one hand wiped across his eyes. And then he passed sentence: for the murder of Joyce Aparo, thirty-four years in state prison, for conspiracy to commit murder, twenty years in state prison, the sentences to run concurrently. "Dennis,'' he concluded, "do what you can. Use your mind to survive up there. There is hope.''

Two deputies moved quickly to Dennis, one on either side. They marched him out through a side door in the courtroom. A few hours later he was in a prison van on his way to the state penitentiary at Somers.

31

The trial of Karin Aparo was supposed to begin a few weeks later. It didn't. It was rescheduled for early January 1990. It was postponed again. It was scheduled for late spring. Santos asked for another delay. He had another case to try in New London that would take most of the summer. Would the court agree to reset the date for the Aparo trial in early fall? Judge Thomas Corrigan made a phone call to the court in New London. That trial was put off.

Finally, in late April, the time had come for Karin Aparo to face and be judged by her peers. Court convened on the third floor of the criminal court building in Hartford, diagonally across the atrium from the courtroom in which Dennis Coleman had spent his last moments of freedom five months before. The first order of business, perhaps as important as any, was the picking of the twelve men and women and the alternates who were the ultimate judges of the facts. Santos estimated it would take him at least a month to find a panel that could hear this case without bias. What he did not want, he said, were jurors who lived in cocoons, who isolated themselves from the world and knew nothing about anything. He wanted an intelligent group, he said, men and women who were concerned about events around them but whose opinions were not forged in cement, who could listen to the evidence with open minds and make independent judgments. It would not be easy to find such jurors, considering all the publicity that had surrounded the murder, and though he still thought that he should have gotten a change of venue, that the trial should have been held in some other part of the state, in Stamford, say, he would try.

He tried. He succeeded. And as he had guessed, it took him nearly a month before he had a jury of the kind he wanted, the kind he hoped to get or perhaps the best he could hope for: eight men, several in their thirties, a few older, and four middle-aged women. Most were white, and they were a cross section of the area's middle class. Santos was satisfied.

Jim Thomas, the prosecutor, didn't seem to care much. On the state's attorney's staff for a dozen years, about six feet, a little thick in the middle, dark hair immaculately groomed, though it grew shaggy as the trial went on, his mustache neatly trimmed, he was an orderly, unexcitable man with a reputation for preparing well, though with little flair for courtroom dramatics. He was supremely confident, certain that he had a case he could not lose, that any jury, once it had heard the evidence he would present, could come to only one verdict. His major concern, he told someone, was overkill. He was not going to parade scores of witnesses before the jurors to recite variations on the same stories, the same details over and over again, and perhaps bore the jury and even turn it against him and the state. He wanted to lay out the evidence rapidly and tellingly, with as little redundancy as possible. It was a surprising game plan to many who heard it. Overkill is a thing most prosecutors fear not at all; the more witnesses telling the same story, the better, for it makes those stories and details impregnable. If judges, defense counsel, spectators and even jurors get tired of hearing the same evidence from a dozen different mouths, get bored, begin to know what the witnesses will say even before they say it, so much the better. Most prosecutors will pile the evidence on with the trowel, will call a halt, and then reluctantly, only when a judge tells them, enough, it's not necessary to hear that story again.

The jury, one to which Santos had few objections and about which Thomas did not seem much concerned, was finally in place and ready to hear testimony at ten in the morning on Monday, May 21, 1990. The jurors peered with interest at the defendant, some of the younger men on the jury with what seemed more than passing interest. The Karin Aparo who sat at the defense table across the well of the court was hardly the same Karin Aparo who had been arrested nearly three years before. Then she had been sixteen, a teenager with short dark hair, a little plump, the plumpness accentuated by tight jeans and tight jacket. Then her manner had been arrogant and self-confident; then her face had borne an expression of superiority. Now she was nineteen, and in the intervening years she had been groomed and coached well by Santos and his legal assistant, Hope Seeley, and others. Now she was a slight, almost fragile young woman, who sometimes looked about twelve. Now she wore long, loose print skirts, white blouses and flowered sweaters or long, flowing dresses. Now she wore little makeup and large, nearly rimless glasses that covered much of her face. Now her hair was long, partly gathered in a ponytail held by a large white ribbon tied in a huge bow at the back of her head. Now she seemed vulnerable, even a little frightened, biting her lower lip often, her smile, which

came now and then, nervous. She was the picture of innocence. Miss Goody-Two-Shoes, somebody called her.

Thomas began, as prosecutors must, by calling witnesses to prove that a crime had been committed, that Joyce
Aparo was dead and had been murdered. There was Dr. Peter
Adams, the Massachusetts medical examiner, who did the
autopsy on the body of Joyce Aparo, to testify that she was
killed by "ligature strangulation." In cross-examination
Santos tried to suggest that Joyce had been raped or had had
sex before her death, something nobody before had ever suggested. Adams would have none of it.

There was Police Chief Peter Brulotte, beside whose
house in Bernardston the car was found.

There were Glastonbury police officers who told about
their initial investigations, the searches of the Aparo condominium, how they had sealed it once they learned of the
murder, who talked of their initial meeting with Karin and
her lack of reaction to the news her mother was dead.

There was Charles Revoir of the state police, the only
member of the major crimes squad to appear; Thomas decided not to call James Cavanaugh, who had headed the
investigation for the state police, or any of the other state
cops who had conducted separate and overlapping investigations into a dozen or more areas, who had roamed from
the hills of New Hampshire to the lakes of upstate New
York to Fairfield County and into Manhattan and beyond in
search of leads, in search of evidence. Cavanaugh had since
retired; besides, the prosecutor thought one state cop was
enough. Why inundate the jury with repetition or with testimony that might not seem relevant? Revoir appeared not
once but several times, to tell how the investigation was
conducted, to tell of how Karin had turned the "I will 'do
the deed' " note over to him and Cavanaugh, of how she
had come to them the night of her mother's funeral with
Dennis's confession, and a lot more, until the day he arrested her.

There was the Glastonbury police secretary, Beverly

Warga, to relate the conversations she had overheard, the phone call from Karin to Dennis and then their discussions in her office when they were returned for more questioning that first night.

There was a security agent from the telephone company to read into the record the number of calls between the Markov residence in Rowayton and the Tallwoods Country Club in Hebron and the Coleman home in Glastonbury on August 5.

There was Michael Zaccaro, to talk about Karin's actions those first days, of the discovery of Dennis's note, of how he and Jeff Sands had gone with her to the police when she related Dennis's confession, and to discuss his own role as executor of Joyce's estate. It was during Santos's cross-examination that the first signs of a possible defense arose, as he questioned Zaccaro about Joyce's penchant for inventing stories, particularly about Karin's brilliance as a violinist. And it was then that another element entered.

"Did you know if Mrs. Aparo permitted Karin to attend church?" Santos asked.

"We never talked about that," Zaccaro replied.

"You knew that Mrs. Aparo was a Roman Catholic?"

"Yes."

"Did you see religious articles in the condo when you were cleaning it out?"

"Yes. When we were cleaning it out, we found a replica of a bishop's hat in the nightstand in Joyce's bedroom."

"At Mrs. Aparo's funeral, did any priest preside?"

Before Zaccaro could answer, Thomas was on his feet with a sharp objection. Judge Corrigan sustained it.

John Whealon's name had not yet entered the record. But it was apparent that Santos was going to keep trying to get it in and that before the end of the trial he would find a way. That there had been some kind of relationship between the archbishop and Joyce Aparo was, at that moment, something of an emerging secret, though becoming more open all the time. Those involved with the case were well aware of stories and the rumors, as were many people around the courthouse and most members of the media. But word was only just beginning to leak beyond those confines to the general public. Santos was determined that before he was done, the rumors would have wide currency, would be known by anyone who bothered to read a newspaper or listen to the news on radio or television. They would be, if not the opening wedge, certainly a central element in his defense, in the portrait he planned to paint of Karin as a child abused beyond measure, not merely physically but, more important, psychologically, by a pathological mother. What could be more devastating to a Catholic child than tales that her mother had had an affair with a priest? He would accomplish this by trying to bring that priest's name to the surface with questions to any and every prosecution witness who might have some knowledge. He repeated his question to Detective Revoir: "Did a priest preside at the funeral of Joyce Aparo?" Thomas objected before Revoir could answer, and the objection was sustained. When Karin's onetime friend Lori DeLucca was called to testify about Karin's behavior at the funeral and about her observations of Karin and Dennis at the Duboises' house later, Santos once again asked about a priest at the funeral. Another objection sustained. Every time he posed a question relating to the priest, Thomas objected, and Corrigan sustained the objection. It became clear that if Santos were to succeed, he would have to do so with his own witnesses during the defense case.

Still, he got some unexpected help in spreading the word and preparing the public at large for what was to come. The evening before Zaccaro's appearance, this writer appeared on a local television news show. The show's producer asked if I had heard the rumors about Whealon and Joyce. I had. She asked if I might find some way to air them. She and a lot of others, she said, were very tired of the way the newspapers and television and radio stations were hushing this thing up. It was time to get the stories into the open and let Whealon or others have the opportunity to respond. During the program I responded to a question by saying I had heard the rumors from a great many people and had no way of knowing if they were true, but to me the importance lay not in whether they were true but in the effect such stories told to her by her mother must have had on Karin Aparo all through her life. There was, naturally, an immediate and angry response, a torrent of phone calls to the station from outraged listeners. Santos, though, was not upset. The next morning he had a wink and a broad smile when he saw me.

On the fourth day of testimony, at just before three in the afternoon, Dennis Coleman was called to the witness stand. The courtroom was packed. Among the spectators was Dennis's brother, Matt, who had left Connecticut within hours of Dennis's sentencing and gone to the West Coast and had recently returned. With him was Margaret, proclaiming that she and Dennis were now engaged and planning to marry if and when the state gave them permission. There were crowds lined up outside the entrance hoping for a seat, hoping that someone would leave so they could enter.

Dennis Coleman was much changed from the moment at the end of November, when he was marched out of a nearby courtroom to go to prison. The six months had not been good to him. His hair was longer and fuller. He had grown a mustache, red like his hair, perhaps in an effort to make himself look older. It didn't help. He had put on weight, had filled out some, but there was a puffiness, a flabbiness about his face. And his eyes were lifeless, devoid of anything. He was wearing a white shirt, open at the neck, and black pants, gathered at the cuffs. He was imprisoned now not at the maximum security facility in Somers but at the correctional center in Hartford a few miles from the courthouse, a jail used mainly to house prisoners waiting for trial, waiting for sentence, waiting to be sent somewhere more permanent, serving short terms. He had been moved in anticipation of his testimony, to have him at easier access to the courthouse than Somers, nearly an hour's drive to the north. But he had been moved for another reason. He wrote to a friend a few weeks after his arrival at Somers that things were not as bad as he had expected. The other convicts were pretty much leaving him alone, he was not being hassled and he expected that it would work out. He was wrong. He was different from most of the other prisoners. For one thing, he was white; for another, he was middle-class; for yet another, his had not been a crime growing out of poverty, out of need. Within a few more weeks he was the target of the other convicts, particularly the hard-core, violence-prone inmates. He was assaulted and beaten, for reasons known only to those who beat him. His arm was broken. He was battered. And then he was threatened. The word spread that he was going to testify for the state against Karin Aparo. It mattered not that he had good reason to testify against her. By testifying, the reasoning held, he was siding with the state, and at Somers it was always us against them, the cons against the state. He was, then, a traitor or worse. If he testified, he was told, he would be killed. So he was moved to Hartford, for the state's convenience and for his protection.

He entered the courtroom with his wrists overlapped in front of him, as though he were manacled. Karin watched him from the moment he appeared through a side door. She could not take her eyes off him. He glanced at her, then quickly looked away. Over the next hours, as she stared at him, he looked at her and then away in a moment. Their eyes rarely met.

He was on the witness stand for five days. He had been coached well by Reese Norris and Jim Thomas, and he told his story—from his meeting with Karin through the murder of Joyce and beyond—fluently and, it seemed to most observers, with conviction and convincingly, though in a voice rarely tinged with emotion. As he came to the moment of the murder, as he described how he strangled Joyce Aparo, Karin began to weep. There was a brief recess so she could gather herself. Then, as he picked up the details and proceeded through them, she put her head on the defense table, and her body shook with deep sobs. There was another recess. (Later, when the jury, during deliberations, asked for this testimony to be reread, she broke down again at those precise points.)

"Why," Thomas asked as he concluded his direct examination, "are you testifying against Karin?"

"I had my story to tell," Dennis said. "It was the right thing to do, considering all the circumstances."

"Have your feelings toward Karin changed?"

"Yes, but not in a single day."

"What are your feelings toward her now?"

"Well," Dennis said, "for a long time after I'd been found out . . ." He shook his head, not finishing his thought. Then: "Today, more or less my feelings are apathy, not hate."

It was Hubert Santos's turn at him now. Santos struck in a dozen different directions. He asked about the deal Dennis made with the state so that his sentence would be reduced from a possible eighty years to thirty-four. "And the board of pardons can reduce that sentence to whatever it wants, correct?"

"I believe so," Dennis said.

"And you can appeal to the board of pardons to have that sentence reduced after you serve four years, and you can make such appeals every year after that, isn't that right?"

"Yes."

"And you intend to do that."

"I most certainly do."

Santos turned in another direction. "Do you believe in God?"

"Yes."

"Did you ever tell people that you were an agnostic?"

"Yes. Many people. That was true at the time. It's not true anymore."

"And when did you find God?"

"In January."

Dennis did not say how he found belief then, nor did Santos ask. Santos's point was to say that if Dennis did not believe in God, then his oath to tell the truth, "so help me God," was meaningless.

"Why," Santos asked, a question to which he returned again and again, "did you murder Joyce Aparo?"

"There were many, many reasons. It all really comes down to that Karin said it had to be done."

"Was that the sole reason?"

"There were many factors. But it all comes to that."

"She asked you to do it?"

"No, she begged me."

"There was no other reason? What about the life insurance?"

"The life insurance was not my concern. That was Karin's reason. We were going to split the money and live in the condo. But the insurance had nothing to do with my motivation."

"When you murdered Joyce Aparo, did you have suicidal thoughts?"

"They were not suicidal thoughts. They provided an alternative. The choice was suicide or murder."

"Was it a cold-blooded murder?"

"No. It was not cold-blooded. It was a crime of passion. It was for Karin and for life. It was not against Joyce. I liked Joyce Aparo."

"Did you ever express a dislike of Joyce Aparo to Karin?"

"I may have."

"Did you ever tell Karin that you considered her mother unstable?"

"Yes."

"That you considered her self-centered?"

"Yes."

"That you considered her ignorant?"

"Yes."

"That you considered her close-minded?"

"Yes."

"What opinion did she have of you?"

"I don't know. She never expressed anything to me but a good opinion. All I knew about what she felt was told to me by Karin."

"Did you go out with Joyce Aparo socially in the summer of 1987 when Karin was in Rowayton?"

"Occasionally."

"Did you have conversations with her? And did those conversations center around Karin?"

"Mostly about Karin, yes."

"Did she tell you that Karin was having a good time in her relationship with the Markov family?"

"She may have."

"What did they center on, these conversations?"

"Karin's future, mainly."

"Did that future include you?"

"No."

"Did it bother you that Karin was with Alex Markov?"

"Yes, it did."

"Did you have a good time when you were with Mrs. Aparo?"

"Yes. It was pleasant."

Santos turned to the reason why Dennis had finally agreed in September 1987 to cooperate with the police and tell his story about Karin's involvement. "Is it not the real reason that you decided to cooperate because you looked at

Karin's last diary entry and then you were informed that she
wanted to get rid of both you and her mother? When you
heard that, you wanted to kill yourself?''

"Yes, briefly."

"And kill Karin?"

"Yes, briefly."

"On August third, you went into the Aparo condo?"

"Yes."

"Did you go into Karin's room?"

"Yes."

"Did you see pictures on her dresser?"

"Yes."

"Of her with Alex Markov?"

"Some with, some without."

"You knew that she kept diaries and papers in her
bedside table in a drawer. You opened the drawer and held
the diary. You read it, and you learned the number of times
she had sex with Alex Markov. Isn't that true?"

"I did not read the diary."

"Well, were you read the last page of the diary before
you agreed to cooperate?"

"Portions of it."

"What part?"

"That she had sex with Alex Markov twenty-six
times."

"And you said you murdered Joyce Aparo out of love
for Karin?''

"Yes."

Just what kind of love Dennis had for Karin was
Santos's next tack. "You were in love with her throughout
the relationship?"

"Yes."

"Was the act of tying her to the bed with nylons and
having sex with her love?"

"It was love and passion."

"You tied both arms to the top of the bed and her legs to the bottom and then had sex. This was love?"

"It was love and passion."

"Did you buy a pair of handcuffs?"

"Yes."

"And did you drill holes in your bed and attach one set of handcuffs to the holes and the other to her wrists?"

"Yes."

"And this was an act of love?"

"It was an act of passion."

"Did you buy a metal dildo to have sex with Karin?"

"Yes."

"And this was an act of love?"

Dennis turned bright red. "I'm trying to recall the circumstances" was all he could say.

"Was it love to ask Karin to write you obscene letters?"

"I don't recall asking her to do that."

Santos grilled Dennis for more than two hours about various letters of late July and early August 1986, demanding that he put precise dates on them since most of them were undated. The questioning went back and forth, Dennis uncertain about which letters came first or second or third, becoming more and more lost and confused, and the spectators and jurors becoming just as confused. (Later Matt Coleman commented, "I learned one thing listening to all that. I'm never going to write a letter again without putting a date on it.")

Finally, when Judge Corrigan tried to put a stop to it, asking, "Is there a point to be made in all this?" Santos's answer brought down the wrath of the court.

"The point," he replied, "is that the witness is lying."

Corrigan was furious. He glared at Santos. "You are out of order, Mr. Santos," he raged. "You are not to characterize the witness's testimony. The court is not interested in your opinions, and they have no place in a court of law. Another outburst like that, and this court will be forced to take some action.''

Santos bowed his head. "I apologize, Your Honor," he said meekly. But he had made the point he wanted to make.

Now Santos wanted to know whether Karin really had the kind of influence over Dennis that he said she had, really had that overwhelming effect on him. "You were not eating, you were not sleeping, you were not feeling well, you were walking around like a zombie, isn't that what you said? What did you mean by that, feeling like a zombie?"

"I meant basically that my life revolved around her and she was removing herself from my life. There was no way I could resist doing whatever she asked."

"If she asked you to jump off the Brooklyn Bridge, would you have done that?"

"No."

"If she asked you to go to Washington and kill the President, would you have done that?"

"No."

"If she had asked you to kill your mother, would you have done that?"

"No. There would have been no point in doing any of those things."

"But you say she asked you to kill her mother and you did that."

"Yes."

There was not an area of Dennis's testimony that Santos did not probe, not try to impeach with questions that were often rambling and confusing, not just to Dennis but to the spectators and the judge as well, who broke in more than once to wonder just where Santos was going.

There was even the inevitable question about the Catholic Church and the immediate objection from Thomas, sustained by Corrigan.

When Dennis Coleman finally left the stand, most of those who had listened to those five days of testimony, to all the cross-examination by Hubert Santos seemed to think he had made a credible witness, that he had borne up well under the intense strafing from the defense counsel, that there had been little hesitation in saying he couldn't remember precise dates and times of letters and phone calls, even some events and that he had inflicted major, perhaps fatal, damage to the defendant.

Even Santos was not pleased with his own performance. On the sidewalk outside court at the end of that last day, he asked an acquaintance what he thought, how he thought it had all gone. The acquaintance said he thought Dennis had made a believable witness, that he had been direct and forthright, obviously well rehearsed. What, Santos asked, was the opinion of his own performance? The acquaintance said he thought Santos had been uncertain of where he was going, had struck out wildly and often blindly, and it had shown. There had been, for example, that strange demand that he be allowed to show the move *Friday the 13th* to the jury because Dennis had watched it hours before committing the murder, a demand Corrigan rejected out of hand. The general feeling among spectators and the press was that Santos probably had done little damage in his cross-examination.

Santos shook his head sadly, gloomily. "I know," he said.

Finally there was Shannon Dubois. She was a little nervous, but she told her story directly and with few hesitations, remembering the details with almost total recall. She told of Karin's phone call informing her of the murder on the morning after and the plea that Karin needed her. She told of the moment when she asked Karin outside the Coleman house, "Who could have done it?" and then, "Do you know?" and Karin's reply, "Yes, I know. It was Dennis."

And then Shannon described how Karin led her up to Dennis's room and showed her the evidence in the duffel bag and how Karin told her "that on five different nights they had planned to kill her mother."

"Why," Thomas asked, "did you ask Karin if she had anything to do with it?"

"Because," Shannon answered, "she told me that Dennis had done it and she knew how he had done it."

"What else did she say?"

"She said she had talked to Dennis on Monday night before the murder. She said she told him she didn't want to be there when it happened and that she would come home early on Wednesday and clean everything up and then call the police."

Then Karin left with the people from Athena, and Dennis arrived home from work and asked her if she knew what had happened, and she said yes, because Karin had told her. And that night, with Karin staying at her house, Karin asked if she had talked to Dennis and she said, "Yes, and he told me in detail everything," and sketched out what Dennis had said.

"Oh," Karin replied, "that's what he told me last night."

She had finally gone to her parents and to the police when "I was all by myself for the first time and I got very upset and it all came out."

Santos was gentle with her on cross-examination, as he tried to shake her testimony and score a few points. She was not to be shaken, though. His only score dealt with Karin's transportation back to Glastonbury. Shannon had told the police that Karin had told her that she had been delayed in getting back to Glastonbury because her car was blocked in the Markovs' driveway. Santos noted that Karin did not have a car then.

Late in the morning of Friday, May 31, the state rested. It had called sixteen witnesses. It had not called Kira Lintner or Christopher Wheatley. Thomas apparently thought that both were impeachable, that any testimony they gave would be suspect and self-serving. He decided to pass them by. He had not called many others who might have supported and amplified the testimony presented. He had not wanted to go in for overkill. Still, he had presented a strong case and, many thought, a convicting one. Dennis Coleman might be a suspect witness, a convicted murderer and so, perhaps, not to be believed, as the credibility of felons is invariably in doubt. Yet his testimony seemed direct and persuasive, far from self-serving, for he did not try to shirk his own responsibility for what he did. And so one was forced to ask the questions, Did he have a reason to lie? How would lying possibly help him? Santos maintained that he had invented his story to help the prosecution and in so doing help himself; if Karin were convicted on his testimony, then perhaps the board of pardons might look more kindly on his applications for early release. Further, Santos held, Dennis was seeking revenge on Karin for what she had done to him, for all her lies, for all her ill use of him, for cuckolding him with Alex Markov by attempting to implicate her in the murder. Still, one was forced to wonder: If he had not done the murder at her urging, how would killing Joyce Aparo have helped him win back Karin and sideline Alex Markov, especially if he had read that July 1987 diary, as Santos insisted he had, and discovered what she was writing there about him and Markov?

But Dennis had not been the state's only witness to put Karin at the center of the conspiracy, to point to her as an accessory to the deed. Dennis might be suspect, his word doubted, but could one doubt the testimony of Beverly Warga regarding the overheard conversations or, especially, the testimony of Shannon Dubois, Karin's best friend, a young woman who had nothing to gain by telling anything but the truth?

32

What would Santos offer as a defense? Most of the spectators who filled the small courtroom day after day, who lined up early in the morning in hopes of seats on one of the hard benches, who remained in line outside throughout the day, praying that someone would leave and a seat become vacant, those who had heard the state's case firsthand and most newspaper readers, television viewers and radio listeners who tuned in for reports about it all during the day and viewed daily with avid fascination pictures from inside the courtroom on television news in the evening seemed convinced now of Karin Aparo's guilt, convinced that conviction was inevitable. How would Santos deflect and turn that feeling? Would that even be possible?

His initial intention was to lay out for the jurors and

spectators, those in the courtroom and those beyond, the tragedy of Karin's childhood and youth, the abuse physical and psychological. He planned to do this by parading before the court a succession of witnesses who would testify to what they had seen or heard over the years, the neighbors, teachers, friends and mere acquaintances who presumably would have unbiased views. By the time they were through, the court, and the world beyond, would be awash in sympathy for Karin Aparo.

There was just one problem with this strategy. It was not going to be offered as mitigation, enabling the defense to change its plea to, perhaps, guilty of a lesser charge, manslaughter. Karin and Santos had no intention of abandoning their stand that she was not guilty of any involvement in her mother's murder. The testimony about abuse would be offered only to explain why she had acted as she had in the summer of 1986, when the original and aborted conspiracy to murder began, and to explain why she had acted as she had in August 1987 after the murder, to show her state of mind.

But if Santos followed this tack, Thomas was certain to object and to object strenuously, with some strong legal reasoning to support him. It was one thing if Karin was admitting guilt and offering this testimony in mitigation. It was another entirely if it was to be used for another purpose, merely to show state of mind and to buttress the claim of innocence. For the court to allow this, Santos had to have laid a groundwork. But if he pursued this strategy, he would not have done that. And there are many legal experts who think the court would have been legally justified in blocking him.

Hope Seeley, the young and gifted attorney who was helping Santos with the case, who had become a staunch supporter of Karin's, came up with an alternative plan. Lead off with Karin, she suggested. Her testimony would show that the defense was not changing its plea and was not citing abuse as mitigation. The plea would remain not guilty, but Karin's testimony about what she endured would reveal her contentions on why she had acted as she had and would lay the essential groundwork for the witnesses about abuse to support her allegations.

Santos bought the idea.

His defense began on the ninth day of the trial, Monday, June 4, with the defendant herself, Karin Aparo. As she stepped slowly toward the witness box, she appeared frightened, nervous, biting her lips. Santos led her through her version, which at the beginning at least jibed with Dennis's, of the meeting of the two and how they became lovers, led her to the beginning of August 1986, where the stories diverged.

Her diary entry "We have a plan"? The plan had nothing to do with murder. "Dennis and I wanted to run away," she said.

The diary entry "Dennis and I have our plot" and the note at the end "Update: will not carry out our plan"? That had nothing to do with murder either. It had to do with running away, and the note at the end meant "I was totally unrealistic, and there was no way I could do it."

When she wrote to Dennis that "I will do whatever is necessary," she wasn't writing about murder. "I was telling Dennis that I was going to tell my mother that I wanted to leave. But there was no way it could have happened."

That, she said, running away with Dennis, was what all those letters were about; they had nothing to do with a plan to commit a murder.

Yes, she had crushed some pills and put them in her mother's sandwich, she admitted. But that was because Joyce was angry with her and Dennis because she had found a note from him in Karin's window and was demanding that they stop their affair. So Karin had taken just two pills Joyce used for migraines and mixed them with the relish. Just two pills. Just enough to calm her down.

"Was it your intention to kill your mother?" Santos asked.

"No, it wasn't."

"What were your feelings toward your mother?"

"They were mixed. At times I really loved her, and at other times I was very afraid of her."

"Why did you want to run away?"

"Life with my mother was very difficult. She was very mean, psychologically, emotionally and physically. She'd tell me things and I'd find out they weren't true. She told me that my dad wasn't my dad, that it was somebody else."

She talked about Dennis, and she talked about Alex Markov and how Joyce told her, "I wouldn't mind if Alex got you." By the end of June 1987, she said, "my relationship with Dennis was falling apart. I was sleeping with Alex in the middle of June. I felt I had to break up with Dennis. He didn't want to. So I decided to separate." By July she was spending ever more time with Alex and her feelings toward Dennis were very mixed. She still loved him, but he was too possessive.

She gave her version of the events of late July until the murder, saying she had never asked Dennis to murder Joyce and had nothing to do with it. During all those calls the morning after the murder he never told her that he had killed her mother, nor did she ask him if he had.

The call to Dennis from the Glastonbury police station that evening, overheard by Beverly Warga? "Did you know, or had Dennis told you by then, that he killed your mother?"

"No. He did not tell me then."

At Dennis's house, in his room that night, she was feeling a little uneasy because she had just learned that her mother was dead, and her stomach was bothering her, so they went right to bed and went to sleep and never talked about anything. It was only in the morning that Dennis took her down to his car, the Triumph Spitfire, and opened the trunk and showed her the plastic garbage bag with her mother's car license plates and other papers. Even then he did not tell her he had murdered her mother, though now she believed he had. She said to him, she told the court, "Throw all that stuff out. If I didn't see it, I don't know about it." She said those same words to him when he took her back upstairs, opened his closet and showed her the duffel bag with Joyce's purse and the black clothes.

About then, she said, she asked him why, "and he said because she was making me go with Alex."

She called Archbishop Whealon to tell him of the murder and ask him to conduct the funeral service. She called Shannon, "who used to be my best friend." When Shannon reached the Coleman house, Karin testified, she told her everything she knew. Shannon asked, "Were you involved in it?"

Karin replied, "No."

Shannon said, "Did you have any idea this was going to happen?"

Karin said, "I had no idea."

"Do you know who was responsible?"

"No."

"Was it Dennis?"

"No . . . yes."

Shannon said, "I don't believe you."

Santos proceeded to take her through the by now familiar ground of how she found Dennis's note and turned it over to the police, through the funeral, where she had seen her mother's body for the first time, seen the marks and the bruises and the distorted features, and had gone into shock, and how afterward, in the Duboises' bathroom with Dennis, "I wanted to tell him what I had seen on my mother, and I wanted him to explain." That was the first time, she said, that Dennis told her the details of the murder.

"Seeing my mother made me decide I was going to tell the police about Dennis. I didn't want to be the one to turn Dennis in. I still loved him. I was so confused. I had conflicting feelings regarding Dennis. He said he killed my mother because I was sleeping with Alex. I loved my mother because she was my mom, but I was afraid of her and I didn't know how to put all of that together.''

She had gone with him and had sex with him twice after he was released from prison, and she did so, she said, because ''he was all I had left and I didn't want to lose him.''

''Why did you show so little emotion after your mother's death?''

''Because it didn't hit until later.''

''Why did you lie and cover up for Dennis Coleman?''

''I was afraid and I was still in love with him and I didn't know what to do.''

''Did you conspire with Dennis Coleman to kill your mother?''

''No.''

''Did you beg Dennis Coleman to kill your mother?''

''No.''

''Did you entreat Dennis Coleman to kill your mother?''

''No.''

''Did you solicit Dennis Coleman to kill your mother?''

''No.''

''Did you ask Dennis Coleman to kill your mother?''

''No.''

Santos took her this far. Now he was preparing to take a crucial step, the gamble that would be the main thrust of his defense. If it worked, he could change the whole course and tenor of the trial. He had nothing to lose. He had been laying the groundwork for it day after day, with those questions, to which answers were not permitted, about a priest, about childhood abuse, about other aspects of Karin's life with her mother. Now he tried to swing wide the door and get it all in.

''Where did you grow up?'' he asked.

''In East Hartford.''

"What did your mother do?"

Before Karin could answer, Thomas rose and objected. It was as though he suddenly understood what Santos was attempting. This line of questioning, he said, was not relevant.

It was absolutely relevant, Santos said, and he asked that the jury be sent out so he could explain why. The jurors filed out. Now Santos showed his hand. What he intended to do, he said, was go into the history of Karin's relationship with her mother and father, to develop in detail the psychological and emotional abuse to which she had been subjected from her earliest age until the day of the murder and beyond. His purpose was to explain Karin's conduct in August 1986, when those first discussions of murder arose. "What Karin did," he said, "when she made that sandwich and when the lights were flicked was not with intent to commit murder, but rather she was acting out all the frustration that developed over the years of child abuse." By showing this, he said, he would be able to rebut the state's claim that she was engaged in any conspiracy at all, and he would explain why she acted the way she did after the murder, why she covered for Dennis and why she had sex with him.

He intended, he told Corrigan, to have Karin testify to everything she remembered about her mother through all the years, and then he would corroborate her stories of all the abuse with the testimony of teachers and others who were witness to it, or its results, and with hospital and social service reports. And then he would bring in the psychiatrists, who "are prepared to testify that the defendant suffers from a mental disease or defect. She fits the profile of a battered child, and her conduct before and after the murder was consistent with the result of that abuse. We will show that she did not have the mental state to commit the crime nor the specific intent to conspire and participate in it. The experts will rebut the state's claims that she did. The whole history of mental and physical abuse is essential to our defense. And the centerpiece is the lie that someone else was her father, and not Michael Aparo.''

Thomas was outraged. He didn't see what such testimony, or evidence, had to do with this case. ''She says, 'I didn't do it,' so how is this relevant? What Mr. Santos is trying to do is present a mutually exclusive defense, and that is not permissible. She is not entitled to this defense. She could have pled not guilty and not guilty by reason of insanity, and then she could present this testimony. But she took the witness stand, and she denied everything.''

Corrigan asked whether Santos was preparing to offer an insanity defense.

Santos said, ''We might. We don't have to make that decision at this point. We will decide at the time of Your Honor's charge to the jury.'' At this point all he wanted to do was lay out the relationship with Joyce Aparo and show how what Karin did in 1986 was the culmination of that relationship and why she was acting it out. ''Our purpose is to show that she never conspired and that her conduct after the murder was consistent with and the result of the years of abuse and the effects that had on her. If the testimony we offer is credible, then it has the possibility of raising a reasonable doubt whether she actually conspired and helped Dennis Coleman plan and commit the crimes charged between August 1986 and August 1987. The state says, if she didn't conspire and didn't abet, then why cover up? The defense says, this is a troubled young girl who did some things that can be construed as consistent with guilt but are actually the result of abuse.''

By not committing himself to a particular line of defense, Santos was keeping all his options open. If Corrigan refused to allow this testimony, Santos was sure he would have solid grounds for an appeal should Karin be convicted. If Corrigan permitted him to put everything he wanted on the record, let the jury hear it all, then at the end Santos could judge the effect and decide where he wanted to go. He could continue to maintain that Karin was not guilty of any crime because she had done nothing. This would compel the jury to decide only on the counts of the indictment whether or not she was guilty of the crimes charged. If she was guilty, she would be sentenced, at Corrigan's discretion, to up to eighty years in prison, and Corrigan had the reputation of a fair trial judge and a very stiff sentencer. Or Santos could decide to use the evidence as mitigation. This would allow the jury to acquit her on the murder and conspiracy counts and to find her guilty of a lesser offense, manslaughter, as it could not do if the original plea stood; she would then be subject to a much less severe term in prison. Or Santos could decide to change the plea to not guilty by reason of diminished capacity, mental disease or defect, the insanity defense.

He would have, then, very wide latitude to make a decision once that testimony was on the record. It was an audacious step, one the prosecution did not seem to have anticipated or prepared for. But it was one that Santos had obviously been planning to take, without revealing it to anyone before, and in so doing put Joyce Aparo on trial in place of her daughter.

Thomas tried his best to prevent Santos from following along this path. It seemed as though he suddenly realized where this might be heading, and he wanted to stop it before it got out of control, before all his careful planning for the state lay in ruins. So he argued vehemently that the testimony Santos intended to present was irrelevant unless the defense changed its plea. To no avail. Corrigan thought about it, called a recess and then, when he returned, announced that he was going to permit Santos to pursue this line, to lay out for the jury Karin's story of the history of Joyce Aparo's abuse of her, to bring in Archbishop Whealon's name at last and the effect all that abuse and all those lies had on her; he was going to let Santos call witnesses to back up Karin's story and then, perhaps, allow him to call his experts to give their psychiatric opinions.

*   *   *

So the case turned, and it was Joyce Aparo, not Karin, who was now on trial in the public mind—on trial and soon convicted as the tales of abuse, the tales of lies and deceit, the tales of Archbishop Whealon filled a packed and sometimes stunned and certainly appalled courtroom and newspaper columns and the television screens over the next ten days. The stories came from Karin herself, from all those teachers and neighbors and friends and from the psychiatric experts. They were chilling. It was possible to feel the sympathy grow and swing. At the beginning Karin had been an object of scorn. Now she was turning into an object of pity.

In the corridors outside the courtroom, on the sidewalk outside the courthouse, one could hear voices saying, "She should have killed that woman herself. Then she could have pleaded justifiable homicide and gotten off." There was, though, an inevitable "but." "But she didn't. She got that poor jerk to do it for her, and now he's in prison for thirty-four years." No matter the testimony that Santos was managing to enter onto the record, the public perception of Karin's guilt remained unchanged, though not the views about what punishment she might deserve, which had once been that whatever Dennis got, she should get as much if not more. Punished she should be, people said, but nobody was sure just how.

When Santos was finished, it remained to be seen how and if Thomas would manage to rebut and deflect the impact. First came his cross-examination of Karin. It was a trying time for both of them.

"What," he asked, "were your feelings for Alex Markov from August fifth to August twelfth?"

"I don't remember."

"Did you ever intend to marry Alex Markov?"

"Maybe."

"Have children with Alex Markov?"

"Maybe."

"Tell people after you met Alex Markov that you and Dennis were just friends?"

"Yes."

"Now you say you loved Dennis?"

"Yes."

"Why did you lie to Dennis?"

"I didn't want him to know."

"Did you go off with Alex Markov in the Coleman house to Dennis's room and discuss having him as your guardian?"

"After what happened, I didn't know what to do."

"What was to be Dennis's role?"

"I didn't know."

"Did you love Dennis when you called him from Woodstock and asked him to buy you a ring on July fourteenth and you were sleeping with Alex Markov?"

"Yes."

"Why did you turn Dennis in?"

"It was seeing my mother's body for the first time."

"That's all?"

"It was the pressure. Knowing everything and not knowing what to do with it."

"There was no agreement between you to cover up your participation in the murder?"

"No."

"Why did you lie to Dennis then?"

"I didn't want him to know I had gone to the police."

"Why?"

"I was afraid he would get mad."

"What does that mean to you?"

"I didn't know how he would act. Not then, but later, when we were alone. I was not sure what I felt."

"Did you see Dennis after he got out of jail?"

"Yes."

"You went and saw Dennis and you say you were afraid of him because he had killed your mother, yet you had sex with him?"

"Yes. I was afraid. The way he was acting and asking questions."

"You felt compelled to have sex?"

"I didn't feel in a position to say no. I didn't want to do anything to upset him."

"But you had just turned him into the police. Did you discuss that?"

"Yes."

"What did you say?"

"I don't remember."

"You saw him once more. Were you afraid of him then?"

"I think so."

"You had sex with him then?"

"Yes."

"And you were afraid of him?"

"Yes."

"Why did you lie to Shannon about how the police got the note Dennis left in your bed?"

"I don't know."

"What did you mean in your letter to Dennis about crucial papers?"

"I don't know what that refers to."

"The plot you wrote about, that refers to running away and getting married?"

"Yes."

"That was the extent of the plot?"

"Yes."

"Why did you need a guardian if you were going to run away?"

"So my mother couldn't get me back."

"About the pills. You say you did that to calm your mother down?"

"Yes."

"Did you tell Dennis this?"

"Possibly."

"What did you tell him?"

"I don't remember."

"How could Dennis help you run away?"

"I don't remember."

"What's the distinction between running away with help and without help?"

"I'm not sure."

"Did you have the logistics worked out?"

"I don't remember now."

"In your letter, you mentioned unfulfilled promises. What were the unfulfilled promises?"

"They were his promise to take me away from my mother and get married."

"But what did you mean by the reference to unfulfilled promises?"

"I don't remember."

"You said you crushed the pills into her sandwich to calm her down. What does calming her down have to do with running away?"

"I wanted to get away from her because she could be so difficult to be with."

"But how could that help you run away?"

"It couldn't."

"Why did Dennis write to you that he would kill for you?"

"It was just a general expression of his feelings for me."

"This is the same man who was upset by the flicking of the lights?"

"Yes."

"What did he mean by writing that he was giving his soul to something black?"

"I don't know."

"On the night of July thirtieth, what were your intentions regarding Dennis?"

"After the trip to Binghamton we would have the rest of the summer together. Really, my intentions were that because Alex was going away, I was not using Dennis."

"You were not using him when you were sleeping with others and leading him to believe it was not so?"

"That was not my intention."

"Did you tell Shannon Dubois that you had a role in the murder?"

"No."

"Did you tell her you were supposed to clean up?"

"No."

"Did you tell her about other plans to murder your mother?"

"I can't remember. But we did have discussions."

"You didn't tell her about the discussion with Dennis about the flicking lights and that plan to kill your mother?"

"I don't specifically remember."

"Were you misleading Shannon?"

"No."

"Why did you tell Shannon the same story you told Dennis about the finding of the note?"

"I don't remember."

"The note you wrote Dennis after he was arrested, where you said, 'Don't worry about what others say.' What were you afraid he would hear?"

"I don't remember."

"What did you mean by telling him, 'I forgive you for loving me'?"

"I was telling him how sorry I was that he thought he did this for me."

"What did you mean by the reference that you didn't want to go to jail?"

"I thought that would happen if I refused to testify."

"For twenty-five years?"

"That number just came out."

"You still say you had no part in the murder?"

"Yes."

"Why did Dennis lie?"

"Obviously, he was in jail and he said he didn't want me to be with other men. That was one of his motives. He told me that one night. He didn't want me with anyone else. That was it.''

"You betrayed him?"

"Yes."

"Did you use him?"

"Yes."

"Did you use him to get rid of your mother?"

"No."

Despite what appeared a damaging cross-examination of Karin, Thomas was still faced with somehow dealing with the impact of the total defense and the portrait that emerged of Karin as the victim. What did he do? Did he summon rebuttal witnesses, if he could find any, to restore some of the sheen to Joyce Aparo's tarnished image, to turn her back into the victim? He did not. Did he call those missing witnesses Christopher Wheatley and Kira Lintner to put the focus back on the crime itself and on Karin as the instigator and the collaborator? He did not. Did he call Shannon Dubois's parents or Dennis Coleman's parents to corroborate at least part of their children's testimony? He did not. Did he call Alex Markov to tell whatever he knew or whatever he was willing to tell, or even Albert Markov? He did not. Did he call others who had what might have been pivotal knowledge of Karin's role? He did not.

He did try, though, to refocus the case on the murder and on Karin. To do so, he called two rebuttal witnesses. One was Ann Marie Murray, the partner in Athena, to testify to her walk with Karin on the morning after the murder during which Karin told her how much insurance and how large an estate Joyce had, thus refuting Karin's claim that she had no knowledge of either.

The other was Jill Smith, with whom Karin lived for a few months in the winter after the murder. She was in court to relate how that winter she had driven Karin back and forth between her home and Santos's office and how during those rides she and Karin talked about the case. In one of those conversations they discussed the phone calls between Dennis in Glastonbury and Karin in Rowayton the night of the murder, of how upset Dennis was that Karin was not at home and, according to Karin, he told her he was going to kill Joyce.

"Then you knew he was going to kill your mother," Jill Smith said.

"Yes," Karin answered, "but I really didn't think he was going to do it, because he had told me before that he would and he didn't."

On another ride they talked about the poisoned sandwich, and according to Smith, Karin told her she had emptied a bottle of sleeping pills into the relish. "Karin," she said, "you could have killed your mother with that act."

And Karin said, "I know. I know."

Hubert Santos had a good time with Jill Smith on cross-examination. "While Karin was in your house," he asked, "did you have someone come in and try to get rid of the evil spirits that Karin was generating?"

"No."

"Do you belong to a charismatic church?"

Thomas objected, Corrigan sustained, so the witness did not have to answer.

"Was there another woman staying there?"

"Yes. Shirley stayed there briefly."

"Did you tell Karin that Shirley had supernatural powers?"

"No."

"Did you tell Karin that Shirley was going to perform a service to rid the house of the evil spirits that Karin was generating?"

"No."

"Did you have prayer services in your house?"

"Yes. We prayed for you."

"You prayed for me?"

"Yes."

It had its effect. Santos smiled in bemusement, and the courtroom erupted with laughter.

33

A trial is a secular ritual, its forms codified, its manners precisely dictated. It passes from the reading of the indictment through the selection of the jury to the presentation of the evidence and the rebuttal of that evidence. It proceeds then to the closing arguments and the judge's charge and at last to the jury's deliberation and verdict. We had come to that moment when prosecutor and defense counsel, reaching for all their oratorical and legal skills, attempt to sway and convince the jury, those ultimate judges of the facts, and so carry the day.

Jim Thomas had the first word and the last, as the ritual prescribes. "It is not my job," he began, "to convince you but to lay out the evidence for you. My opinion doesn't make any difference. It's not proper for counsel to state his opinions on what the evidence means. That's for you.''

The issues of this case, he said, were very limited. "Who's telling the truth?'' Dennis Coleman, Shannon Dubois and the other witnesses for the state, or the defendant? Who has the most to gain? Does Dennis Coleman really have an interest in the outcome? Does he have something to gain? Perhaps he feels used and betrayed. Perhaps he feels anger. But did he really waver until cross-examination? Perhaps there were things he couldn't remember. But three years have gone by since the event.

"But the case does not rest on your assessment of him alone. There is all the other evidence and all the other testimony. There is Shannon Dubois. Why did she take the stand? Would she perjure herself against her best friend? Was there any motive for her to come in here and testify? The only way she could get into trouble was to perjure herself. It is the same problem we all face. Her best friend told her she was involved and would return the next morning and clean up. What kind of a burden is that to put on a sixteen-year-old?

"The defendant was not obliged to take the stand. But she did, and look at what she said about all the letters and about Dennis Coleman's testimony. Does it ring true? What was her response to the questions about the crucial papers, about all the letters? 'I don't know, I don't recall, I don't remember.' Does that ring true? Her case rests on two things. 'I wasn't involved, it was just fantasies, and the reason I may have fantasized was because my mother abused me. I didn't do it, and anything you may think I did wrong was because of what my mother did to me.' ''

The mother. "Joyce Aparo,'' Thomas said, "is not the issue in this case. Am I going to stand here and say Karin was not abused? No. But to what degree was she abused? Sure, some of the stimuli on Karin was [*sic*] not good. You shouldn't do to a child what was done to her. You shouldn't tear a child down constantly. Part of the picture is what she did in response to her mother. I submit that her explanation is not so. The psychiatrists explained her actions after the murder. But ask yourselves how impartial were the psychiatrists? Everything they said was based on what she told them. There is a flaw in the posttraumatic stress syndrome diagnosis, and Dr. Cigalis brought it out. Her conduct was consistent with someone who was involved in a murder. And does the testimony of the psychiatrists really count for anything? To accept it, you have to reject Dennis Coleman and Shannon Dubois and all the letters and all the rest.

"She manipulated and used Dennis Coleman and then wasn't quite sure what to do with Dennis Coleman, to keep him on the hook or to turn him in. She decided to make a preemptive strike and go to the police. Dennis said she used him. Others said she used him and others. She wanted the police to misrepresent where she found the letter. She lied to Dennis, and she lied to Shannon about that. If you believe the evidence, you will see that the defendant played on Dennis's emotions like she played on the violin.

"This is a sad and tragic case. The woman who was murdered loved her life. She had her problems. She was pleading for help. Look at those letters to Archbishop Whealon. But she loved her life.

"Dennis Coleman gave up a life of promise. Should you feel sorry for Joyce Aparo and for Dennis? Yes. Should you feel sorry for Karin? Yes. And I do. I wish there was something we could do for her, and for Dennis. If only someone that night had slapped him, and the others, on the side of the head.

"But they were talking murder, and not stealing apples. Though we feel sorry for the defendant, the law must apply. Abuse does not excuse what Dennis did or what she did. It may explain it and mitigate it, but it doesn't excuse it. It has no place in this case. Abuse does not impact on your decision. What we all feel in here does not matter. The evidence is what matters. Decide this case on the basis of the evidence.''

In substance, it was probably an effective argument. But Thomas is not a ringing orator. He spoke dryly and with not much emotion, and perhaps that substance was lost.

Not so Hubert Santos. He pulled out all the stops, played on all the emotions.

''Yes,'' he said, ''there was a conspiracy that ended when Joyce Aparo was murdered. It was a conspiracy between Dennis Coleman, Christopher Wheatley and Kira Lintner. Karin was not part of it. And anything that happened after the murder is not evidence of Karin's part in a conspiracy. The same is true of the count that she was an accessory. Once the murder was over, she could not be an accessory afterwards. What happened afterwards is not substantive proof. Karin testified that she was guilty of hindering prosecution. But that was after the murder.

''Think that after you reach your verdict, when you go home and go to sleep, can you be comfortable with what you did? Better that ten guilty persons go free than that one innocent person be convicted. Everyone makes mistakes. Juries make mistakes. They are human beings. There must be proof beyond a reasonable doubt. We are talking here about liberty, not about an accident case.

''Dennis Coleman is a troubled young man, seriously mentally ill. He sat here for twenty hours and described in detail how he killed Joyce Aparo as calmly as going to McDonald's and ordering a Big Mac. He was as cold as ice. We said lots about Joyce Aparo, but we never said she deserved to die. Dennis Coleman was not a farmhand hired to do this. He has an IQ of one hundred thirty-seven. Dennis Coleman was prepped to be a witness. Dennis Coleman was charged with murder. The same crime Karin is charged with. He faced a twenty-five-year minimum mandatory sentence, a sentence that cannot be overturned or reduced or suspended by a judge no matter how he feels. And Dennis Coleman knew that. And the maximum sentence in this state for murder is sixty years and twenty years for conspiracy, so Dennis Coleman faced in essence twenty-five to eighty years. He asked himself, 'How do I get out of this jam?' Let's make a deal. Shannon Dubois and Christopher Wheatley and Kira Lintner had already made deals, so who was left to give them to make a deal? The only person who never tried to make a deal. Karin. So Dennis had to make a deal, and he did, and the state recommended that he get forty-two years. But Dennis didn't like that deal. He wanted to sweeten it up. So he starts to say, 'I was mentally ill,' and so he ends up with thirty-four years, only nine years above the minimum mandatory sentence.

"Do you want to believe that kind of witness beyond a reasonable doubt? He's got everything to gain now. There's the board of pardons. It's the oldest game in the book. He's going to the board of pardons in four years, and it has the power to reduce a sentence. He's going to try to get them to do it. He's going to show them a piece of paper with Karin's conviction, and he's going to say Karin made him do it. 'I was a sex slave and she made me, she begged me to do it, and now she's convicted. The jury bought my story. She begged me, and she made me.' Is that the kind of witness you want to believe beyond a reasonable doubt?

"Dennis was manipulated, yes. But not by Karin. By Joyce Aparo into her own murder. She took him out to dinner, to the movies, shopping, in July while Karin was in Rowayton. What do you think he and Joyce talked about? Only Joyce Aparo and Dennis Coleman know what was said between them, and one is dead and the other is trying to get out of prison. But we may be sure they talked about a thing they had in common. Karin. And Joyce said, Karin is so happy; she's seeing Alex Markov. She's going to Rowayton. Her violin is getting better. She's so happy. She did a head game on this young man. We know what this woman was capable of.''

In ringing, melodramatic tones and phrases Santos recapitulated the events of the spring and summer of 1987, when Dennis's "life was falling apart. He had a terrific job and he loses it. By June he's a short-order cook at a country club. His life is falling apart. And at the end of May Karin tells him they should halt their relationship for a month, 'and I'm in love with Alex Markov,' and she's spending more time with Alex Markov in Rowayton. On June twenty-sixth, the anniversary of their first date, Joyce has an accident and Alex Markov drives Karin to the hospital and he drives her back to the condo and Dennis comes over and Alex is there, in the shower, and he's going to spend the night. His anger is building up.

"On July fourth Karin tells Dennis that she's had sex with Alex Markov, and from July seventh to July fourteenth she goes to Woodstock with Alex Markov. Dennis is frantic. He wasn't sleeping; he wasn't eating; he's walking around like a zombie. And he learns that Joyce is promoting Alex Markov and Karin, and his anger is uncontrollable. On July twenty-eighth Karin tells Dennis what if she had more sex with Alex, and he explodes and says, if it's true, he'll drive off the road and kill them both. That's why she wrote in her diary that he was suicidal. And two days later he's crying and begging outside her window for her not to go to Binghamton. He was beyond obsession.

"But she goes to Binghamton. And on August fourth he goes into the house, and he sees pictures of Alex Markov on her dresser, and he opens her drawer and pulls out her diary, and he reads of all the occasions she had sex with Alex Markov. That's when he wrote the 'I will "do the deed" ' note. He's frantic and hysterical, a zombie at that point.

"On August fourth, eight hours before the murder, he calls Karin and he hears her breathing heavily and he hears Alex Markov in the background and he assumes he's interrupted sex. Eight hours later he murders Joyce Aparo. And what does he do that evening? He goes to look for beer and he goes to Kira Lintner's house and they sit around and drink beer and watch horror movies, they watch *Friday the 13th*, with its scenes of teenage sex and the murderer who kills all the kids and who turns out to be a mother. And then he decides to do the murder, and he goes out and buys the panty hose and the black stuff and everything else. Did Karin tell him to do these things? Poppycock.

"This kid is in a major jam, and he's looking for a way out. He says it was self-defense, either him or Joyce. But then he goes back to Glastonbury and he brushes his teeth and he goes to work. But he never calls Karin to tell her. She calls him at work about the missing car being found. He did it for her and he doesn't call her? He doesn't tell her this is the ultimate expression of his love for her? She begged him to do it? The only begging outside her window is his begging her not to go to Binghamton.

"And Karin's motive? Things had improved with Joyce because she had a relationship with Alex Markov, the same way they improved when she was with Alasdair Neal. Joyce told everyone about Karin and Alex Markov. Is this the diary of a girl planning to murder her mother or a girl who has a relationship with her mother she always wanted and is happy about? This is not the diary of a young girl intent on murdering her mother, but living an imaginary life with Alex Markov and the concert scene and the dinner scene.

"Shannon Dubois is a nice young girl. But she was sixteen. She talked to the police three or four times before and never mentioned Karin. Then her parents get her a criminal defense lawyer who gets her immunity. We've got a frightened young girl of sixteen. We don't basically disagree with what Shannon said. She said Karin told her of four incidents. We admit it. They were fantasy talk with her boyfriend, brought on by the abuse of her mother, not to kill her mother. Shannon Dubois didn't tell about the time they talked about wanting Joyce dead and Shannon said she wanted to push her out of the car. This is teenage talk, anger at the mother, and it isn't serious.

"The only issue in dispute is the testimony that Karin was going home to clean the house. Shannon Dubois said that Karin had a car. But Karin didn't have a car. Don't forget, Shannon had a two-hour conversation with Dennis, and he told her all the details from his demented mind. And don't forget that Joyce had left a list of cleaning on the refrigerator door.

"This is the state's case. If they didn't have Dennis on the witness stand, she wouldn't be here. There is a sickness in this case. Everyone focuses on this little kid and calls her every name in the book. It's sad.

"And where are Kira Lintner and Christopher Wheatley? Did Dennis tell them that Karin had begged him to do it? Do you think they wouldn't have called them if he had? Kira Lintner, Christopher Wheatley, Shannon Dubois and Dennis Coleman, they were on the bandwagon to get this little kid.

"Why did they focus on this kid? Because Officer McKee said she only shed one tear. This is the great manipulator. Don't you think she would have fallen on the floor and become hysterical and shed tears by the bucket?

"Did anyone bother to find out about this kid? This kid showed no emotion, so she had to be part of the plot. Now, after all these years, Karin has been able to tell her story. This kid has been ripped apart. With all the criminals loose on the streets, all the power of the state has been focused on this kid.

"The great manipulator? Why didn't she throw the note away when she was alone in the condo? You know one thing about Karin. She's not stupid. She's smart. This kid was a product of abuse, so terrible she was ripped apart.

"Manipulated Dennis Coleman into murdering her mother? She should have turned Dennis Coleman in sooner. Why didn't she? You must understand Karin, and to understand Karin, you must understand Joyce. We called the witnesses to help you understand why she did what she did after the murder. The kid was filled with guilt, not for being involved in the murder but for introducing Dennis and Joyce and for other things. How desperate does someone have to be to convict this girl on the kind of evidence they introduced here?

"What this child has suffered. Karin never had a chance to be loved by her mother and father, to be the little child, to play with other children, to practice her religion, to return love in a spontaneous way. Ladies and gentlemen, please give Karin a chance to go on in life and get the help she needs to prosper as a young adult. Isn't it time to stop the abuse of Karin Elizabeth Aparo?"

Santos sagged a little, nodded to himself and returned to the defense table. He had spoken for an hour and twenty minutes.

James Thomas now had the final word. He spoke briefly. Santos, he complained, had attempted to mangle the case in his closing argument. "Giving Karin a chance is not relevant. Did she conspire to kill her mother and aid and abet Dennis Coleman is what this is all about. She made a choice. It was her choice. If Mr. Santos's argument was not an attempt to get sympathy, I don't know what is. This kid isn't here because of that but because she was involved in a murder. You must decide on the basis of the evidence, not on sympathy. As much as a human part of us might like to do that, it destroys the whole criminal justice system. The crime here cannot be justified. Can it be understood? Perhaps.

"Is there any evidence for half of what Mr. Santos said? He acted like he was at dinner with Joyce Aparo and Dennis Coleman. It is not proper to argue, to interpret things that are not part of the case.

"There is ample evidence that Karin Aparo lied about many things. Was she formulating a plan to turn in Dennis Coleman? I don't know. But she knew there was a plan to kill Joyce Aparo, and she was involved in it.

"Mr. Santos closed by telling you about abuse. The abuse is very sad, and I don't know to what extent it existed. But it's not a defense. Joyce Aparo was not on trial, and it's not my job to defend her. Karin set herself up as the judge and the jury of her mother, and she sent out the executioner. There is no death sentence in Connecticut, and Joyce Aparo didn't deserve to die.

"Much as your hearts may go out to the defendant, you must decide on the facts and the evidence presented in this court. Whether or not you convict, I wish I could take a different position with this young lady, just as I wished I could have with Dennis Coleman. But I can't.''

And then it was up to Judge Corrigan to explain the law to the jury. He warned the panel that it was not to speculate about evidence or witnesses that were excluded or not presented. He took a moment to castigate Santos for some of the things he said during his close. Asking the jury to give the kid a chance was a blatant appeal for sympathy, and it was not proper. It was not proper to discuss who had made deals and who hadn't; it might be true, but it must also be remembered that neither the state nor the defense had put into evidence what negotiations may have taken place between the defendant and the state. Santos should never have talked about possible sentences for the crimes charged; that is something for the judge to decide, and the jury is not to consider it.

The jury, he instructed, was to give equal weight to eyewitness testimony and circumstantial evidence. "If a fact, a piece of circumstantial evidence is logical or reasonable, it can be as weighty as direct evidence and can be credited. For example, if you go to bed at night and the sky is clear, and when you wake in the morning, there is snow on the ground, though you did not see the snow fall, it is logical and reasonable to assume that it snowed during the night. Remember, a crime is not usually committed before eyewitnesses; therefore, circumstantial evidence may often be the only evidence available.''

The rules the jury must follow, he instructed, were that

the defendant is presumed to be innocent until and unless
the jury was satisfied about her guilt; her past had no bearing on the deliberations. If there are two reasonable con-
structions to a piece of evidence, the jury is to take the one
that favors the defendant.

As for reasonable doubt, "It is not a slight doubt, or a
possible doubt, or a surmise, conjecture, or guess, or sympathy, or pity. It does not arise because a fact has been
contested. It flows from the evidence or the lack of evidence, and it must be based on reason."

He proceeded to summarize the evidence, telling the
jury to examine closely the testimony of conflicting witnesses, especially Dennis Coleman's since he "is a self-
confessed criminal and all things being equal, you would
not believe him in relationship to others who gave conflicting testimony."

If the jury found that the state had proved that Joyce
Aparo was murdered, that Karin intended to kill her, that
she solicited Dennis to do that deed and that she joined him
in the murder by helping him plan it and do other acts in
concert, then the jury must convict her of accessory to murder.

If the jury found that Joyce Aparo was murdered, that
there was an agreement between Dennis and Karin to cause
that murder and that one of them, Dennis, carried out that
agréement even though the other, Karin, was not present
and did not play a role in the actual commission of the
crime, she was, nevertheless, guilty of conspiracy to commit murder, and the jury must return that verdict.

At eleven-thirty on the morning of June 18, 1990, on
the eighteenth day of the trial, the jury retired to deliberate
on a verdict.

34

—————

The jury deliberated, and deliberated, and did not reach a verdict, and the days passed.

Hubert Santos was, he said, not optimistic. He looked dour. He wandered the corridor, back and forth between the empty courtroom and the locked small office a hundred feet away where his client waited. He had taken a big chance. He had not used an insanity defense; he had not used all that evidence on abuse as mitigation, to ask that the jury be allowed to consider a lesser charge, manslaughter. He had decided to go for broke, either conviction on the indictment or acquittal. Now he was worried.

John Bailey kept coming up from the state's attorney's office and paced nervously about the area around the court. He couldn't understand what was taking the jury so long.

There was no question in his mind what the verdict ought to be and would be. If he had been on the jury, he said, it would have taken him ten minutes. He was confident, but he was puzzled.

Reporters and court personnel sat around, read books and newspapers and magazines, engaged in idle conversation and waited. And speculated. Like much of the public outside, they were nearly unanimous in the view that Karin was guilty. Most thought a conviction would come. Some thought Karin would go down on both the accessory and the conspiracy counts. Others weren't so sure. All that testimony on abuse, despite Corrigan's charge, would have an effect. The jury, they said, would not want to send Karin away for sixty years; that was what conviction as an accessory would probably mean. Not after all those stories. It might acquit her on that. But surely it would convict on conspiracy. After all, there was all that testimony, and even if one had hesitations about Dennis, who could not believe Shannon, or Warga, or the meaning of all those letters?

By the end of the first week there was still no verdict, and the jury was sent home for the weekend. It was to resume deliberations on Monday. An acquaintance remarked to Santos that he found this practice a little odd. In New York, in other states, once a jury begins deliberations it continues to deliberate, weekends included, until it reaches a verdict or is hopelessly deadlocked, and it is usually sequestered during the process, taken to lunch and other meals by a bailiff, the food and lodging on the state. In Connecticut the jurors go home every night, take weekends off, join the crowds of spectators, reporters and court personnel for lunch at fast-food wagons parked outside the courthouse or at other fast-food joints down the block, the neighborhood lacking good restaurants, and pay their own way.

Santos replied that he thought the Connecticut method the right way. Unbroken deliberations and sequestering, he said, might lead to a verdict but not necessarily to justice.

Since when, the acquaintance said, did courts and trials have anything to do with justice? That might be a by-product, but in reality they had all to do with what evidence got in and what was kept out and with the relative abilities of opposing counsel. Courts were a stage on which the lawyers played the leading roles and vied for the best reviews.

Another week passed, and still no verdict. Now and then the jury asked for rereading of testimony, for rereading of Corrigan's instructions. But that was all. There was little sense that the jury was coming close or even that it might be so deadlocked that it would never reach a decision. Observers began to try to read meaning into the way the requests were framed, into the way this juror or that looked at Karin during those brief court appearances. Was that young juror actually ogling her? Was the scowl on that one's face indication of displeasure with her or with something else? Were the yawns and fidgeting yet another indication of boredom or impatience or what?

At midafternoon on Thursday, June 28, the third week of deliberations nearing an end, the word suddenly resounded. The jury was coming in. There was a verdict.

Thomas and his assistants took their places. Santos, his assistant, Hope Seeley, and Karin moved to the defense table. Reporters and spectators rushed in to grab every seat. Judge Corrigan in his black robes appeared and settled behind the bench.

The door opened. The jury filed in. The foreman, a burly man in his late thirties, an engineer for Northeast Utilities, looked at Karin, gave her a smile and a wink.

"Has the jury reached a verdict?" Corrigan asked.

"We have, Your Honor," the foreman said.

"As to count one of the indictment, accessory to murder, how do you find?"

"Not guilty."

Karin Aparo let out a gasp, clutched Santos's hand, began to cry.

Among the spectators there was stunned silence, heads began to shake in disbelief.

"As to count two, conspiracy to commit murder, how do you find?"

"We are deadlocked. We are unable to reach a verdict on that charge."

The vote on conspiracy, jurors later said, was seven for acquittal, five for conviction; among those five were three of the four women on the panel. A few days later one of the jurors who had been for acquittal on the conspiracy charge said he thought that he had made a mistake, that he should have voted for conviction, but "Well, I guess I'll have to live with that."

On the sidewalk outside the courtroom later the jury foreman and several of his younger male colleagues gathered before microphones to talk about what they had done. The foreman said he had decided that Karin was not guilty even before the state had finished its case. Dennis Coleman, he said, "was a very self-centered individual. This boy was already twisted. To turn around and say he felt no animosity toward her, that is to me a direct lie." He was convinced, he said, that Dennis Coleman was a liar who had tried to implicate Karin Aparo in order to get his own sentence reduced. The case, he added, should never have been brought to trial in the first place, and the state should not even consider retrying her on the charges on which the jury hung because any reasonable jury would acquit her on those as well. The other jurors nodded their agreement.

Somebody asked if the jurors thought Shannon Dubois was lying. No, they just believed she was confused, so much so that she mixed up what Dennis told her and thought it had come from Karin.

And then suddenly Karin Aparo appeared in their midst. The foreman saw her coming. He grinned at her. "Did you catch my wink?" he asked.

She nodded and smiled back. "Thank you so much."

She gestured toward the other jurors. "I just owe them my life," she said.

The foreman put his arms around her and hugged her, stroked her hair and her shoulders. One of the other jurors grinned and said, "We read your diary."

"I'm so embarrassed," she said.

The whole thing was a spectacle no one, not even the oldest and most jaded courtroom veteran, could remember having witnessed before. An acquitted defendant might nod and smile at his jurors in the courtroom. But a gathering on the street outside? A physical embrace?

That night, Karin and several friends went to a popular Hartford restaurant to celebrate. The festivities were on the house.

By that night, too, public outrage was reaching a crescendo. Callers were flooding the switchboards of the local television and radio stations, of the newspapers and of State's Attorney Bailey's office. Those calls were nearly unanimous in condemning the verdict as a miscarriage of justice and demanding that she be retried on the conspiracy counts. The majority of those calls came from women. No one in the area could remember such a public reaction to a trial and a verdict before. "We've had people let us know what they thought on cases before, but never anything like this," said an attorney in Bailey's office. "It was absolutely amazing. We've gotten so many calls, a hundred in one day alone. What really stands out is the anger. They don't want this to be dropped."

The Glastonbury police chief was "shell-shocked. I never would have believed it."

A former neighbor of the Aparos on Butternut Drive shook her head. "I can't believe she could have got off. We're all so upset."

While some who had testified in Karin's behalf were relieved and pleased for her, they had mixed emotions. "It's about time the abuse of Karin Aparo stopped and this

evil woman is put to rest where she can't hurt anyone,''
Sandra Yerks said. ''Joyce Aparo was an evil, vicious lady
who hurt a lot of people. The only thing I feel badly about
is the young boy, Dennis Coleman.''

Dennis Coleman. Some reporters rushed to the Hartford Correctional Center the day after the verdict to find out
what he thought. ''My reaction was shock,'' he said. Karin,
he said, had learned from her mother ''how to manipulate
people. She did that with me. In a very subtle way, she did
that to the jury, too. There's a very strong urge in me to let
people know what happened. I'm not some kind of monster.
She was just as guilty as I was. If there was any justice, she
should have been found guilty.''

Over the next weeks the public outcry over the verdict
did not let up. It grew. The pressure on John Bailey to retry
Karin on the conspiracy count was unrelenting. After hes-
itating, he announced that indeed, the state was going to do
just that.

Hubert Santos was indignant. His client had been subjected to enough. She should be free to pick up her life and
go on. To retry her would be double jeopardy.

Into court went Bailey and Santos. Santos demanded
that the charge be thrown out. He lost. He demanded that if
she were tried, it should be as a youthful offender, behind
closed doors, the record sealed, because she had been fifteen when the alleged conspiracy began. Again he lost. Just
before Christmas 1990 the court ruled that because of the
seriousness of the charges, Karin Aparo's peers would judge
her once more, as an adult, on the charge that she conspired
to murder her mother. Santos, though, brought forth more
appeals on more grounds, to more and higher courts. He
was not sanguine about the possibility of blocking another
prosecution. Nevertheless, he was determined to take every
legal step on Karin's behalf.

But at some point, no one is quite sure when, Karin
Aparo will go on trial again, to hear once more the stories

of how she conspired with Dennis Coleman to have her mother killed. Once more a jury will decide her fate. In the meantime, she will spend her time going to school during the day and working at the bank in the evening, trying to live some kind of life with her future still in doubt. While she waits in this limbo, there is at least the comfort of knowing there are some who believe in her and upon whom she can lean. There are new friends, from the bank and from school. There is a new boyfriend, a young man who appeared with her during the final days of her trial and whom she sees often. There is Hubert Santos who, after his initial doubts and uncertainties, came to believe implicitly in her and her innocence and, going far beyond what one would normally expect of an attorney, has sought every possible means in his efforts to protect and defend her. He has become, in many ways, something of a surrogate father, a role he has accepted willingly.

But she can no longer look to Archbishop John Whealon for the advice and counsel he gave all her life, who was at the center of her life from childhood, and at the center of Joyce Aparo's fantasies. At the beginning of August 1991, the intestinal cancer that had afflicted him for decade, leading to numerous hospitalizations and surgery, sent him once again to the hospital. He died during another operation.

One day in the fall of 1990 I was sitting with Dennis Coleman in a private conference room at the Hartford Correctional Center. He was still there. The state had not yet found a place to move him. He could not go back to the state penitentiary at Somers. He had been told, and the state knew, that a posse was waiting for him. Because he had testified for the state, the other convicts had sentenced him to death. If he appeared there again, the sentence would be carried out. So he remained for a while in this limbo. He had begun to study, to take college courses leading to a degree. He wanted to be moved to a more permanent place where he could use what he knew. He had ideas, he said, about revamping the state's computer system, and if he got a chance, he would like to put them into practice. He had other plans as well. Before Thanksgiving he was to marry. Margaret, the young woman who had become his constant companion in his final months of freedom, who had sat with his family at his sentencing hearing, who had appeared again when he was called to testify against Karin, would become his bride, would wait for him on the outside while he spent however many years the state of Connecticut decided were essential to serve the ends of justice, fitting punishment for the crime he had committed. There would be conjugal visits, but there would be no hope of a real life for them until he reached middle age.

The conversation came around to Karin and all that had happened. He had put her behind him now, he was sure. She had been his past, and she had been his ruin. Margaret was his present and his future, whatever that held for him. But he could never truly escape Karin Aparo no matter how long he lived. She would cast her shadow across his life.

Did he really mean, he was asked, what he had said in court, that what he felt for her now was only apathy?

He thought about that for a time, then slowly shook his head. "Not really," he said.

What did he feel?

He took his time. "I feel sorry for her," he said at last. "I feel pity for her. And I'm the last person who should ever feel pity for anyone."

Afterword:
A Note on "Fair Use"

Throughout this book, and especially in Part Three, the reader came upon mention of various letters and diary entries written by Karin Aparo and Dennis Coleman. During their trials many were offered as exhibits and read in open court to spectators and jurors, most often by the defense. They became part of the court record, printed in the transcripts available to the public, and many were also printed in full in various newspapers and other publications in Connecticut.

It was my desire, and it had been my intention, to quote extensively from those letters and diaries. More eloquently than I could, they express the emotions, hopes and aspirations of both Karin Aparo and Dennis Coleman and the pressures they were under during these years. Their own words, I believed, were essential if the reader was to gain insight into them and what lay behind their actions. In the past this would have presented few problems. Such extracts, especially from court documents, were covered by what was known as the fair use doctrine applied to unpublished materials, though such materials are protected by a so-called statutory copyright. Despite popular belief, exhibits and other evidence offered in a court of law, though published in court transcripts and available to anyone who seeks to read them, are considered unpublished works.

Times have changed, however, and what was once standard practice for writers of nonfiction, both scholarly and popular, became impossible following several federal court decisions, one by the United States Supreme Court and two by the United States Court of Appeals for the Second Circuit.

Those decisions, which overturned lower federal court rulings upholding a broad concept of fair use, were rendered by the Supreme Court in *Harper & Row* v. *Nation Enterprises* in 1985 and by the court of appeals in *Salinger* v. *Random House* in 1987 and in *New Era Publishing Company* v. *Henry Holt & Company* in 1989. The Supreme Court refused to hear appeals from those lower-court decisions; as a result, they were allowed to stand. The impact was to strike down the age-old doctrine of fair use.

In *Harper & Row* the Supreme Court ruled that the *Nation* magazine's publication of long excerpts from an autobiography by former President Gerald Ford before the book's publication by Harper & Row had violated and infringed upon Ford's copyright. "Under ordinary circumstances," the Court said, "the author's right to control the first public appearance of his undisseminated expression will outweigh a claim of fair use."

The court of appeals extended this doctrine far beyond merely protecting the contents of books about to be published or in the process of being written from being excerpted at length, which conceivably could damage the financial and other interests of the author. It ruled that without the express permission of the person who wrote them, or his or her estate or heirs, nothing anyone had written at any time, no matter how distant in the past, including letters, diaries and other private papers, could be quoted or excerpted in books or in any other media.

The reclusive novelist and short story writer J. D. Salinger had brought suit against the author Ian Hamilton and his publisher, Random House, seeking to block their use of quotations from a number of Salinger's unpublished letters in a biography scheduled for publication. It mattered not that those letters were on deposit in the Harvard University library and available for public examination. The appellate court held that since the words in all unpublished works, as in published ones, remain the property of the writer, not of the recipient, without Salinger's permission nothing in those letters could be quoted. It granted an injunction against publication of the biography until all quotations from Salinger's letters were removed.

A similar ruling was forthcoming from the court of appeals when suit was brought against the publisher Henry Holt and the author Russell Miller to bar the use of quotations in a critical biography from unpublished letters of L. Ron Hubbard, the founder of Scientology. The court said Miller had relied too heavily on these unpublished materials, though it gave no definition of what it meant by "too heavily." The book, as it happened, was published anyway because of a legal technicality: New Era, which controlled rights to the Hubbard letters, had waited too long to file its suit; the statute of limitations had lapsed. But the chilling impact of that and the other decisions remained in force.

The potential result was a serious, some thought even fatal wound inflicted on the writing of history and biography, of all nonfiction, scholarly and popular, as we have come to know it, perhaps even on the dissemination of news in any medium no matter how vital to the public interest. Copyright lawyers insisted that unless and until Congress and/or the courts acted to redefine "fair use" broadly, authors of works of nonfiction could not quote more than a few words from unpublished diaries, letters and other documents, even if they were part of court records and widely available, even if they were written in the distant past, even if they had previously been published in newspapers, magazines or other periodicals, without the express permission of the writer of those letters, diaries and other works or, if the writer was dead, of his or her estate or direct heirs.

Yet such permissions are not always easily obtained. The direct heirs to a deceased letter writer or diarist may have disappeared, may not be easily found, or, if found, may, for one reason or another, refuse to grant the requested permission. The letter writer or diarist may decide to dictate what may be said about him or her either by refusing to grant permission or by selectively giving permission—that is, this may be quoted and that may not. Or the letter writer or diarist may demand payment in exchange for permission.

Throughout the spring of 1991 writers and representatives of the Authors Guild met on a number of occasions with members of both the House of Representatives and the Senate and with committee staff in an effort to draft federal legislation that would restore the concept of fair use to near where it had existed in the past. Initially these efforts were resisted strenuously by the American computer industry, which believed that the old concept of fair use posed a serious threat to its control over the software used in computers. If a fair use doctrine were enacted into law, the computer industry maintained, it would permit wholesale piracy of its programs—that is, allow foreign competitors to break its unpublished software codes, make a few revisions and then sell those programs as their own. Late in the spring, however, representatives of the authors and the computer industry reached a compromise that would, in essence, protect software from piracy and at the same time permit authors fair use of unpublished documents. Legislation reflecting that compromise was introduced in both the Senate and the House, and passage seemed assured.

However, publishers are still concerned that such legislation will be challenged in the courts, and so before fair use can again be established as a viable doctrine, the courts will have to rule. Until such decisions are forthcoming, from the courts of appeals or the Supreme Court, most publishers continue to restrict severely what may be quoted from court documents, letters and other unpublished materials without the express permission of the writer or heirs.

Dennis Coleman, understanding that only his own words could adequately express his state of mind and all the pressures upon him, agreed to grant me permission to quote extensively from what he wrote, and for this I am most grateful.

Karin Aparo refused to grant permission to quote from her letters and diaries in this book, though many excerpts previously appeared in newspapers in Connecticut and are part of the court record of her trial, read into that record not by the prosecution but by her defense. It has been necessary, then, for me to try to give the reader not the words as she wrote them but, rather, the substance and sense, as I see them, of what she wrote. I would have preferred it otherwise, as I am certain the reader would have, but until and unless the courts act in a positive manner to permit the unfettered and fair use of documents in the public record, there is no other choice. Would it were not so.

Compelling True Crime Thrillers
From Avon Books

BADGE OF BETRAYAL
by Joe Cantlupe and Lisa Petrillo

76009-6/$4.99 US/$5.99 Can

GUN FOR HIRE:
THE SOLDIER OF FORTUNE KILLINGS
by Clifford L. Linedecker

76204-8/$4.99 US/$5.99 Can

LOSS OF INNOCENCE:
A TRUE STORY OF JUVENILE MURDER
by Eric J. Adams 75987-X/$4.95 US/$5.95 Can

RUBOUTS: MOB MURDERS IN AMERICA
by Richard Monaco and Lionel Bascom

75938-1/$4.50 US/$5.50 Can

GOOMBATA:
THE IMPROBABLE RISE AND FALL OF
JOHN GOTTI AND HIS GANG
by John Cummings and Ernest Volkman

71487-6/$4.99 US/$5.99 Can